Beyond Innocence,

or the **Altersroman**

in **Modern Fiction**

Beyond Innocence, or the **Altersroman** in **Modern Fiction**

Linda A. Westervelt

University of Missouri Press
Columbia and London

Copyright © 1997 by
The Curators of the University of Missouri
University of Missouri Press, Columbia, Missouri 65201
Printed and bound in the United States of America
All rights reserved

5   4   3   2   1   01   00   99   98   97

Library of Congress Cataloging-in-Publication Data

Westervelt, Linda A.
    Beyond innocence, or, The altersroman in modern fiction /
    Linda A. Westervelt.
        p.   cm.
    Includes bibliographical references (p.   ) and index.
    ISBN 0-8262-1137-2 (alk. paper)
    1. American fiction—20th century—History and criticism.
    2. Middle age in literature.   3. Life change events in literature.
    4. Midlife crisis in literature.   5. Experience in literature.
    6. Memory in literature.   7. Aging in literature.   I. Title.
    PS374.M49W47   1997
    813'.509354—dc21   97-15907
                                                           CIP

∞ ™ This paper meets the requirements of the
American National Standard for Permanence of Paper
for Printed Library Materials, Z39.48, 1984.

Designer: Kristie Lee
Typesetter: BOOKCOMP
Printer and Binder: Thomson-Shore, Inc.
Typeface: Galliard

The University of Missouri Press wishes to acknowledge the
generous support of the Limited Grant-in-Aid Program of the
University of Houston in the publication of this book.

For **Donald** and for **Austin**

Contents

Preface

The idea for this study occurred when I noticed that in three of the novels I was teaching in my course in contemporary U.S. fiction, characters in their fifties were engaged in the process of looking back over their lives. The male and female protagonists in Wallace Stegner's *Angle of Repose*, Joan Didion's *A Book of Common Prayer*, and Toni Morrison's *Jazz* feel forced by circumstances to review their past decisions. Particularly startling to me was that, while very different in tone and mood, style, and setting, these three books all portray characters going through a process of discarding some previously valued version of their life and constructing a new version, one that makes the long-held view seem like a delusion. Not only are the stages of the process similar—shock, consideration (at first resisted), and revision—but two helping characters recur to provide some part of the shock that causes the protagonist to review his or her life. A young person of the same sex as the protagonist causes him or her to feel old, and a guide, usually of the opposite sex, offers an instructive insight that helps the protagonist to see his or her life in a different way. These three novels present the character's psychological development in some detail, although *Jazz* does not necessarily observe other conventions that we have come to expect in a realistic novel. What differs is the degree of resolution. The protagonists in *Angle of Repose*, *A Book of Common Prayer*, and *Jazz* reach closure when they accept their revised view of themselves, but, in comparing them, the reader sees that the characters are more or less thorough in their review, more or less honest, and more or less courageous in their response to what they learn.

Following my observation about the resemblances among *Angle of Repose*, *A Book of Common Prayer*, and *Jazz*, I proceeded in three directions, searching for other similar novels and for relevant psychological and critical scholarship. My search for other examples, first among twentieth-century U.S. novels and then among earlier and contemporary novels generally, was rewarded with numerous discoveries, going as far back as *Don Quixote* part 2. I began my search for U.S. fiction by reflecting that if other novels that shared the structure and concerns of *Angle of Repose, A Book of Common Prayer,* and *Jazz* were to be found—if these three were members of a larger group and not exceptional—then seeking novels with middle-aged protagonists written by authors who present detailed psychology seemed a logical place to begin. The work of Henry James came immediately to mind. *The Ambassadors* is the fullest example of the kind of novel that I am defining: the focus is almost exclusively on the process in Strether's mind, and James presents Strether's thoughts and feelings in great detail. James also makes more explicit than Stegner, Didion, or Morrison that, in the process of assessing one's life, a second shock occurs. This shock destroys the protagonist's resistance and precipitates the resolution, removing the delusions that the character has about his or her life.

Studying James provided another insight into these novels as well. In looking at other work he wrote during the same period, when he was in his fifties and early sixties, it becomes clear that James explored the process of life assessment in several stories, as he brings to his reader's attention when he groups the protagonists of these stories and names them his "poor sensitive gentlemen."[1] This recurrence, evident also in Stegner's work, is important because it shows the deep investment by the writer, which may be taken to indicate the therapeutic nature of portraying such a transition. In fact, while puzzling over the apparent similarities in *Angle of Repose, A Book of Common Prayer,* and *Jazz,* I read interviews in which both Stegner and Didion admit that the concerns of the characters in these novels are close to their own personal dilemmas at the time of the writing.[2]

In continuing to search U.S. fiction, especially novels written by authors in their fifties, I found Wharton's *The Mother's Recompense,* Cather's *The Professor's House,* Faulkner's *The Mansion,* and Marshall's *Praisesong for the Widow* to be four examples of the kind of novel I am describing. At this point, confident of the wide presence of stories of life assessment, I made the decision to limit the number of novels I would consider, rather than attempt a broad survey. I made my selection partly by preference and partly because each of

1. James, preface to *The Novels and Tales of Henry James,* 17:ix.
2. Wallace Earle Stegner and Richard W. Etulain, *Conversations with Wallace Stegner on Western History and Literature,* 98, 15; Joan Didion, "Cautionary Tales," 23.

the texts I have chosen highlights a different aspect of the definition. Thus, I have included Cather's novel in order to have a text that explores resignation as a valid outcome of assessing one's life. Faulkner's less familiar novel, one less typical of his other work, expands the discussion by situating two characters' evaluations of their lives within an assessment of the community. He places the intensely personal and private activity within a larger context. Working with *The Mansion* made what is true of all these novels more obvious: the characters have a strong sense of place. Although the focus is on their interior life, the characters achieve authenticity within a culture at a particular time. While they are all similar in portraying middle-aged protagonists who are reviewing their lives, *The Ambassadors, The Professor's House, The Mansion, Angle of Repose, A Book of Common Prayer,* and *Jazz* allow me to present the tremendous variety that the category allows: differences in period and place, style, gender of author and protagonists, and degree of resolution.

I might have stopped with these six texts and fashioned this as a book about twentieth-century U.S. fiction exclusively, but doing so would have left me unable to consider, except theoretically, the possible broader implications of my discovery for the study of the novel. That is, I wanted to see whether novels in other cultures and times portray a protagonist's development during adulthood, as well as whether similar characteristics might emerge. Searching widely, I found examples in seventeenth-century Spain (Cervantes's *Don Quixote* part 2), nineteenth-century Germany (Stifter's *Der Nachsommer [Indian Summer]* and Fontane's *Unwiederbringlich [Beyond Recall]*), as well as twentieth-century Britain (Woolf's *Mrs. Dalloway* and Lessing's *The Summer before the Dark*). Again, rather than write a survey, I have chosen just one of these, *Don Quixote* part 2, the most remote, to make the point that the process of assessing one's life that is increasingly prominent in our time is not new to the novel.

At the same time that I was reading novels, I also investigated the scholarship by psychologists and psychiatrists who describe development during adulthood, building on the model envisioned by Erik Erikson, in order to learn the tasks and goals of the process. Roger L. Gould formulates the transformation in late middle age as the process of coming gradually to "live by a world view generated out of personal experience" rather than one based on "false assumptions, . . . the rigidly interpreted rules of childhood, and the fantasies we impose upon life."[3] I will explore this literature in Chapter 1, and it buttresses the discussion throughout the following chapters.

Finally, I looked at the literary criticism of a similar category of novel, the bildungsroman, which also traces the process of a character's growth from one age to another, for its defining characteristics. Aware of the current challenges to the idea of genre as well as the difficulties of attempting a classical rhetorical definition and classification, which may seem reductive and prescriptive rather than descriptive, I sought models of thoroughness in definition. I have been encouraged that thoughtful definition is worth pursuing by the recent feminist scholarship on the female bildungsroman, such as Susan Fraiman's *Unbecoming Women: British Women Writers and the Novel of Development* and the essays in *The Voyage In: Fictions of Female Development,* edited by Elizabeth Abel, Marianne Hirsch, and Elizabeth Langland. This recent scholarship revises the earlier definition of the bildungsroman, contained in the work of Susan Howe and Jerome Buckley, for example, expanding without demolishing a helpful model.[4]

Thus heartened, I felt that it would be useful to name this kind of novel the *altersroman,* or age novel.[5] The word *altersroman* has the strength of naming the essential concern of the protagonists—confronting mortality toward the end of middle age—without specifying the particular matters that challenge them and without adding an emotional association. Thus, the name *altersroman* allows the possibility of exemplars that end with affirmation as well as those that end with the protagonist's feelings of disgust or despair that so little time is left. Altersromane are books about seeking wisdom, although not everyone of this age becomes wise. Using a German word highlights that the altersroman is a classification equivalent to the bildungsroman,

3. I have consulted Erikson's *Childhood and Society,* 268–74; *The Life Cycle Completed: A Review,* 32–33, 55–66; *Identity and the Life Cycle,* chapter 2; *Adulthood* (which he edited); and *Insight and Responsibility,* 132–33; Gould, *Transformations: Growth and Change in Adult Life,* 38–39. See also Bernice L. Neugarten, ed., "The Awareness of Middle Age," 97–98; and "Adult Personality: Toward a Psychology of the Life Cycle," 139, 147. Gould and Neugarten have been my two primary sources for the expansion of Erikson's model.

4. Susan Howe, *Wilhelm Meister and His English Kinsmen: Apprentices to Life;* Jerome Hamilton Buckley, *Season of Youth: The Bildungsroman from Dickens to Golding.*

5. I am indebted to Karen P. Danford for helping me find an accurate German word, *altersroman,* for the equivalent to the word *bildungsroman.*

which also portrays characters' making a transition from one stage of life to another.

One further point about selection to be made is that, while I have purposely sought the greatest variety in the matters of period, style, and gender, I *have* slanted the discussion with my decision to emphasize the completion of the life assessment or resolution. By resolution I mean the thoroughness and honesty of the self-examination, the changes (physical or psychological) that the protagonist decides to make in the time remaining, and the extent to which the protagonist is able to affirm the life he or she has lived. Examples of the altersroman may be placed on these three scales. The three aspects of resolution are not so tightly interdependent that one predicts the other, however. Also, the decision to change is not necessarily positive, as thoroughness, honesty, and affirmation are, but may be simply an indication of the dissatisfaction the protagonist feels with his or her life thus far. In the seven novels that I have chosen, the protagonists accept their age and reach some resolution, at least for the time, whether that is affirmation or despair. That is, of the characteristics that these novels share, completing the process is crucial, as I discuss further in Chapter 1.

Acknowledgments

I am grateful to the College of Humanities, Fine Arts, and Communication at the University of Houston for offering me a Faculty Development Leave as I began this project and a Limited-Grant-in-Aid to help with the preparation of the manuscript. I want to thank Dorothy Baker, Harmon Boertien, Elizabeth Brown-Guillory, Terrell Dixon, Lucille Fultz, Marlene La Roe, William Monroe, James Pipkin, Patty Sloan, Lorraine Stock, Roberta Weldon, Patricia Yongue, and Lois Zamora, who have provided advice and encouragement. Beth Rigel Daugherty, Terrence Doody, and Sherry Lutz Zivley made particularly helpful contributions during the course of writing the manuscript. I am also indebted to my research assistant, Karen Dodwell. Special thanks to my husband, Donald Lutz, and to our son, Austin.

Beyond Innocence,

or the **Altersroman**

in **Modern Fiction**

1

The Changing
Circumstances
of Life

By the time most people reach their late forties, external and internal changes make them feel sufficiently vulnerable that they experience an irresistible urge to reflect upon the life they have had thus far. The changing external circumstances that heighten their awareness that they live in time may include the death of a parent, illness, or a reminder that one is in the generation with authority.[1] Psychiatrists and psychologists do not agree on the age at which the midlife assessment begins, but most discuss people who are between 45 and 55. Else Frenkel-Brunswik says that late middle age begins at 48.5 years of age and ends at 63.8 years of age. This turn to introspection has no single social cause, such as a job change or children's growing up, nor is it directly tied to a biological event in the same way that changes in adolescence are linked to puberty.[2]

Whatever the external circumstances, internally, resistance to change and the desire for continuity and the status quo give way to the urgency

---

1. Gould, *Transformations*, 220–21. Based on extensive research, Gould's study is the most complete. He, more than other psychologists and psychiatrists, relates the tasks of development in late middle age to those of earlier stages of adulthood. The psychological literature credits Erik Erikson as the originator of the model of adulthood as a period of continual development. See *Childhood and Society*, 266–74, as well as his expanded discussion in *Life Cycle Completed*, 32–33, 55–72. I have also consulted Erikson's *Identity and the Life Cycle*, chapter 2, especially 104–5, and *Insight and Responsibility*, 132–33.

2. For discussions of the age of the midlife review, see Gould, *Transformations*, 217; Neugarten, "Awareness of Middle Age," 94, and "Adult Personality," 140; Frenkel-Brunswik, "Adjustments and Reorientation in the Course of the Life Span," 80–81. For discussions of causes, see Gould, *Transformations*, 229; Donald Wolfe, Dennis O'Connor, and Marcy Crary, "Transformations of Life Structure and Personal Paradigm during the Midlife Transition," 960–61, 971; Neugarten, "Adult Personality," 142; and Frenkel-Brunswik, "Adjustments and Reorientation," 82.

to find out what one wants out of life and to act while time remains.
The impetus comes from the sense that time is running out, not fear
of *imminent* mortality. While the pressure of time fosters the urgency
to complete the process, introspection is resisted because relinquishing
the fundamental illusion that absolute safety is possible, that death will
not come, constitutes a tremendous threat to security. The nature of
the task, looking honestly at oneself and questioning the values that
have provided stability and consistency for approximately three decades,
makes this transition more tumultuous than some others.[3] Not yet
facing death, but with death as a reality on the horizon and no protector
in between, one feels less reason to keep the deepest passions quiet
to please others or to gain protection. The emotions and desires that
surface may include less admirable ones, such as greed or anger or the
craving for acclaim and vindication. Too, by the late forties, enough life
has been lived that one can measure the self one is against the early vision
of what one's life would be like. Examining where the two do not match
helps a person to distinguish what has occurred due to circumstances
from what has occurred due to his or her own choices, actions, and
omissions. One acknowledges responsibility and failings as well as good
qualities. One decides how one will handle old grievances and how one
will atone for perceived wrongs done to others. The review of the life
one has had thus deepens and personalizes the initial insights that the
sinister and death exist. In sum, what has been known intellectually is
understood emotionally. What literary critics have described as the fall
from innocence to experience at the beginning of adulthood proceeds
further at this stage when one sees that the sinister is present not only
in the world, but within the self as well.

Other previously unexpressed qualities that emerge may be admirable, although Gould suggests that these behaviors have been avoided
because the individual regards them as weak or frightening. Psychologists observe that men often become more open to what the dominant
culture considers "feminine" traits, such as expressing feelings freely.
They experience "relief from masculinity." Women become more assertive and more independent. In novels in which middle-aged characters look back over their lives, this exploration shows up, in part, as

---

3. For discussions of the turbulence of this stage, see Gould, *Transformations*, 307,
and Wolfe, O'Connor, and Crary, "Transformations of Life Structure," 966. Other
information in this paragraph relies on Gould, *Transformations*, 217–19, 294–95, 25.

willingness to accept guidance from someone of the opposite sex. The guide offers a different way of approaching life that the protagonist has not valued before. While they do not usually become lovers, several of the female guides help the male protagonists to experience intimacy, for example. If, as in *Don Quixote,* the guide is not an actual person but an idealized woman whose wishes Don Quixote invents, it is easier to see that the guide represents an element of one's own character, unexpressed until now. Although introspection is private, an individual does not experiment with different attitudes and emotions in isolation. This behavior affects one's closest associates and is, in turn, shaped in response to the collective values of one's culture, which are also changing.[4] Erikson stresses culture and time:

> Although aware of the relativity of all the various life styles which have given meaning to human striving, the possessor of integrity is ready to defend the dignity of his own life style against all physical and economic threats. For he knows that an individual life is the accidental coincidence of but one life cycle with but one segment of history; and that for him all human integrity stands or falls with the one style of integrity of which he partakes.[5]

Psychologists report that people experience a sense of closure when they have looked thoroughly at their lives (or as thoroughly as they have the courage to do) and have experimented with values and behavior. Introspection over time, along with reactions from others, allows individuals to see their life as an integrated whole, with their contributions to where they are now fully understood. At this point, people feel that continued reflection will confirm but not change what they have come to see about themselves.[6] By this time, too, individuals have determined

4. Gould discusses social context in section 7 of *Transformations,* 321–34, and on 236 and 241–43. See also Neugarten, "Adult Personality," 140; and Ravenna Helson and Paul Wink, "Personality Changes in Women from the Early 40s to the Early 50s."

5. Erikson, *Childhood and Society,* 268.

6. Closure is discussed in Wolfe, O'Connor, and Crary, "Transformations of Life Structure," 958–60, 969, 971; Gould, *Transformations,* 309–36, especially 311; and Frenkel-Brunswik, "Adjustments and Reorientation," 80. The psychological literature assumes that reflecting on one's life is a gradual process, taking several years. See Wolfe, O'Connor, and Crary, "Transformations of Life Structure," 960–61; Gould, *Transformations,* 218, 243; and Frenkel-Brunswik, "Adjustments and Reorientation," 80–81.

for themselves which duties or ideals will receive their attention. They feel less inclined to act according to some notion of what is right or what is expected by society or by others. While reaffirming some former values, attitudes, and activities, people may rearrange priorities in an effort to fulfill the self they have come to know. This reconfiguration sometimes requires major changes, such as the frequently cited example of Gauguin's leaving his family and his position as a broker in Paris in order to pursue painting in Tahiti, although more often it results in changes in attitude perceived only by close associates. Overall, psychologists observe that people tend to achieve greater balance in their investments in career, family, and leisure activities.[7]

A third aspect of resolution, being able to affirm one's life, follows from and depends upon the first two, reviewing the life one has had and determining which, if any, changes one will make. The psychological studies all assume introspection as the necessary component of assessing one's life, and all mention reconfiguring one's present life. Further, this literature acknowledges that closure implies that people find a way to make peace with and, if possible, to affirm a more accurate and fuller picture of their identity. However, psychologists and psychiatrists deal less directly with the way this crucial aspect of assessing one's life comes about. Why do some people affirm their lives, despite regrets, while others cannot, but end in disgust or despair? Neugarten says that consolation comes from the mastery humans feel when they act based on *conscious* experience, but she does not discuss why some people become tolerant and wise in response to wide experience while others become rigid. The study by Wolfe, O'Connor, and Crary establishes a correlation between having the freedom to adapt one's life and achieving satisfaction. Gould agrees that a complex series of behavior contributes to fulfillment in later middle age. Discarding outworn assumptions about life; seeking redress and asking forgiveness of oneself and others, as they are appropriate; and expanding one's repertoire of emotions, including previously forbidden ones, all help people to be more "authentic" or more fully themselves. Gould says that the thorough exploration of one's passions prevents bitterness, rote responses, and the sense that

7. For discussion of these various aspects of self-determination, see Wolfe, O'Connor, and Crary, "Transformations of Life Structure," 960, 966–67, and table 2D; Gould, *Transformations,* 235–36, 243, 265–66, 310–19; and Frenkel-Brunswik, "Adjustments and Reorientation," 83.

life is meaningless during the next phase of life. Erik Erikson links "the acceptance of one's one and only life cycle" with inevitability.[8] That is, it may be sufficient for affirmation that people understand that their character and circumstances have conspired so that they have made the only choices they could and still have been themselves. As a character in James's "The Middle Years" says when he is urging another to affirm his life, " 'What people "could have done" is mainly what they've in fact done.' "

The psychologists do not explore this final aspect of assessing one's life systematically, and the novelists concur that the leap to acceptance is mysterious and difficult to predict. Don Quixote is one character who goes beyond acceptance to affirm his life, and he attributes his doing so to God's grace. At the end of *Don Quixote* part 2, Don Quixote proclaims, " 'Blessed be Almighty God, who has shown me such goodness. In truth his mercies are boundless, and the sins of men can neither limit them nor keep them back! . . . The mercies . . . are those that God has this moment shown me . . . .' "[9] With these words, " 'by God's mercy,' " Alonso Quixano affirms that part of his life in which he thought he was most authentic and for which he earned " 'the name of Good' " (826). He asks forgiveness of God and his family and friends for the time he spent away from his estate, believing that he had a noble title and a lover and trying to impose his ideals on others. Many readers agree with Sancho Panza's plea that Don Quixote not renounce knight-errantry.[10] However, when *Don Quixote* is considered

8. Neugarten, "Adult Personality," 139–40; Wolfe, O'Connor, and Crary, "Transformations of Life Structure," 960, 966–67; Gould, *Transformations,* 245, 298, 318; Erikson, *Childhood and Society,* 268. The quote from Erikson refers to the eighth stage in his model, maturity, which Erikson implies is the end of the life cycle. Psychologists and psychiatrists now consider Erikson's seventh stage, generativity, to describe development in the thirties and forties, while the task of the last stage begins in late middle age rather than at the end of life. See, for example, Frenkel-Brunswik, "Adjustments and Reorientation," 80–81; and Robert C. Peck, "Psychological Developments in the Second Half of Life." This study uses *maturity* to refer to the goal of development in late middle age.

9. Miguel de Cervantes, *Don Quixote,* 826. Subsequent references are cited parenthetically by page number in the text.

10. Carroll B. Johnson also reviews the psychological literature that deals with the life cycle and cites Erikson and Gould, but concludes that Alonso Quixano "chooses to die" and regards his death as "an admission of failure" (*Madness and Lust: A Psychoanalytic Approach to "Don Quixote,"* 32–55, 194, 196). Johnson identifies Don Quixote's not

as a story about assessing one's life in late middle age or an altersroman, the reader is asked to rejoice at the protagonist's affirmation of his life over his dream. *Don Quixote* part 2 shows both the energy required to maintain one's illusions, once they become suspect, as well as the pain of giving them up.

Except for Alonso Quixano's dissatisfaction, which begins in part 1, he engages in assessing his life in part 2, the focus of this discussion.[11] Cervantes does not show what precedes Alonso Quixano's decision to rename himself and become a knight-errant. He may not have a shock that precipitates this drastic change. However, his leaving his household and his comrades, the priest and the barber, to take a new role and embark on a journey implies that he has sensed that a part of what he wants from life is still unfinished or missing. Since he names "renown" and the "service" of his country as his goals, Don Quixote, presumably, finds his life thus far to have been too quiet and private, and he wants some other kind of experience (27). Seeking adventures that will test his courage, he also seems worried that he is timid. In part 2, his sensitivity to an ecclesiastic's heated rebuke to him may indicate that his lack of intimacy and family is another of Don Quixote's concerns. The priest tells him to " 'Go home and bring up your children if you have any,' " to which Don Quixote angrily responds, " 'For which of the stupidities you have observed in me do you condemn and abuse me, and bid me go home and look after my house and *wife and children,* without knowing whether I have any?' " when the priest has not mentioned a wife (601, emphasis added). At the same time that he seeks different experiences, becoming Don Quixote also permits him to escape the life of Alonso Quixano: a bachelor of late middle age, without wife or children, a hidalgo or member of a class with repetitious, minimal duties along with declining means and status in that era.[12] As Don Quixote, he tries to avoid assessing his life, which his feeling of dissatisfaction might begin and his ample leisure time at home might make difficult to

---

having a wife as an important issue, as I do, but he argues that Alonso Quixano transforms himself because he is threatened by his own "middlescent-incestuous desires" for his niece (193).

11. Sabrina Hassumani first called my attention to the significant differences between parts 1 and 2. Ellen M. Anderson also focuses on part 2 of *Don Quixote* and offers a reading of his deathbed conversion that agrees substantially with mine, in her "Dreaming a True Story: The Disenchantment of the Hero in *Don Quixote,* Part 2."

12. Johnson describes Alonso Quixano's cultural milieu (*Madness and Lust,* 56–59).

suppress but which his quest will force upon him nonetheless. Indeed, the irony is that, far from allowing him to avoid assessing his life, the very quest that Don Quixote embarks upon at the outset of part 2— meeting Dulcinea—confronts him with his chief delusion, that he is a successful courtly lover, intimate with a beloved.

That Don Quixote does not say he feels old, which so often precipitates looking back over the life, is not surprising, since he habitually ignores his bodily needs, particularly in part 1, as if to deny the physical, including his age. The narrator, of course, makes the reader aware that Don Quixote has reached midlife when he pokes fun at Don Quixote's age, "bordering on fifty," as an inappropriate one for setting out on such a journey (25). Don Quixote seems unaware of reminders of age until the last third of part 2. Whereas being around younger people might force him to recognize that he belongs to a different generation, he does not see himself as older than others. He acts as lovesick in the wilderness as the youthful Cardenio and the other lovelorn shepherds. In part 2, however, as he responds more realistically to physical evidence, Don Quixote shows clearly that he feels old. In part 1, he makes several rhetorically skillful speeches, such as the one championing arms over letters, and he tells the prisoners specifically what to do after he releases them. In contrast, in part 2 he offers fatherly advice about life in general, based on his long experience and wisdom. For example, he urges Basilio and Altisidora to find suitable work (544, 676), and he counsels the Knight of the Green Coat about his son's career. He also seems to consider himself old in relation to Sancho Panza, whom he calls "my son" in part 2, rather than "friend Sancho," as he does in part 1. More important, in part 2 Don Quixote does not ignore his bodily need for food and sleep and refers to this time as his "latter years" (686). He feels full of cares (800), defeated and in despair (787, 789, 813, 825), and says that he wants to die (750, 802). Contradictory evidence certainly exists—he does not hesitate to joust with the Knight of the White Moon on the beach, nor is he surprised that he has inspired the love of a younger woman, Altisidora—yet, in general, Don Quixote is increasingly aware of his actual age and feels the pressure of time passing in part 2.

His three sallies allow Don Quixote to explore his values and attitudes, away from his household and his usual companions. He experiments with new behavior when he seeks a beloved, apparently for the first time. That Don Quixote may never have spoken to Dulcinea, his name for Aldonza Lorenzo (469), and that he certainly never sees

Aldonza Lorenzo during the course of parts 1 or 2 make her a most unusual beloved. The narrator describes her as "a very good-looking farm-girl with whom he had been at one time in love, though, so far as it is known, she never knew it nor gave a thought to the matter" (29). Although in the present time of the novel, Don Quixote has confidence that he is attractive to women (Maritornes and Altisidora), in the past, as Alonso Quixano, he has somehow never proposed to the woman he loves during the twelve years he has admired her (183). Even in her absence, however, as Dulcinea, she functions as the guiding figure who helps Don Quixote understand reality and explore his emotions because of the hopes that he entertains in relation to her.

Dulcinea's increased importance to Don Quixote is a crucial difference between parts 1 and 2.[13] Choosing her to be his lady and naming her Dulcinea are Don Quixote's last preliminary business before setting out on his first sally, but he considers her as an afterthought, only when he remembers that a knight must have a lady and after he has armor and a new name for his horse and himself. Since his idea of Aldonza Lorenzo is more important than the real person at this point, Don Quixote can transform her at will: " 'I picture her in my imagination as I would have her to be, as well in beauty as in condition' " (185). He expands his idea of Dulcinea's role gradually and in response to questions from Sancho Panza and others. However, Don Quixote does not risk trying to speak with her directly, just as he has never declared his love for Aldonza Lorenzo earlier. His goals in part 1 of achieving fame and serving Spain have the secondary result that he sends those he has helped or vanquished to El Toboso to appear before Dulcinea as his ambassadors. He also sends Sancho Panza to her to declare his love in case she should reject him (186).

In part 2, however, visiting Dulcinea is his reason for setting out. He has been emboldened at the end of part 1 by the barber/enchanter's prediction that he and Dulcinea will marry and by his belief that

---

13. Though working within the context of Jung's stages of self-discovery, Ruth El Saffar's discussion of Dulcinea, the feminine ideal, as the goal of Don Quixote's third sally in part 2 has been helpful (*Beyond Fiction: The Recovery of the Feminine in the Novels of Cervantes,* chapter 4, on *Don Quixote,* part 2, especially 85–91, 122–26, and 3–15). El Saffar sees Don Quixote's quest in part 2 as a journey into his unconsciousness and as the stage of self-discovery in which he develops a relationship with the anima, the "undesired, undesirable female," who helps the male protagonist to self-understanding, whereas I stress his becoming more aware of the real world, including time and his physical limitations.

Dulcinea has been made aware of his new heroic identity because of Sancho Panza's (false) report that Dulcinea " 'told me to tell your worship that she kissed your hands and she entreated . . . you . . . to set out at once for El Toboso, . . . for she had a great desire to see your worship' " (366–67, 238). Thus, he wants to speak to her himself and pursue their relationship. Rather than letting Rocinante choose the path, as his custom has been, he begins his third sally with a definite destination: " 'I am resolved to go [to El Toboso] . . . in order to obtain the blessing and generous permission of the peerless Dulcinea. That being granted, I expect and feel assured that I shall conclude and bring to a happy termination every perilous adventure, for nothing in life makes knights-errant more valorous than to have gained their ladies' favor' " (463). Don Quixote discovers what he needs and wants as knight-errant by trial and error as he goes along. Having added companionship by inviting Sancho Panza on his second journey, he now wants Dulcinea's direct affirmation and "favor" as he begins his third. Performing courageous deeds for her without knowing whether she appreciates his service was satisfactory in part 1 (87), but no longer. In making her more important to him and to his worth as a knight, Don Quixote unwittingly takes a risk that threatens his fantasy altogether.

As he tries to establish a relationship with her in part 2, Don Quixote's version of Dulcinea is challenged at every turn, beginning with Sancho Panza's "enchanting" her, their first adventure after setting out the third time. Cervantes is playing with identity when he has Sancho transform Dulcinea from a lady into a peasant, when she is really a farmer's daughter, but Don Quixote's having finally gathered his courage to speak to Dulcinea makes Sancho's trick devastating. In part 1, Don Quixote believes the enchantments that he invents, such as the windmill and the barber's basin. In part 2, he has more trouble overriding the physical evidence before him, particularly when he has not invented the enchantment. (A notable exception occurs when Don Quixote does not accept what his eyes tell him when he lifts the helmet of the Knight of the Mirrors and sees the face of the bachelor [500].) Thus, here, he accepts Sancho's identification of the peasant girl as Dulcinea and his explanation of her appearance, but he cannot deny what he sees, hears, and smells: a common girl on a donkey, speaking coarsely and smelling of garlic rather than perfume. Don Quixote is horrified that the person whom he strives to honor has, solely because of her connection to him, been tormented by enchanters, as he believes he has been (477). Even more shocking than her unenchanting/enchanted appearance is her rude refusal to acknowledge him. Don Quixote reinterprets her running away so completely, however, that he acts instead as if her appearance proves that *a definite bond exists between them*, recognized by Sancho and the enchanters. Thus, he takes full responsibility for her state: " '*I alone am to blame* for her misfortune and hard fate' " (478, emphasis added). He ties his career more firmly to hers by making her disenchantment and coming to thank him not only his main goal but also a crucial test of his ability as a knight, since this failure overshadows any other great deeds he might accomplish. As he later tells the Duke and the Duchess: " '[I]n her have my enemies revenged themselves upon me, and for her shall I live in ceaseless tears, until I see her in her pristine state' " (608). Don Quixote has attempted to make his fantasy real by meeting his lady, only to be cast further into his delusion by Sancho Panza's trick, the first of many impositions others make on him throughout part 2. Not even his most affirmative adventures—his victories over the lions and the Knight of the Mirrors and his reception by the Knight of the Green Overcoat and the guests at Basilio's wedding, episodes that follow immediately after the meeting with Dulcinea—can console Don Quixote for his failure with her. This first adventure in part 2 plagues him until he reaches home, as reflected in his imagining the peasant girl as part of the disastrous scene in the cave of Montesinos, in his repeatedly referring to her enchantment, and, later, in his pressing Sancho Panza to complete her cure. The number of times that Don Quixote begs or orders Sancho to give himself the prescribed number of lashes to disenchant Dulcinea—at least eight times during their journey home—indicates the extent to which her condition is on his mind (751–821).

Cervantes makes clear that during the crisis of assessing one's life, tension exists between what one can admit consciously and what one struggles not to see. The episode in the cave of Montesinos shows that Don Quixote is aware, at some level, that he can imaginatively transform neither the current condition of knights and ladies nor his relationship with Dulcinea into whatever he wishes, as he has in part 1.[14]

---

14. The cave episode has received a great deal of critical attention. El Saffar discusses what the episode reveals about Don Quixote's psyche (*Beyond Fiction*, 103–10). Ellen M. Anderson notes, "It is through the fiction of his vision [in the cave] that he can begin to dream the truth of his identity as the creator of the life-story he wishes to read through his living" ("Dreaming a True Story," 180). She sees his deathbed recovery as

Furthermore, the *un*ideal aspects of real life—ugliness, money, the exchange of sex and money, frustrated expectations, and distortions of time—are all present. In his visionary adventure, Dulcinea again rudely rejects him, except to send her companion to ask him for money, the very commodity that Don Quixote has tried to ignore as beneath his attention, neglecting to bring it on his first journey and letting Sancho Panza handle it thereafter. Not only has he been ineffective in disenchanting her, but he cannot even come up with the amount of money her emissary says she needs. Thus, as she enters his thoughts or dreams in the cave, Dulcinea refuses both to conform to Don Quixote's idealization of her as beautiful and demure and to accept his attention or devotion, except through offering to exchange her skirt, sometimes translated to a more intimate garment, a slip or petticoat, for *reales*. He resists impropriety by refusing to accept her clothing, thus denying her sexual overture, and he resents being asked for a loan. He wants to be her knight, " 'enjoying her discreet conversation,' " a description that stresses private and proper communion, not her banker dealing with her emissary in public or one who buys her favors (557). Don Quixote's later questioning of the reality of the cave episode may show his resistance to the vision of Dulcinea as farm girl whose relationship to him is not ideal. Still, his description of what happened in the cave reminds the reader that Don Quixote has been greatly affected by Sancho Panza's trick. This conglomeration, Aldonza Lorenzo/Dulcinea/peasant girl, guides Don Quixote, for, when his quest for Dulcinea fails toward the end of part 2, he can no longer sustain his delusions that he is a knight and that he has a beloved.

That Don Quixote sets out in part 2 to speak with Dulcinea makes his disappointment and disillusionment seem inevitable, for as the reader of part 1 knows, she is his own idealized creation. At the same time, however, that Cervantes prepares the reader to expect the failure of Don Quixote's quest, he also plays with complex ironies. For example, Cervantes shows that recognition by others, which should foster Don Quixote's delusion, undermines it instead. While Sancho Panza, the

---

"a reversal of his experience in the Cave of Montesinos" (184). Helena Percas de Ponseti discusses the symbolism in *Cervantes y su concepto del arte*, 420–29. John G. Weiger, *The Individuated Self: Cervantes and the Emergence of the Individual* (61–65), and Manuel Durán, *La ambigüedad en el "Quijote"* (216), both discuss the sexual implications of the adventure.

bachelor, the Duke and the Duchess, and Don Antonio seem to validate Don Quixote as a knight, they actually hinder him from acting freely by imposing their own extravagant adventures on him. Thus, he can describe his stay with the Duke and the Duchess as " 'captivity, . . . the greatest evil that can fall to the lot of man' " (741). Knighthood does not consist of " 'remaining shut up and inactive' " in comfortable homes and having to accept that Altisidora returned from the dead and that he and Sancho flew on Clavileño, but in seeking his own adventures (738). Although Don Quixote is pleased when treated as a knight by the aristocrats, he considers being under obligation to them a high price for recognition (595). More important, he must also resent others' hemming him in by constructing scenarios for him precisely when, after Sancho's enchantment of Dulcinea, he is struggling to maintain his imaginative vision. As evidence of his struggle, he accurately perceives inns as inns, is aware of danger, and is uncertain enough to consult oracles. Deliberately and elaborately playing with his role, the aristocrats call attention to it as an object for their sport. The pain and doubt that others cause by affirming Sancho's hoax reveal a vulnerability that makes Don Quixote need Dulcinea's affirmation even more.

In addition to Dulcinea's elusiveness and the imposition by Sancho and the aristocrats, a third threat to his delusion is the recognition of time and money that circumstances force upon Don Quixote. In part 1, he sets out twice on open-ended journeys without intending to return home by a certain date, and he believes that Sancho has made a journey of thirty leagues in only three days' time (239). In contrast, besides having definite destinations in part 2, Don Quixote has three reminders that he lives in calendar time: the one-year retirement to begin upon his return home agreed to as the terms of his engagement with the Knight of the White Moon, the moment when Sancho Panza completes the thirty-two hundred lashes decreed by the Duke's major-domo (posing as Merlin) to disenchant Dulcinea, and his illness. Don Quixote has become "puffed up and conceited" with his success and fame, so that his defeat in arms by the Knight of the White Moon is a devastating one, which he cannot attribute to enchantment but only to "the special preordination of heaven" (768, 792). Not only does the year's retirement remind him of calendar time, but Don Quixote also sees that he now has only the period it takes him to return from Barcelona to La Mancha in which to disenchant Dulcinea. With this defeat and the pressure of time it brings, Don Quixote redoubles his reminders to Sancho to lash himself. However, Sancho's last stroke will be an end point in time, a goal that Don Quixote therefore seeks and resists. He says that he is " 'dying of hope deferred' " because Sancho will not whip himself (757), yet he backs off easily each time Sancho makes an excuse because once the lashing is complete, Don Quixote will know whether Merlin is trustworthy and whether his lady will join him. Finally deciding, Don Quixote stoops to a bribe by offering to pay Sancho to lash himself, again connecting money with Dulcinea and moving their affair from the realm of the ideal.

At this juncture of time and place, less than a day's journey from home, Don Quixote enters the final phase of assessing his life, namely finding a way to be reconciled to a more accurate version of the life he has had. The sequence of events is worth scrutinizing in some detail. Both desperate and confident enough to risk the outcome of his quest, Don Quixote actively seeks Dulcinea along the road: "as he pursued his journey there was no woman he met that he did not approach to see if she was ["his already disenchanted"] Dulcinea del Toboso, as he held it *absolutely certain* that Merlin's promises could not lie" (821, emphasis added). Later on the same day, with the first glimpse of their village, Sancho emphasizes that they are returning home when he falls on his knees to exclaim: " 'Open your eyes, *beloved home*, and see your son Sancho Panza returning to you . . . ! Open your arms and receive also your son Don Quixote, who, if he comes vanquished by the arms of another, comes victorious over himself, which, as he himself has told me, is the greatest victory anyone can desire' " (821, emphasis added). Anxious, trapped by the rules of knight-errantry into returning to the town he escaped, and feeling far from victorious over himself, Don Quixote's response is understandably harsh: " 'Leave off this foolishness.' "

Just hours after the high point of his confidence, precisely "at the entrance of the village" and at the last moment that he can conduct himself as a knight, according to the terms of his encounter with the Knight of the White Moon, Don Quixote admits defeat. He interprets an overheard remark, " 'You'll never see it again as long as you live,' " and a hare's escaping from the greyhounds who are chasing her as bad omens that confirm the failure of his own "hunt" (822). Choosing to see these random events as relevant to him and denying Sancho Panza's attempts to revise them with words and money, Don Quixote abruptly concludes that he is " 'never to see Dulcinea again' " (822). If his quest for Dulcinea followed the pattern of the search for the absent beloved in the romances, then Don Quixote's *not* possessing her should allow him to continue as her knight. Instead, as part of the process that the story of assessing one's life traces, relinquishing Dulcinea at the threshold of the village is a step toward acknowledging that he has been deluded.

In his second encounter, his conversation with the priest and the bachelor, Don Quixote presents his plan to become a shepherd, a pitiful grasping at straws. He makes being home bearable by consoling himself with thoughts of escaping as far as he can, spending his time out of his house, while still honoring his promise to remain in the village. Hiding behind another adopted identity, Quixotiz, he plans to put another pattern borrowed from literature between himself and life. However, Don Quixote lowers his expectations, for he no longer hopes to see Dulcinea, only to "give range to his thoughts of love" for her (823).

During his third conversation after his return, his practical niece and housekeeper criticize Don Quixote's plan to be a shepherd with reminders of his age. His niece says that he is too old, for " ' "the barley stalk is too hard now to be turned into shepherd's pipes." ' " His housekeeper adds that it is too late for him, since shepherds are " 'bred and seasoned to such work almost from the time they were in diapers' " (825). Don Quixote cannot continue to " 'give free range to [his] fancies,' " because, as he feared, reality intrudes (821). He acknowledges the mundane in the form of responsibility and physical reality: " 'I know very well what my duty is; help me to bed, for I don't feel very well; and rest assured that, knight-errant now or wandering shepherd to be, I shall never fail to care for your needs, as you will see by my actions' " (825). After this point, he never speaks Dulcinea's name again, even when Sancho and the bachelor try to entice him to return to his delusion by invoking her name (825, 827, 828).

What Don Quixote's leaving at the beginning of part 1 means to him now becomes clearer as Cervantes explains what being home means to him. Leaving home has allowed him to substitute action for reviewing his life and remaining in the place he finds unsatisfactory amid people who have known him all his life and to whom he is accountable. Don Quixote has expended a great deal of energy to forestall confronting his situation, because he feared that he would have to judge that life as empty as well as nearing its end. His gains at first are numerous. Away, Don Quixote is able to experiment with a wide range of novel emotions and to test his values. Activity also pushes aside thoughts of mortality.

The strenuous activity and fasting he is capable of in part 1 reassure him that he can hold off death a while longer. Don Quixote may be physically vulnerable day-to-day, but he is courageously seeking the risks appropriate to a man-at-arms in his prime, not waiting for death like a middle-aged man whose time is gradually and uneventfully running out. Defying death with each adventure, he tries to decrease his fear and to rob death of its awesomeness. Desiring Dulcinea is a quest for youth as well, for the barber/enchanter's prophecy of marriage and children makes having a second chance at life seem possible (366–67).

Don Quixote's formulation of knight-errantry not only provides an escape and some proof that he is hearty, but it also enhances his worth. He believes that he has made a pact with life that allows him to consider himself special. Over time, if he does all he can as a knight, according to the models in the books of chivalry, working for the good of humanity and Spain, then he will be rewarded with Dulcinea, who increasingly becomes, in his mind, a source of affirmation. Until that time comes, other aspects of knight-errantry bolster his ego. The code of chivalry offers the security of having a model of what to think and do, as well as a clear rank in society. At least in part 1, his squire looks up to him, and he can imagine his beloved receiving those he has vanquished in her honor. Don Quixote is innocent, for he assumes, on the authority of his books, that he can make such a bargain.

Don Quixote strives to feel secure and in control, but, even with acclaim from the Duke and the Duchess, events in part 2, especially his failure to experience Dulcinea's sanction, prove that he cannot have his way, despite hard work, the help of others, desire, and magic. Thus, returning home, where reality is more difficult to disguise, looks like the ultimate defeat. However, while his return marks the defeat of his quest, it brings his dismantling of his delusion to a rapid conclusion. At the threshold of his village/reality, he himself destroys his quest for Dulcinea's affirmation, the one victory that he thought would fulfill him. His own recognition of the inevitable failure of his attempt to be someone he is not provides a deep shock. He connects this second shock, which deepens his initial insights about his worth and the limits of the time remaining, to his guide, but it comes from himself. However desperately he plans to become a shepherd during the next few hours, this moment on the threshold is the point at which Don Quixote loses his innocence and understands the impossibility of making a bargain to gain protection. Having relinquished his own construction, he is prepared to decide for himself whether his life has been worthwhile. The question then becomes whether Don Quixote's return to reality and his responsibilities will be accompanied by despair or acceptance.

At first, "sadness" and "melancholy" prevail, as Don Quixote mourns for the loss of his dream (825, 826). The narrator again emphasizes that Don Quixote lives in time: "Since human affairs are not eternal but all tend ever downwards from their beginning to end, and above all man's life, and as Don Quixote's enjoyed no special dispensation from heaven to slow its course, its end and close came when he least expected it. For—whether from the melancholy his defeat produced, or by heaven's will that so ordered it—a fever settled upon him and kept him in his bed for six days" (825). The narrator coyly refuses to name the cause of Don Quixote's physical illness here, but Don Quixote decisively attributes his psychological and spiritual cure to divine intervention in the passage quoted at the beginning of this discussion: " 'Blessed be Almighty God, who has shown me such goodness. In truth his mercies are boundless, and the sins of men can neither limit them nor keep them back! . . . [N]ow, by God's mercy, in my right senses, I loathe [the "profane stories of knight-errantry"] . . . that until now have been real, and have done me such harm' " (826–27). All of part 2, which is far more plotted than part 1, has prepared the reader for Don Quixote's seeing through his delusion. Cervantes has even foreshadowed the means by which the change occurs. The references to God during the meetings with the Parliament of Death in chapter 11 and the men from the braying town in chapter 27 and his discussion with Sancho Panza about the preordina-tion of heaven in chapter 66 make Don Quixote's commending divine providence believable. Saved by grace from the fate of the Don Quixote of the false version, who dies in an insane asylum, Alonso Quixano dies peacefully, confessed and surrounded by family and friends.

The working of grace is mysterious, and Cervantes does not detail Alonso Quixano's thoughts before he affirms his life, just as he has not revealed details of his dissatisfaction before he transformed himself into Don Quixote. Still, putting sadness behind him, he reaches this goal, since he sees the identity of Alonso Quixano, recognized by his community as honorable, as one worth having: " 'I am no longer Don Quixote of La Mancha, but Alonso Quixano, whose way of life won for him the name of Good' " (826). His statements, "I am no longer . . ." and "I am Alonso Quixano," not merely "I was called Don Quixote," stress both the seriousness of his intention to change his identity in pursuing his ideal and the depth of his recovery. Psychologists recognize that during a time of change, a person feels drawn back to his or her former way of thinking. Here, Don Quixote's male friends, especially Sancho Panza and the bachelor, tempt him three times to return to his delusion, because they believe that a return will restore his will to live, but Alonso Quixano resists each time by affirming his lifelong identity and rejecting his assumed one. His denouncing for his niece in a legal document the kind of suitor he has been for Aldonza Lorenzo, one who sought a woman as an ideal, further underscores his conviction. His assessment is, finally, that the person he wanted to be, and tried to be for a time, does not measure up to the person he was for most of his life. No longer innocent, he gives up his attempt to make his life fit a literary pattern and affirms the self he has been. He considers his real life, with the mundane and the unexpected that occurs unshaped by a design, to have been better than the life with imposed identity, even though real life includes death. This act of courage redeems his fear that he has been timid.

While Alonso Quixano's last confession is private, his will is public and detailed. Consoled now that he *has* responsibilities to discharge, he makes thoughtful provisions. Once again, his actions involve money. His will is not merely benevolent, but also tries to control the future according to his recovered value of practicality. He silences any future claims against Sancho Panza and reasserts himself as the master who grants favors. He tries to provide protection for his niece after his death and ties his prohibition to money. If his niece's betrothed has been encouraged by romances to view women as ideal, then his knowing that he will marry a woman without a dowry will force him either to choose to marry anyway, despite this harsh reality, or to break the engagement.

Novels in which a character looks back over his or her life often contain autobiographical echoes. In an interpolated tale in part 1, Cervantes includes some of his experience when captured by pirates, but this kind of factual autobiographical reference is not what is crucial in the altersroman. It is more to the point that Cervantes and Don Quixote both feel they are mortally ill, one at the end of writing part 2 and the other at the end of his adventures.[15] El Saffar traces another significant

15. Manuel Durán, *Cervantes*, 27–29.

autobiographical echo in *Beyond Fiction,* where her thesis is that his last four works—*La Galatea, Don Quixote* parts 1 and 2, and the *Persiles,* written one year after part 2—reveal Cervantes's personal, psychological process of moving away from ideals (the pastoral and chivalry) and becoming more comfortable with reality.[16] She documents this process primarily by showing that in the four works, Cervantes increasingly portrays women as autonomous and realistic, rather than as ideals to be pursued. After having his main character give up his quest for an idealized Dulcinea and be reconciled with reality at the end of *Don Quixote* part 2, Cervantes is able to begin the *Persiles* with the hero and heroine traveling together as equals and to conclude with their marriage. In the context of the age novel, El Saffar's reading substantiates that, for author and hero, replacing illusory ideals with reality and becoming comfortable with people of the opposite sex as well as with the traits of the opposite sex within oneself are a primary part of reaching maturity.

Cervantes shows most clearly the discrepancy between an illusion one may have about one's identity and the self one actually is, for his protagonist has two distinct names for these two versions of himself: Don Quixote and Alonso Quixano. Seeing each version more clearly for what it is in order to assess the life one has lived is the primary task of the protagonists in this study. The discussion of *Don Quixote* part 2 presents seven characteristics that recur in the six U.S. novels included here. Other quite different distinguishing features might be discovered in other works, but variations of these seven are shared by the novels studied here, as well as by the additional examples mentioned. (1) The protagonist suddenly feels old and (2) experiences a shock that disturbs some customary view of himself or herself. Together, these circumstances precipitate a period of introspection during which the protagonist reviews his or her life. (3) A younger person, usually of the same sex, offers another reminder of age. Often, the protagonist becomes a mentor to this young person. (4) A guide, usually of the opposite sex, presents an unwelcome truth and helps the protagonist to (5) a moment of deeper insight, a second shock, when he or she sees the delusion—usually about intimacy or involvement or power—

16. El Saffar, *Beyond Fiction,* 1–15.

as such. The second shock has an element of the uncanny, because the protagonist has unwittingly contributed to some aspect of it. Don Quixote, for example, has only imagined Dulcinea's responses to him, yet he is stunned when she does not come to meet him on the road. In psychological terms, these characters come to understand more deeply what they have already partially known at some level.

(6) Resolution occurs after the protagonists have faced all that they have learned from their introspection, including flaws, and have accepted responsibility for their contributions to their life. The revised version of the life reached after the second shock does not depend upon the opinion of others; it is felt to be true. At the same time, an individual achieves integrity within his or her culture as it is at that time, not in isolation. After facing the discrepancy between the closely guarded and cherished, distorted version of the life and what now is seen as a fuller, more accurate assessment, the protagonist may be able to affirm the life he or she has had, although resignation and despair are also possible responses. The joy evident in Alonso Quixano's prayer of thanksgiving and praise is echoed at the end of *Jazz* and at the end of *Mrs. Dalloway,* by Virginia Woolf, in Clarissa Dalloway's thought that "she had never been so happy. . . . No pleasure could equal, she thought, straightening the chairs, . . . this having done with the triumphs of youth, lost herself in the process of living, to find it, with a shock of delight, as the sun rose, as the day sank."[17] Physical change may occur (marriage or divorce, change of location), but psychological change is the defining feature. While reevaluating the assumptions and values one has lived by and experimenting with different behavior during the course of the assessment, the protagonist may already have begun these changes, but they are confirmed as part of the resolution. In these works, the drama of reviewing one's life is the central focus, occurring in the present time of the novel. The reader learns about the protagonist's earlier life, but only what he or she recalls as relevant to the assessment.

(7) Autobiographical echoes suggest that telling the story of assessing one's life at late middle age serves a therapeutic purpose for the author.[18] The author and protagonist may have a similar family

17. Woolf, *Mrs. Dalloway,* 282.
18. Buckley's including autobiographical echoes in his definition of the bildungsroman caused me to consider it here (*Season of Youth,* 26, 250). Buckley quotes Maugham's view of his bildungsroman, *Of Human Bondage,* in Maugham's preface to the 1963

structure. More often, they share age, gender, geographic allegiance, cultural milieu, and sensibility. The authors of the altersromane considered here portray assessing one's life in more than one way, whether that occurs in multiple plots in one work, as is the case in Faulkner's *The Mansion* and Morrison's *Jazz,* or in multiple works, as is the case in Cervantes's last four works, in James's series of "unlived life" stories, *The Ambassadors,* and a later story, "The Jolly Corner," and in Stegner's *All the Little Live Things, Angle of Repose, The Spectator Bird,* and *Recapitulation.* This repetition suggests that the process of development in late middle age is at least as difficult and complex as the earlier initiation into adulthood.

The concerns people have in later middle age identified by psychologists are accounted for by the seven distinguishing features. These characteristics are sufficiently present in each of the seven novels studied here to warrant calling a novel with a middle-aged protagonist who assesses his or her life an "age novel" or altersroman, although the characteristics emerge with different emphasis. Stegner's character studies his female guide's advice throughout the novel, whereas Didion's character's male guide gives his lesson in one crucial sentence. James devotes two books of *The Ambassadors* to Strether's thoughts after his second shock, whereas Faulkner ends *The Mansion* shortly after his character experiences his. Thus, while a list of seven characteristics may seem restrictive, the range of possible representations within each is enormous.[19]

Penguin edition: "The book did for me what I wanted, and when it was issued to the world I found myself free from the pains and unhappy recollections that tormented me" (325).

19. Two recent books that consider aspects close to my interest here are Barbara Frey Waxman, *From the Hearth to the Open Road: A Feminist Study of Aging in Contemporary Literature,* and Margaret Morganroth Gullette, *Safe at Last in the Middle Years, the Invention of the Midlife Progress Novel: Saul Bellow, Margaret Drabble, Anne Tyler, John Updike.* Waxman uses the German word *reifungsroman,* or "fiction of ripening," as an extremely broad, positive term to describe the aging experience of female protagonists aged forty to ninety, from middle age to young old age to frail old age in works by Doris Lessing, Alice Adams, Elizabeth Taylor, Paule Marshall, May Sarton, and Margaret Laurence. Gullette proposes that beginning in 1975, with the publication of Bellow's *Humboldt's Gift* and Drabble's *Realms of Gold,* writers have felt able to revise the common view that middle age is a time of decline and substitute plots that emphasize the progress a protagonist may make in the middle years. See also Annis Pratt's "Novels of Rebirth and Transformation." Pratt uses Jungian terms to discuss novels by Woolf *(To the Lighthouse),* Nin, Lessing, and Atwood in which middle-aged protagonists abandon

This study features seven novels in which the characters get far enough with the process of assessment that they reach acceptance or despair, but a word about another type is in order. Some altersromane portray closure only in the sense that the characters are satisfied that they have examined their lives and have decided on changes to make. In comparison, however, these protagonists fail to assess their lives thoroughly or to question habitual responses or to reach acceptance, so that these novels seem barely to belong to the category. However, just as the term *bildungsroman* means that the character experiences some psychological change but does not stipulate the extent of his or her self-knowledge, so too the term *altersroman* as it is used here means that the character is engaged in the review that comes with the recognition of mortality in later middle age but does not stipulate the extent of the reconciliation. Although numerous, these curtailed examples are less interesting because the protagonists do not seem as wise.

John Barth's *Chimera* tells the stories of three men who disentangle themselves from old relationships only to begin new ones that look, to the reader, to offer more of the same rather than significantly deeper self-knowledge. As Barth's Genie says in *Chimera,* " 'My project . . . is to learn where to go by discovering where I am reviewing where I've been—. . . but I'm going in circles, following my own trail!' "[20] Through a play on words, the last sentence in the book replicates this image by sending the reader back to the beginning of the book: " 'It's no *Bellerophoniad*. It's a ' " (320). The best response to fill the gap in this text is "chimera," the book's title and a mythical creature. "Going in circles," perpetual repetitive motion is an attempt to put off, endlessly, looking at the end. Characters such as the Genie, Perseus, and Bellerophon alternate between anger and grief. They seem to be scrupulously introspective, but their talk about themselves is vacant. These stories do not show their characters' deeper understanding of life, but only their frenetic attempts to have a second chance and to avoid confronting the reality that youth and early middle age are past. Feeling that they have not gotten all that they can out of life thus far, they do not forgive themselves and resolve to do better with what

---

their social connections in order to understand themselves better. Among the steps in the process, Pratt names having a male guide, who may also be a lover, but is not the protagonist's goal, and confronting figures in memory, especially parents.

20. Barth, *Chimera,* 18.

they have, but feel cheated and resolve to try again. In a variation, *Paradise,* by Donald Barthelme, the fifty-three-year-old protagonist, Simon, accepts the blame for his numerous affairs and divorce, but he uses his paralyzing guilt and scrupulous conscience to avoid having to look more closely at the reason he resists intimacy and changing his behavior.

Although Faulkner's *Absalom, Absalom!* is not an altersroman, one of the stories in the novel is an example of an assessment that concludes with even less resolution. "Impelled" to hurry because he feels that time is running out, Thomas Sutpen reviews his life when he is in his mid-fifties and wonders why his "design" for his life, "to establish a dynasty," has failed twice.[21] He tells his story to General Compson, " 'the only friend he had' " and " 'in whose confidence and discretion he trusted,' " in order to ask, " ' "Where did I make the mistake in [my design]" ' " (274, 272, 263). The general tells Sutpen that his problem is his " 'innocence,' " that he is so devoted to his design that he does not realize how deeply he insults people. Other characters frequently use the word *innocence* to describe Sutpen as they replay his assessment of his life in the novel as well.[22] More listener than guide, the general does not state his judgment that Sutpen's inquiry is not genuine and that Sutpen " 'was not listening, did not expect an answer, who had not come for pity and there was not advice that he could have taken, and justification he had already coerced from his conscience . . .' " (273). Trusting only his reason, " 'his code of logic and morality, his formula and recipe of fact and deduction,' " Sutpen does not change his attitude or behavior after this conversation, but tries to establish his dynasty twice more and ends as a " 'mad impotent old man' " (275, 180). Although the Genie, Perseus, Bellerophon, Simon, and Sutpen all remain engaged with life,

21. The quotations in this sentence are Faulkner's comments in answer to students' questions, in Frederick L. Gwynn and Joseph L. Blotner, eds., *Faulkner in the University: Class Conferences at the University of Virginia, 1957–1958,* 35, 198. Subsequent quotations in the paragraph are from *Absalom, Absalom!* and will be cited in the text parenthetically. Narrators within the novel also report Sutpen's worry that time is running out (261, 278). See David L. Minter, *The Interpreted Design as a Structural Principle in American Prose,* 192–219, to whose discussion of Sutpen I am indebted.

22. See 220, 226, 229, 232, 233, 234, 240, 246, 250, 252, 263, and 265. In *William Faulkner: The Yoknapatawpha Country,* Cleanth Brooks says that "Sutpen never really acquires wisdom, for he never loses his innocence" (308). Moreover, Brooks says, "in his innocence," Sutpen asks the wrong question, " 'Where did I make the mistake . . . ?' " when he should be asking, " 'Where did I do wrong[?]' " (297).

the assessments in these novels are incomplete, with the protagonists' repeating their past, "going in circles, following their own trail," barely holding off despair and fear of death.

The drama in the present time of *Absalom, Absalom!* is not Sutpen's assessment, but the attempt by others to interpret it forty-five years after his murder. The novel thus provides insight into the link among generations that is relevant to the altersroman, since a younger person is often the recipient of a lesson or a story offered by the protagonist as a legacy of personal and community values. Here, Sutpen does not intend this legacy, and it embodies values about which his primary interpreter, Quentin Compson, is ambivalent. Quentin is troubled by Sutpen's story partly because it is a story of failure, as is the history of his own family.

More often, a story of *Bildung* is a subplot within an altersroman, and it shows the differences between the way older and younger characters explore values. The German novel *Der Nachsommer,* or *Indian Summer,* written by Adalbert Stifter when he was fifty-two years old, focuses on the reminiscences of the older person, Baron von Risach, that are presented to a younger person, Heinrich, in a series of lengthy lessons. As much a treatise as a novel, *Der Nachsommer* details the baron's coldly rational view of life and the results of his experiments on his estate, which Heinrich receives with attention and gratitude. Indeed, Heinrich's full and confident endorsement of the baron's way of life constitutes part of the baron's affirmation of his own life. In his preface, Wendell Frye states that Stifter has written "one of the most complete statements of the 'Humanitätsideal,' . . . traditional values and culture," which will make the young man "a more complete and fulfilled human being."[23] Stifter names the novel for the baron's time of life, but he has Heinrich narrate the story. However, *Der Nachsommer* merely exaggerates what nearly every altersroman has: a young person who reminds the older person that he or she must accommodate the rising generation and who, as protégé, receives the legacy of personal and cultural values that the older person, as mentor, passes on.

Several further refinements of the definition of the altersroman are best made by considering what it is not. Not every novel in which a middle-aged character affirms his or her life resembles other works in

23. Stifter, *Der Nachsommer,* 5.

this category. For example, the widower Newland Archer in Wharton's *The Age of Innocence* reviews his life at the end of the novel before deciding not to visit Ellen Olenska, the woman with whom he was in love as a young man. Readers construe his decision and his sense that their chance for intimacy has passed as his affirmation of the life he has had. However, that review occurs in one scene, while the plot of the novel traces his adult life and does not focus on his evaluation. A novel that tells a chronological life story has a wider scope than development in later middle age, so that it seems more precise to exclude novels such as Wharton's *The Age of Innocence* or Mann's *Buddenbrooks* and to include novels in which the present time is the time of the assessment. The altersromane considered here trace the protagonist's early life only as he or she recalls incidents from the past as part of the process of assessment. For example, in *The Professor's House,* the reader learns about those aspects of Professor St. Peter's career and marriage that matter to his review of his life, but his recollections seem haphazard, as he proceeds by association, not in chronological order. Whether the narration is first or third person, the altersroman is more likely to have a central consciousness and not move among several characters, as in *Buddenbrooks*, although *Jazz, The Mansion,* and *Mrs. Dalloway* are exceptions.

The altersroman is also not simply a deathbed story, even though the protagonists in two of the novels considered here, *Don Quixote* part 2 and *A Book of Common Prayer,* die soon after they have their insights. Don Quixote does not expect to die so soon. Death comes suddenly. Grace Strasser-Mendana knows that she is dying two years before she finishes writing her narrative, but her illness is not the primary cause of her reflection. She finds the courage to reconsider her life in response to what Charlotte and Leonard Douglas teach her. She writes about her illness only twice and is involved enough in life to speak with everyone who knew Charlotte, even to travel from Central America to Buffalo to meet Charlotte's daughter. Characters in late middle age assess their lives in anticipation of the time remaining. Death is much closer for Iván Ilých in Tolstoy's *The Death of Iván Ilých,* for example.

Another advantage of defining the altersroman or "age novel" by focusing on the protagonist's psychological stage is that it allows the distinction to be made between novels that portray characters engaged in assessing their lives and those that trace development at an earlier stage, the subject of the bildungsroman. In their introduction to *The*

Voyage In: Fictions of Female Development, Elizabeth Abel, Marianne Hirsch, and Elizabeth Langland point out the limitations of the classic definition of the bildungsroman that specifies the age, education, work, and relationships of the protagonist.[24] Their expanded definition is helpful in allowing for differences between male and female development at the beginning of maturity, whether these are differences of degree, such as rate, or differences of kind, such as education and attitude toward relationships. At the same time, however, their claiming every novel that portrays development, even in memory, as a bildungsroman threatens the definition from the opposite direction, by making it too inclusive. In their introduction, Abel, Hirsch, and Langland group Flaubert's *Madame Bovary,* Fontane's *Effi Briest,* Chopin's *The Awakening,* Woolf's *Mrs. Dalloway,* and Lessing's *The Summer before the Dark* as examples of bildungsromane that portray development delayed until adulthood. Similarly, in other contexts, male characters who are older than is usual for the protagonist of a bildungsroman are considered to have delayed development. In "The *Bildungsroman,* American Style," C. Hugh Holman groups Strether, the protagonist of James's *The Ambassadors,* with the younger male protagonists in *Moby Dick, The Blithedale Romance, Daisy Miller,* and *The Great Gatsby,* among others. Critics point out that Don Quixote's embarking on his quest is inappropriate for his age. However, the reflections and development of Emma Bovary, Effi Briest, Edna Pontellier, Miles Coverdale, and Nick Carraway, all in their late twenties, resemble those of younger protagonists more than they resemble those of Clarissa Dalloway, Kate Brown, Lambert Strether, or Don Quixote, all in their forties or fifties.[25] Their age and the circumstances of the protagonists' lives should make it unlikely that *Don Quixote, The Ambassadors, Mrs. Dalloway,* and *The Summer before the Dark* are examples of the bildungsroman. However, duration of life does not ensure maturity. The distinction needs to be made on the basis of the protagonist's psychological development.

24. Abel, Hirsch, and Langland, *Voyage In,* 3–19. For another view, see Susan Fraiman's reservations about "the notion of a 'female *Bildungsroman*'" in *Unbecoming Women: British Women Writers and the Novel of Development,* ix–xiv, 1–13, 143–45.

25. Holman, "The *Bildungsroman,* American Style," 179–83. See also Elizabeth Abel, "Narrative Structure(s) and Female Development: The Case of *Mrs. Dalloway.*" For a view of Mrs. Dalloway's maturity that is closer to mine, see Blanche H. Gelfant, "Love and Conversion in 'Mrs. Dalloway,'" 234, 241–42.

Calling *Don Quixote, The Ambassadors, Mrs. Dalloway,* and *The Summer before the Dark* bildungsromane has some plausibility because Don Quixote, Strether, Clarissa Dalloway, and Kate Smith appear to be engaged in some of the same developmental struggles as characters much younger. Don Quixote sets out to honor his lady, Dulcinea, and acts like the young lovers he meets. Strether has been a husband and father, but, like Don Quixote, he remains naive about relationships and sexuality. Woolf's and Lessing's protagonists are not naive, but their reflecting on their decision to marry years ago has been discussed as "delayed" or "deferred maturation," completed only when they are fifty-two and forty-five, respectively. To explain the situation in the least familiar of these novels, Doris Lessing's *The Summer before the Dark,* Kate Brown reevaluates her marriage. Having been a homemaker and raised four children for "nearly a quarter of a century," Kate feels that she has been "passiv[e], adaptab[le]" and has not grown.[26] She worries that, except for the early intimate years with her husband and the few times recently when she has been spontaneous with her friend Mary Finchley, she has mouthed the platitudes of her culture for so long that she does not know her own feelings or have an authentic voice. During the summer, when Kate acknowledges her alienation from her husband and her anger at him for his series of casual affairs, she is able to say how she feels.

However, despite their trying to have a second chance at life or their reconsidering earlier choices, the reflections of Don Quixote, Strether, Clarissa Dalloway, and Kate Brown reveal that they are engaged in a later stage of development than characters in early adulthood. Although these characters recall choices they have made in the past, their reviewing an earlier crisis of development is not the same as their completing that development. Psychiatrists and psychologists explain this apparent reemergence of issues that were resolved at an earlier stage by saying that every developmental crisis takes earlier development into account. Erikson's "epigenetic" model of the life cycle rests on the underlying assumptions that individuals develop in "steps" and that each stage depends upon what has gone before. Although every culture stipulates

---

26. Abel, Hirsch, and Langland, *Voyage In,* 11–12 (their use of *maturity* to refer to earlier development differs from the use of the term in this study to mean development in late middle age); Abel, "Narrative Structure(s)," 177; Lessing, *Summer before the Dark,* 18.

its own "variations in tempo and intensity," a time frame exists for each stage, and at every stage an individual reviews earlier achievement.[27] Erikson notes, "[E]ach critical item of psychosocial strength discussed here [in his model of the eight stages of psychological development] is systematically related to all others . . . . Each comes to its ascendance, meets its crisis, and finds its lasting solution during the stage indicated. But they all must exist from the beginning in some form, for every act calls for an integration of all."[28] This observation helps to account for the continuity that the characters feel exists in their lives. Gould's case studies reflect his agreement with Erikson's principle that development occurs in stages and that whatever issue has been troublesome for an individual reappears for review during subsequent stages of development. Since the conflicts of early adulthood and late middle age both deal with identity, it is precisely the conflicts of early adulthood that seem to reappear during the assessment of life in late middle age. Not surprisingly, then, the novels considered in this study as altersromane, including the four by Cervantes, James, Woolf, and Lessing, all portray the process of reexamining not random events from the past but moments significant to the characters' development at an earlier stage.

The telling distinction, however, must be whether these four characters accomplish the developmental tasks of midlife. Are they able to confront their deepest fears and desires and to admit the flaws and decisions that have influenced the course of their lives without being overwhelmed? Are they able to feel secure while discarding lifelong assumptions that now seem wrong? *Mrs. Dalloway, The Ambassadors,* and *Don Quixote* part 2 offer insight into the first question. During her day of reflection, Clarissa Dalloway flutteringly examines what she sees as a major decision that has shaped her life, what others judge to be her faults, and what she is defensive about as her worst failings. She still feels "the grief, the anguish" for having hurt Peter Walsh by rejecting his proposal years ago, but, having been happy with Richard Dalloway, she does not regret her decision (10). Midway through the day, Clarissa feels "desperately unhappy" when she considers the criticism of others, who, she believes, accuse her of giving parties because "she enjoyed imposing herself," is a "snob," or is "childish." She quickly revises what others call

27. Erikson, *Childhood and Society,* 269–74.
28. Ibid., 271. Even in the revised edition, where Erikson stresses the continuity of development, he still insists that resolution occurs.

a fault into one of her two attributes: " 'That's what I do it [give parties]
for,' she said, speaking aloud, to life. . . . They're an offering . . . . An
offering for the sake of offering, perhaps. Anyhow, it was her gift," she
thinks (183–85). Clarissa is also able to dispatch other shortcomings, such
as her "virginity" and her having failed her husband at Constantinople
(46, 178). However, she has trouble acknowledging what she judges to
be her unacceptable private passions—hatred and ambition—as part of
her image of herself. Clarissa's hatred is complicated, being directed
at her daughter's tutor as well as at the judgment she feels the tutor
makes of her as a woman in the upper class. In the morning, she can
distract herself from thinking about "this hatred," which becomes "that
hatred" two pages later, with flowers and preparation for her party. She
banishes her thoughts with a reprimand, "Nonsense, nonsense!" (17,
19). But in the evening, Clarissa feels alive when she is reminded of her
hatred for her daughter's tutor: "That was satisfying; that was real."
She seems grateful for strong emotion: "She hated her: she loved her.
It was enemies one wanted, not friends—" (265–66). Thus, she finds a
way to admit such an improper fury. Her ambition is also tinged initially
with defensiveness, for she has not been the success that she wanted to
be. Later in the evening, moved by news of a young man's suicide and
feeling "forced to stand here" alone in a room, Clarissa acknowledges
finally that "[s]he had schemed; she had pilfered. She was never wholly
admirable. She had wanted success. Lady Bexborough and the rest of
it" (282). She comforts herself by thinking about Richard, and affirms
her life in her exclamation of joy quoted earlier: "[S]he had never been
so happy" (282). Nature and routine help her as they have earlier in the
day. She looks out her window at the sky, the part of nature that has
made her childhood home in the country present to her in her adult
home in the city. "[S]traightening the chairs, pushing in one book on
the shelf," and catching a glimpse of the old lady across the way whom
she has watched for years, Clarissa regains her security. She understands
the suicide, but she returns to her party, her life.

Strether accepts the implied criticism of the younger people in *The
Ambassadors* and holds himself accountable for not having lived more
fully, but in his final conversations in Paris, particularly his exchange
with Madame de Vionnet, he speaks with assurance about his decisions.
His development is the topic of the next chapter.

Alonso Quixano could not have prevented or slowed the social
changes in Spain that have occurred during his lifetime, but he does

hold himself responsible for his choices that have given his own life its shape. He relinquishes his innocence when he acknowledges what he feels has been his flaw, his timidity. Without bitterness or cynicism, in his will, he honors the values of his culture in the present time, not the ideals that he tried to impose as Don Quixote. He faces death with courage and provides a model for his witnesses.

The Summer before the Dark provides insight into discarding outworn assumptions. Kate Brown understands that her choosing to remain in her marriage is different from her twenty-two-year-old friend's deciding whether to marry, if only because the younger woman is " 'looking for . . . a man who knows all the answers and can say, Do this, Do that.' " Having abandoned her own belief that a husband could provide that kind of buffer from life, Kate thinks, " 'There's no such animal' " (243).

Interestingly, whereas many bildungsromane have pessimistic endings, the protagonist of an altersroman often affirms life and avoids despair. Along with their awareness that they are older, that many major decisions are in the past, and that death will come, the protagonists also feel satisfaction. They do not have the same sense of possibility that many young characters have, but the peace from the acceptance of the self they have been and now are is, for some, a great consolation. To return to *Mrs. Dalloway,* at the end of Clarissa Dalloway's party, fifty-two-year-old Peter Walsh tells Sally Seton, fifty-five, "There's Elizabeth [the Dalloways' seventeen-year-old daughter] . . . she feels not half what we feel, not yet." He has just characterized being "mature" (not "old," Sally has corrected him) as the age when "one could watch, one could understand, and one did not lose the power of feeling," as opposed to youth, "[w]hen . . . one was too much excited to know people" (294–95). Although they admire Elizabeth, both Peter and Sally judge that the gains that come from being their own age outweigh the advantages of youth.

2

"A Modest Retreat"

The Ambassadors, by Henry James

Beginning in 1893 when he was fifty years old and ending in 1908, James wrote several stories and a novel in which middle-aged men look back over their lives to assess the choices they have made. In "The Middle Years," "The Altar of the Dead," "The Beast in the Jungle," *The Ambassadors*, and "The Jolly Corner," a middle-aged man suddenly sees that he has lived only in a limited way because he has somehow not taken risks or sought experience.[1] The short stories have been called the "unlived life" series, a term that emphasizes loss.[2] However, in each story, with the exception of "The Beast in the Jungle," the hero feels an emotional release that does not merely lead to remorse, but offers him an insight that he regards as an advantage. Since the first three stories end with the hero's death or approaching death immediately after his insight, they show the insight occurring abruptly without the process of reconciliation that usually follows in an altersroman. Although James's fuller consideration of the process in *The Ambassadors* is the major focus of this chapter, it is appropriate to begin by looking at assessment in the first three stories together because they function like sketches or cartoons for the novel. As short stories requiring selection and compression, they present those elements of the altersroman that they do contain in stark relief. The fourth story, "The Jolly Corner," originally published five years after *The Ambassadors*, finishes the series with greater affirmation than the earlier stories contain.

I

The situations of the three men in "The Middle Years," "The Altar of the Dead," and "The Beast in the Jungle" are remarkably similar. The

---

1. Citations to James's stories and novels are cited hereafter parenthetically by volume and page number.
2. Krishna Baldev Vaid, *Technique in the Tales of Henry James*, 224.

men are alone, they feel old, and they receive a shock. The first condition is peculiar to James's versions of the life-assessment story, but the latter are two of its regular features. Dencombe has been married but has been a widower for many years. Stransom's fiancée died just before their marriage, and he has recently quarreled with his only companion, the woman who mourns at his altar. Marcher has never married, although he has had a lifelong companion, May Bartram. Intimacy turns out to be so frightening to him that, without naming it, he has imagined it as a life-threatening beast. The stories do not show Stransom and Marcher engaged in careers. Although the narrator says that George Stransom has "done many things in the world" (17:4), the reader has no direct evidence of his "immersion in large affairs," always seeing him in the chapel where he lights candles in remembrance of acquaintances who have died or in the rooms of the woman who mourns Acton Hague (17:12). Marcher uses his premonition that some momentous event will occur to him as a reason to excuse himself from experience in every arena. Dencombe has "the sense of ebbing time, of shrinking opportunity" (16:80). George Stransom is fifty-five at the beginning of the tale and perhaps sixty at the end, yet he sees himself as "a quiet elderly man" (17:17) and feels that he has "well reached the age of renouncement" (17:50). Although "The Beast in the Jungle" covers the longest period of time—"year after year" and Marcher's "whole middle life" (17:86)—Marcher's passivity causes the reader to see him as having reached the "age of renouncement" at an early age. Each of these characters might remain unaware without the shock that precipitates his insight: Dencombe has a serious illness, Stransom's plan that his altar devoted to his dead be perpetuated by another mourner is challenged, and May Bartram dies.

As these characters assess their lives in response to the shocks they receive, each finds that he has misunderstood his situation. Unlike the other two, Dencombe has enjoyed his life as an observer and writer (16:81–82). His single regret is that he judges he has only just begun to write well, "to get abreast of" literature (16:95). If he has misjudged anything, Doctor Hugh tells him, he has *under*estimated his accomplishments.

In contrast, circumstances force Stransom and Marcher to acknowledge more fundamental delusions. Stransom has deceived himself into believing that he knows himself and that he shows a "generous heart" (17:6) in remembering the dead, especially his dead fiancée, Mary Antrim. The reader, however, understands from the first two episodes that he is not generous or humble, but petty and self-righteous. Stransom believes that by remembering "his own" dead, he is superior even to those considered "most generous" who still do "nothing" for their dead (17:5). His feeling of superiority becomes especially clear in section 2, when he meets a widowed friend and his new wife: "The frivolity, the indecency of it [Paul's remarrying so quickly, as if his first wife had been a "domestic servant he had replaced"] made Stransom's eyes fill; and he had that evening a sturdy sense that he alone, in a world without delicacy, had a right to hold up his head" (17:10).

Stransom's "devotion" at his altar and his plan that the mourning woman will complete his scheme by lighting a candle for him after his death occupy his emotions and provide him with a view of his life that not only satisfies him for many years but also acts as "an immense escape from the actual" and conceals the truth (17:4). His mourning for Mary Antrim constitutes a celebration of his loss of her, a way of keeping this wound present to the exclusion of what turns out to have been a more devastating wound, the loss of the companionship of his only close friend, Acton Hague, by betrayal. Because he feels like "a stone . . . cold, . . . horribly cold" at the news of Acton Hague's death, Stransom can deny that this death matters or requires commemoration (17:12). Stransom believes that he has limited his emotional life out of devotion to his fiancée, but he discovers that another cause is the pain from his betrayal by Hague. When Stransom learns the coincidence that his fellow mourner has devoted all the candles on his altar to the one person he has excluded, a man who has somehow "wronged" both of them, this information touches the wound he has spent his life trying to deny (17:43). Combined with his quarrel with the woman, the shock of discovering that his grudge against Hague is still so powerful nearly kills Stransom.

Marcher is the most obviously deluded and self-centered of the three men. The narrator undercuts Marcher's calling himself a "man of feeling" (17:79) by revealing that he is isolated and detached (17:78–79, 82, 93). He suppresses his feelings and judges everything in relation to himself. Thus, when he learns that May is seriously ill, he imagines that he shows concern for *her* when he thinks about "the loss she herself might suffer. 'What if she should have to die before knowing, before seeing—[the leap of his beast]?'" (17:94). He fails to understand what May has offered him all along, even during her most direct appeal, when, "all draped and all soft," she approaches him and says, "'It's never too late'" (17:103, 105). However, "he only waited . . . [before] her contact imponderably pressing" (17:106). Not until the end of the story does he understand what May has known, that he is the man to whom nothing has happened.

Works with older male protagonists often include female characters of similar age who act as guides to facilitate the men's insight and help them express their emotions. These works also hold womanly activity, such as ministering at a sickbed, and emotions traditionally associated with women in high regard.[3] In "The Middle Years," Doctor Hugh's ministering and devotion have feminine aspects, and the narrator describes the men's experience as a love relationship: Doctor Hugh talks about his "infatuation" with Dencombe, and he "put[s] into his young voice the ring of a marriage-bell" (16:104, 105). Stransom has two female guides, the mourner of his enemy and his "vision" of his dead fiancée who inspires his act of forgiveness. Stransom takes a lesson from Hague's mourner, who shows him that she has forgiven Hague for what Stransom considers must have been an injury greater than the one he has suffered (17:43). Originating as his own inspiration and resulting in an outpouring of compassion, Stransom's vision is an interesting variation of the female guide. Like the imagined Dulcinea, the guide whom Don Quixote tries to honor and please, Stransom's imagined vision of Mary Antrim inspires him to express an emotion contrary to his usual righteousness.

Marcher's female guide, May, refuses to do more than lightly suggest the possibility of intimacy to Marcher: she asks if his great sense was about "'falling in love'" (17:72). Then, when he fails to respond, out of love and concern for him, she keeps him ignorant that he has missed intimacy (17:111, 113). May touches him only after her death, when her absence accomplishes what her presence could not. Marcher comes to know how much passion has been available to him and how much he has refused only when he comprehends the devastating grief of a stranger. The shock overwhelms him and forces him to revise his version of his life completely. May's telling him that she hopes he will never know about his beast is her coded way of assuring him that she understands

---

3. Gould, *Transformations,* discusses the ways that men and women explore and expand traditional gender roles in midlife (235–36, 278). See also the case studies he reports in section 5 (232–66).

what he has missed and that she forgives him, *should* he ever find out for himself and need such consolation.

Following the shock of seeing their lives in a new way, the men in these three short stories all experience incredible emotional release, an abbreviated version of the reconciliation that the altersroman explores in greater detail. In the earliest of these life-assessment tales, Dencombe reaches reconciliation, but rather quickly and with more direct outside help. Dencombe's ease is appropriate, however, because he has best understood his life all along. He is satisfied with the praise of a discriminating, admiring reader, and he accepts Doctor Hugh's consolation: " 'What people "could have done" is mainly what they've in fact done' " (16:103). "The Middle Years" also lacks the emotional depth that comes from the character's evaluating his life by exploring relationships because it focuses exclusively on evaluating the life by exploring career.

Stransom is fortunate in a different way, in that he has the opportunity to make peace and thereby "open his spirit" even though his enemy has been dead for many years and he himself is about to die (17:56). His emotions when he forgives his enemy do not shatter him as Marcher's revelation in the cemetery does, since the result is that Stransom can be reconciled with the woman who has been "the partner of his long worship" (17:56). Like Dencombe's glimpse of immortality through his novels, Stransom also hopes that his plan for his altar, now revised, will give him a kind of immortality. His seeing Mary Antrim in a vision allows him to affirm his having devoted his life to her memory rather than seeking intimacy with another. (In the later work, *The Ambassadors*, James can allow Strether to consult a sexual woman for such aid, but here the guide is an internal construct and virginal.)

Nurturing companions offer crucial help to Stransom and Dencombe, whereas the only person who could console Marcher and allow him to make amends is dead. At the moment of his insight, Marcher cannot approve himself to say that he has done his best, as Dencombe can, and the story ends without showing reconciliation. In his preface, James calls Marcher's "career . . . a great negative adventure" (17:x). However, the narrator indicates that Marcher's insight is worth any pain he will have, for he now has at least "the taste of life" (17:126). For Marcher, as well as for Stransom, to know, even though it is to know all he has not understood throughout his life, and to feel, even if his chief emotion is regret, are better than remaining naive and cold.

These stories, as well as *The Ambassadors* and "The Jolly Corner," also contain a final aspect of the altersroman: autobiographical echoes, which are common in the bildungsroman as well. In his preface, writing about Stransom and Marcher, James ruefully notes, "[M]y attested predilection for poor sensitive gentlemen almost embarrasses me as I march!" (17:ix). These characters are males, approximately James's age at the time the stories were written or slightly older. All deal with limited personal experience and lack of intimacy as the crucial concerns of the hero. "The Altar of the Dead" and *The Ambassadors* also portray men who have experienced an excess of grief for the death of a fiancée or wife, similar to James's response to the death of his beloved cousin Minny Temple. Critics are confident that James portrayed his cousin at the beginning and end of his career, in *The Portrait of a Lady* and *The Wings of the Dove*. It is reasonable, therefore, to hypothesize that, like Stransom and Strether, the excess of grief that prevented the reinvestment of James's emotions occurred at Minny Temple's death. Other autobiographical elements, particularly the absence of a wife or intimate companion and lack of a business career, as well as the repeated focus on mature male characters who have to face their illusions, seem to indicate that James was working out a personal dilemma. "The Middle Years," about a novelist who, like James, continuously revises his work, explores his vocation. In these stories, he evaluates the choices he had made about his life, especially his decisions to live abroad and be a writer, decisions that for him have meant he has observed more than he has experienced directly. In particular, James's life reflects Strether's belief that insight itself is sufficient to constitute experience.[4]

Despite critics' praise for the short stories as well crafted, the first three men, especially in comparison to Strether and Spencer Brydon, are not complex, nor is there much for the reader to interpret. The narrators present them unambiguously as emotionally limited. However, James's other two "sensitive gentlemen" of middle age, Strether in *The Ambassadors* and Spencer Brydon in "The Jolly Corner," have

---

4. Christof Wegelin notes the temptation to identify Strether, "among all of James's important characters," with his author: "*The Ambassadors* is a story of the making of an American cosmopolitan and in this sense may be regarded as a kind of spiritual autobiography" (*The Image of Europe in Henry James,* 88). Sara S. Chapman notes the autobiographical elements in "The Middle Years" in *Henry James's Portrait of the Writer as Hero,* 54, 135–36.

greater emotional capacity as well as time ahead of them to live with the insights they gain. With *The Ambassadors,* James more bravely explores in detail the hero's reaction to the insight that he has not lived. His most optimistic assessment story, "The Jolly Corner," affirms the hero's genteel, "frivolous" life as a full one (17:450).

<h2 style="text-align:center">II</h2>

Like Stransom and Marcher, Strether also feels "ancient and weary," although he is only fifty-five (22:258).[5] Strether does not seem to be alone, since he is about to marry a woman who feels such confidence in their sharing similar values that she has sent him to Paris as her ambassador to bring her son, Chad, home to Massachusetts and the family business. However, as he describes their relationship, he begins to see it not as one of intimacy between partners but one in which he does a domineering woman's bidding. By financing the Review he edits, Mrs. Newsome confers Strether's " 'one presentable little scrap of identity' " along with his income (21:65). Further, Strether feels that since his wife's death years before, he has lived in "solitude," with "people enough all around" him but only "three or four persons *in*" his life (21:83). He holds himself responsible not only for his isolation but also for its chief result, his son's death: "He had again and again made out for himself that he might have kept his little boy . . . if he had not in those years so insanely given himself to merely missing the mother" (21:84). He feels "remorse" for "an opportunity lost." Like Marcher who waits all his life for the beast to leap, Strether characterizes himself as having "tak[en] things as they came," with the result being "an empty present" and "so much achievement missed" (21:83).

James's concern in *The Ambassadors* is not how Strether comes to his first insight, which occurs in Gloriani's garden, that he has made a "mistake" not to live more fully, but how, with the help of a female guide (Chad's lover, Madame de Vionnet), he understands all that he has missed and then reconciles himself to the life he has had. James needs only the first five of the twelve books in the novel to bring Strether to the insight that Dencombe, Stransom, and Marcher have at the end of their stories. At the outset, anticipating the change marriage will

5. See also 22:102, 148, 306.

make, Strether has already begun to review his life, and the shock of experiencing Europeans and Europeanized Americans spurs his self-examination further. Having had his initial insight, Strether slowly accepts its implications, alternately seeking Madame de Vionnet's company and resisting her, protecting himself by vacillating between seeing and not seeing. This process provides the drama of the middle section of *The Ambassadors,* Books Sixth through Tenth. James repeats this structure a second time. In Book Eleventh, at the beginning of the third section of the novel, Strether has a second great insight that extends his understanding of what he has missed. In Books Eleventh and Twelfth, with Madame de Vionnet's continuing help, he resolves the tension between his trying to find the courage to change and his trying to find a way to affirm the life he has had. Repeating the assessment process at a deeper level and including the confusion and detail of Strether's thoughts are James's contribution to the altersroman.

The Ambassadors follows the process of assessing one's life as described in Chapter 1, including a feature not evident in the short stories discussed, namely, a younger character of the same gender as the protagonist who serves two conflicting purposes. The younger person is the source of the protagonist's first recognition that he or she is older or is in the parents' generation. Strether feels old in relation to Chad, little Bilham, and Mamie Pocock. In particular, he is surprised to find that Chad has matured into an interesting adult. Second, while this insight is unwelcome, the younger character still elicits devotion from the older one. Strether wishes that Chad and little Bilham will enjoy the possibilities he has lost, and his envy and regret generously inspire him to nurture them by giving warnings and advice. At the same time, once he decides to expose his own errors by giving advice, Strether becomes a harsh judge when the younger men do not adopt his plans. The younger person in the altersroman is an unwitting sign of time's passage and teaches the protagonist the lesson that trying to turn back time or to live vicariously by telling another what to do is not possible. Strether realizes that he has no control over Chad's life, that all he has is his own life. He cannot justify his life through Chad, and this disappointment contributes to his "cursing" Chad at the end (22:324).

The protagonist who is assessing his or her life often guides a younger character while being guided by someone of the opposite sex. Maria Gostrey, who has received critics' attention for her role as confidante, introduces herself to Strether as a "guide" (21:18), but Madame de

Vionnet fulfills more of the functions of the female guide.[6] Indeed, Strether ends his role as ambassador as much because of his immediate emotional response to Madame de Vionnet as because of Maria Gostrey's helping him to see Mrs. Newsome differently. Fully engaged in life, Madame de Vionnet is experienced and forceful, circumspect, sensitive, and intuitive. One of the many functions a guide may serve is to teach the protagonist to accept a circumstance about which he or she has been judgmental or intolerant before. In this case, Madame de Vionnet encourages Strether to consider a situation from a woman's point of view while suspending his moral views, "his odious ascetic suspicion of any form of beauty," and his fixed idea of women as threatening (21:193–94). Although she works primarily in her own behalf, Madame de Vionnet cares deeply for others, unlike Mrs. Newsome, who concentrates so exclusively on her own goals that she can be described as " 'all cold thought' " (22:237). After he has met her and has had his insight in Gloriani's garden that he has not lived, James makes Strether's relationship with Madame de Vionnet the main focus of Books Sixth through Tenth, a section in which they have five significant private conversations and one other meeting. Her guidance in this section prepares him first to see and then to accept the life he has had, which occurs during his reconciliation in Books Eleventh and Twelfth.

The repetition of the word *save* in the two scenes that begin Book Sixth and end Book Tenth marks what is in between as the middle section of *The Ambassadors*. James begins Book Sixth with Strether's promise to Madame de Vionnet during his first visit to her home to "save" her and ends Book Tenth with his actually trying to do so

6. For a summary of the help Maria Gostrey gives Strether, see J. A. Ward, "*The Ambassadors* as Conversion Experience," 352, 366, 369, 373. Ward also recognizes the importance of Madame de Vionnet to Strether's growth, naming the moment in Book Seventh when Strether decides to align himself with her as "the exact point" in the novel that "dramatize[s] Strether's conversion" (366). Recent discussions of Madame de Vionnet as Strether's tutor include Julie Rivkin, "The Logic of Delegation in *The Ambassadors*," 829–30; Maud Ellmann, " 'The Intimate Difference': Power and Representation in *The Ambassadors*," 506, 511–13; and Patricia L. Walton, *The Disruption of the Feminine in Henry James*, 115–18. Walton sees women as three models for reading in *The Ambassadors*. Mrs. Newsome imposes meaning, Maria Gostrey "prepares the way for the polysemous Marie de Vionnet and thus helps Strether to evolve away from single referential reading toward polyvocal interpretation" (110). Walton argues that Madame de Vionnet presents herself as a text for Strether to read and form his own meanings (116–17).

by speaking up for her to Mrs. Newsome's daughter, Sarah. The day after he visits Gloriani's garden, Strether honors his promise to Chad to try to like Madame de Vionnet. Initially, Madame de Vionnet's guidance takes the form of giving Strether many new impressions, such as appreciating what her home reveals about her heritage and seeing her "rare unlikeness to the women he had known" (21:244–46). Her rhetorical skill is formidable. By asking " 'for common civility,' " she makes "their encounter a relation," and he realizes not only that "he accepted their relation" but also that it will become "whatever she might choose to make it" (21:249, 252). By the end of that meeting, Strether is sufficiently under her charm to use an "exorbitant word": " 'I'll *save* you if I can' " (21:255, emphasis added). Here, at the beginning of their acquaintance, Strether responds so strongly to a woman whom he finds "remarkably attractive" that he commits his first act of disloyalty to Mrs. Newsome by keeping Madame de Vionnet a secret from her, an important sign of autonomy elsewhere in James's work (21:258).[7] He does not take the same precaution by keeping Maria Gostrey a secret from Mrs. Newsome, for, as Strether's friend Waymarsh observes, " 'I don't know as there's any real harm in her [Gostrey]' " (22:102).

Having begun Book Sixth with Strether's declaring his commitment to Madame de Vionnet, James has him speak up to Sarah Pocock on her behalf at the end of Book Tenth, just after he recalls his promise to "save" her (22:204–6). This occasion is the second time that Strether speaks up to anyone (he has told Chad to stay in Paris in Book Seventh). He is clearly aware of what he is doing and fearful, yet even hearing Sarah Pocock insult Madame de Vionnet as being not " 'even an apology for a decent woman' " fails to shake his allegiance and admiration (22:202). James emphasizes this scene as a climactic point in the novel by repeating "all's at an end" three times in the last paragraph. Sarah is the first to say, " 'All's at an end,' " which Strether repeats twice in his thoughts: " 'It probably *was* all at an end' " (22:206). Between these two scenes, Madame de Vionnet carefully guides Strether, as detailed analysis of this section will show.

---

7. 21:258. Verena Tarrant is disloyal in this way to Olive Chancellor in *The Bostonians* (chapters 24, 25). Nanda Brookenham in *The Awkward Age* and Maggie Verver in *The Golden Bowl* use their knowledge, while keeping it secret, as part of their strategy with others.

Given Strether's resistance to women generally, his appreciating Madame de Vionnet is especially remarkable and is a tribute to her rhetorical skill and the depth of her engagement with others. By revealing how deeply she cares for Chad while counting on someone else to describe her marriage so that she does not have to sound plaintive, Madame de Vionnet shows herself to Strether as both tasteful and vulnerable and thus elicits his sympathy for her position. Unlike Chad and Maria Gostrey, she never enumerates all that he may lose by siding with her. She openly flatters Strether, telling him that " 'No one feels so much as *you*' " (22:126).

However, while acknowledging her merits, Strether understands better than the rest of the Americans (except Mamie [22:151]) that Chad is "the product of [Madame de Vionnet's] genius," in part because he has felt her teach *him* "to take his ease" in conversation with her as well (22:116). Even with beneficial results, this kind of shaping can be sinister, and Strether feels threatened at times, particularly during their luncheon, when he feels he is "diving deep" and has "touched bottom," water imagery that recurs when he feels overwhelmed. Strether's thoughts reflect his sense of losing himself: "the situation was running away with him" and "he could only give himself up" (22:13, 14). Strether quickly realizes that Madame de Vionnet can be ruthless as well as adroit, using him rather than guiding him.[8] When he boldly asks her for the favor of not asking her daughter if she loves Chad, Strether imagines that Madame de Vionnet uses his request as a "golden nail" that she "drive[s] in" to make him "more closely connected" to her (21:276). This image of the nail occurs to Strether again during their luncheon when she reminds him of his promise to "save" her (22:22). When he meets her already visiting the Pococks, Madame de Vionnet "publicly drew him into her boat" and betrays him by calling Strether's friendship with Maria Gostrey to Sarah Pocock's attention (22:94, 100–101). It is remarkable that he does not resist, but more so that he decides to "[take] up an oar" to keep her boat afloat (22:94–95)

8. For a negative view of Madame de Vionnet as actress and jealous mother, see Judith Woolf, *Henry James: The Major Novels*, 95, 99–100. Edwin Sill Fussell pays particular attention to James's association of Madame de Vionnet with Napoleon: she "is inevitably associated with *les gloires* of French Literature and Art, on the one hand, making her the most wonderful person the world has ever seen, and, on the other hand, with the Violent Needless Destruction of Public Buildings and Monuments (which are also art), making her dangerous" (*The French Side of Henry James*, 195).

(although he silently follows her lead here, in contrast to his acting on his own at the end of Book Tenth). The many images of Strether as victim in the middle section—his feeling "on the scaffold now" and " '*used* . . . [t]o the last drop of [his] blood' "—underscore the serious consequences of both his participating with Madame de Vionnet and his reflection.[9]

James emphasizes the pain and confusion of assessing one's life in other ways as well. Strether feels contrary emotions and contradicts himself. He wants to see everything, but he also tries not to see at times.[10] He requires that others be gentle with him, such as when he practically asks little Bilham to deny the sexual aspect of Chad's relationship by calling it a "virtuous attachment" (21:180; compare 22:299). Although Strether believes that he has hidden his illusions, he has conveyed them well enough so that the Parisians, who want to manipulate him, and Maria Gostrey can tell him just as much as he wants to hear. Little Bilham tells Strether, " '[Y]ou're not a person to whom it's easy to tell things you don't want to know' " (21:202; compare · 22:287). Strether also protects himself by claiming that his adventure is vicarious and that, as ambassador, he has a minor role. Maria Gostrey tries to have him admit that he " 'came to find out *all*,' " but he means the "all" that happens to other people (21:189). However, at other times, he says that he is " 'making up late for what I didn't have early' " and having " 'enough [fun] to last me for the rest of my days' " (22:51, 35). He understands early on that his association with Madame de Vionnet is a risk to his engagement as well as to his job and financial security, but he accepts only gradually that the adventure is his, not just Chad's, and that he jeopardizes his way of living entirely. Here again, Madame de Vionnet is a help to him by preventing his denial. When he says, " 'It's not my affair,' " she answers, " 'I beg your pardon. It's just there that, since you've taken it up and are committed to it, it most intensely

---

9. 22:186, 140. Tony Tanner lists the violent imagery in *The Ambassadors* and notes that all the violence is internal, in the characters' consciousnesses, not in the "outer world" ("The Watcher from the Balcony: Henry James's *The Ambassadors*," 39). Tanner reads Strether's position at the end of the novel, "alone, homeless, somehow out of life, but full of a priceless vision," more negatively than I do (51).

10. 22:3–5, 266, 325. See Daniel Mark Fogel, *Henry James and the Structure of the Romantic Imagination*, 28, for a discussion of Strether's "process of vision" as dialectical. Fogel locates the dialectic in Strether's ideas, as well as in the characters' dialogue, the novel's phrases and sentences, and the overall structure of the books.

becomes yours' " (22:22). The altersroman depicts a confused search
for understanding of one's situation in midlife, and *The Ambassadors*
contains a meticulously detailed portrait of bewildered reflection, one
in which the narrator does not clarify each of Strether's contradictory
thoughts. Here, James's ambiguity and fine psychological discrimina-
tion provide realism. Strether's reassessment in Books Eleventh and
Twelfth of his insights in Books Sixth through Tenth clears up some
of his confusion, however, so that he can speak and act decisively in his
own behalf.

Strether's second shock finally destroys his partial version of Chad's
relationship that has allowed him to keep his romantic view of Madame
de Vionnet and his illusions about himself as well. Much has been made
of Strether's squeamishness about sex, but what he learns in the country
in Book Eleventh involves far more. Certainly, Strether is stunned that
Madame de Vionnet and Chad have planned to be together overnight
and embarrassed that he has deliberately not thought about sex: "[H]e
had dressed the possibility in vagueness, as a little girl might have
dressed her doll" (22:266). He admits to himself that he is prudish
when he agrees that Madame de Vionnet is correct to lie for his sake,
although he later believes that her motive is not to protect him but
to observe good taste (22:265, 277). He is also relieved that he does
not have to sanction their going together to the hotel. His insight
has a more significant aspect, however. Strether has understood during
an earlier conversation with Chad that the two are intimate (22:222,
225), but he understands the nature of intimacy, its companionship
and the vulnerability of each partner, here only when he interrupts
their communion. Their communicating without words and the "deep
identities between them" are strong enough for Chad to trust that
Madame de Vionnet will handle Strether in the way that suits the couple
best, and sitting with them Strether feels very "lonely" (22:225). They
have each other, and he has no one. Strether also sees again how much
Madame de Vionnet risks for Chad and how much Chad can hurt her,
because of her passion for him. Her vulnerability scares him more than
sexuality, which is just a sign or an aspect of their intimacy. As he puts it
during their last conversation, " 'You're afraid for your life!' " (22:285).
What he sees in the country has the tremendous effect that it does on
Strether because intimacy is the biggest part of what he has missed in
life. At this point, he understands fully what his own words, "live all you
can," include. With his insight that he has missed such close personal

connection impressed upon him more forcefully, Strether assesses his
life in earnest.

However, Strether feels as if he is "still in search of something that
would work," that would allow him to formulate a more positive version
of his life (22:163). One can come to a realization that there is more to
life than what he or she has had and go in several directions, with these
extremes: change before it is too late or remain consistent and forge
a reconciliation between the new insight and the way one is. Strether
takes the second alternative. He affirms and values the way he has been
in three ways, while resisting major change.

First, he is American. After his visit to the *Postes et Télégraphes* to
reply to Madame de Vionnet, Strether sees himself as being part of a
community in Paris, yet soon after, he rejects that community and will
go home to Massachusetts, even though "everything there [will be]
changed for him" (22:271, 294). He appreciates the French *jeune fille*,
Jeanne de Vionnet, but he genuinely likes the American girl, Mamie
Pocock (22:149, 152, 166). He tells little Bilham to marry Mamie so that
he can be "expiatory": " 'I've been sacrificing so to strange gods that
I feel I want to put on record, somehow, my fidelity—fundamentally
unchanged after all—to our own' " (22:167). The "strange gods" do
not replace his own.[11]

Second, he affirms himself for having been faithful to his personal
rules throughout. For example, he decides that his "mission" is finished
once the Pococks arrive, so that he can now visit Madame de Vionnet
freely and no longer consider himself unfaithful to Mrs. Newsome
(22:60, 70). His inner rules also require that he not "do anything
because he had missed something else, because he was sore or sorry
or impoverished, because he was maltreated or desperate; he wished to
do everything because he was lucid and quiet, *just the same for himself
on all essential points as he had ever been*" (22:294–95, emphasis added).
Thus, it is in character for Strether to reject the two suggestions that
he remain in Europe from Madame de Vionnet and Maria Gostrey

11. Wegelin succinctly states the nature of Strether's American character: "His vision
was formed in Woollett, and he knows what inevitable cast that mold has given to the
'helpless jelly' of his consciousness" (*Image of Europe,* 102). See Fussell for an enumer-
ation of the details of Paris—weather, streets, restaurants, interiors—that Strether as
tourist experiences (*French Side,* chapter 7). He notes the nostalgic aspect of James's
use of French particulars, since James recalls Paris as it was during the year he lived
there, 1876–1877 (185).

in order " 'to be right. . . . Not, out of the whole affair, to have got anything for myself' " (22:326). In one sense he means being "right" with Mrs. Newsome by not having gained anything for himself other than his "impressions," but he also means that he wants to be "right" with himself, the self he has been all his life, which requires remaining consistent. Earlier, during his carriage ride with Jim Pocock, Strether rationalizes his not choosing marriage, saying that it would be to lose himself as Jim has lost himself to Sarah (22:82). With this rationalization, he also affirms his choice not to have remarried thus far. In this way, his decision to say good-bye to Madame de Vionnet and Maria Gostrey makes sense for him and gives him peace. Madame de Vionnet tells Strether that he could not act differently, " 'for this evidently is the way you live, and it's what—we're agreed—is the best way' " (22:283). Soon after, Strether repeats this idea in his own words to Maria Gostrey: " 'That's the way [being right] that . . . you yourself would be the first to want me. And I can't do anything else' " (22:326). To remain true to the self he has been, Strether cannot become Europeanized or marry.

Third, Strether affirms himself in the somewhat negative sense that he sees no one else he would rather be, although he is fond of little Bilham. He is condescending toward Jim Pocock and Waymarsh. Although he envies Chad in Gloriani's garden, he does not wish he were Chad by the end, primarily because Chad lacks imagination, a strong criticism for Strether to make (22:225). Strether also stops envying Chad when he sees him as not so transformed as he thought, able to leave "effort" to others, able to switch allegiance and abandon Madame de Vionnet, able to be intrigued with advertising and a bribe of money (22:315–17). Chad's change has been only superficially civilizing; he has the manners to be "easy" in any situation. Thus, Strether also validates his own values by rejecting as models men who lack imagination and integrity.

Ultimately, Strether does not change much, but before looking further at his consistency, the two major differences he does experience that take him beyond innocence must be examined. Strether characterizes himself as an observer, and he values this activity, even though he understands that he has not been an acute observer until the end of his months in Paris. He seems satisfied to witness intimacy, without having the experience himself. For such a sensitive man, "impressions *are* experience," and seeing *is* his adventure.[12] Seeing others, however, is less important than his seeing himself and his life. His expanded self-knowledge is a tremendous change for Strether.

When he affirms that the activity of seeing is important, Strether also accepts the consequences of seeing and accepts that the observer is visible and has moral responsibility. Once he understands that just his presence as an ambassador, a role that he has consistently downplayed, has increased the intimacy between Chad and Madame de Vionnet (22:278), Strether accepts that even if he wants to be ignored and excused from responsibility, exclusive spectatorship is not possible. He also learns to act and speak for himself and is less anxious to please others. It is Strether who forces the meeting in the country by calling out to Chad and Madame de Vionnet in the boat, when they would prefer to " 'cut' him" and "show nothing" (22:258, 257). Whereas at the outset, he seeks confirmation of his views from several people, Strether later feels so confident in his own judgment that he disregards others' opinions, particularly those of the newly arrived American ambassadors at the climax of Book Tenth. He says that he is no longer "booked" by Mrs. Newsome's vision (22:241). In severing his ties, Strether faces the future alone: " 'I must meet my fate alone, and I *shall*' " (22:165). He exercises his will to choose his stance again, once he has seen what it is and what the alternatives are. He will continue to live outwardly as he has before, although with greater self-knowledge. Because he no longer worries about what everyone else thinks, he also gains freedom. Although he describes himself as a victim and his returning alone to Woollett outwardly resembles the renunciation of other Jamesian characters, Strether's confident assertions and his seeing his life differently argue against such a negative interpretation.

Admiring "a woman like" Madame de Vionnet is Strether's other major change, as his last two conversations with her, which occur in Books Eleventh and Twelfth, show. All the while that he has been accepting that her relationship with Chad is a "virtuous attachment," he has been ambivalent, alternately encouraging and resisting her. When Maria Gostrey calls Madame de Vionnet " 'good,' " Strether

---

12. See 22:185, 228, 233 for instances where Strether values seeing or realizes that he does not see everything. The quotation is from James's essay "The Art of Fiction," in *Partial Portraits,* 389.

corrects her with " 'good for Chad,' " indicating that he has abandoned moral absolutes (22:242). Finally, however, with the full disclosure of her sexuality and her artfulness, which earlier would have caused his revulsion, he instead feels awe at the depth of her feeling. During their last meeting, which is in Book Twelfth and which James called "probably the most beautiful and interesting morsel in the book . . . . really the climax,"[13] Strether praises Madame de Vionnet without restraint:

> [M]emory and fancy couldn't help being enlisted for her. She might intend what she would, but this was beyond anything she could intend, with things from far back—tyrannies of history, facts of type, values, as the painters said, of expression—all working for her and giving her the supreme chance . . . to be natural and simple. She had never, with him, been more so; or if it was the perfection of art it would never . . . be proved against her.
>
> What was truly wonderful was her way of differing so from time to time without detriment to her simplicity. (22:276)

It is now precisely her artful variety that Strether admires more than the rigidity of Mrs. Newsome, which he once held in highest regard as evidence of strong character. Indeed, Strether's biggest disappointment in Mrs. Newsome becomes "that she does n't admit surprises" and cannot even entertain Strether's version of Chad's affair (22:239). Strether treats Madame de Vionnet's love for Chad in the most respectful manner. He tells Madame de Vionnet that she has made Chad " 'the most precious present I've ever seen made' " (22:283). What has seemed like decadence and self-indulgence in New England is civilization, "knowing how to live," in France (22:264). Strether's praise also reflects a change in James's attitude, since, for the first time, with Madame de Vionnet, he portrays a sophisticated, sensuous woman in a favorable way, an adulterer who is not punished.[14]

---

13. James, "Project of Novel by Henry James," 413.
14. In her master's thesis, Sabrina Hassumani offers a favorable reading of Madame de Vionnet as James's most successful mature woman, neither earth mother nor shrew but enabling and independent. See also "The Individual and the Form: Maggie Verver's Tactics in *The Golden Bowl*," in which I trace James's heroines as moving from a less worldly woman (Isabel Archer in *The Portrait of a Lady*) to a worldly but less assertive woman (Nanda in *The Awkward Age*) to a forceful, sexual wife (Maggie Verver in *The Golden Bowl*), a development that corroborates the claim here that James is able to feel more tolerant and less fearful of sensuous women.

Thus, despite the threat she poses to Strether's integrity, Madame de Vionnet is his crucial guide: his three strongest positive acts in the novel center on her. He can speak forcefully on her behalf at the end of Book Tenth, and he can insist upon being acknowledged by the lovers in the boat, as previously discussed. Most important, Strether cares less about deserting or being deserted by the Newsomes at the end than about having Madame de Vionnet's affirmation of him, which is the only outside affirmation that he wants. In Book Eleventh, he imagines that he asks her to like him not for what he has " 'done' for [her]," but for "anything else" she chooses (22:251). That is, he wants her to like him apart from his connection with Chad, not out of gratitude or for anything he does but for who he is. Although he must have some certainty by this time that Madame de Vionnet likes him, Strether's request, unspoken but understood during this conversation, still exposes him before another in a way that he does not allow elsewhere. If he has never resisted Mrs. Newsome's commands, it is unlikely that he has ever asked for this sort of recognition from her or that their communication has been reciprocal. Likewise, he paraphrases Madame de Vionnet's affirmation of him as living the best way that he can to Maria Gostrey, at the same time that he does not grant her the permission he extends to Madame de Vionnet to formulate a version of his life (22:325–27, 283). Madame de Vionnet's response, that she understands the way he lives and that it is " 'the best way' " for him, spoken during their last conversation, gives Strether the means to accept his life (22:283). She shows him that he is desirable, desired. And his asking for her good opinion is not simply a request, but is also his gift to her in return: he says that he respects her enough to care whether she likes him. Most interesting, although he begins his appeal for her good opinion in Book Eleventh, before his great insight in the country, Strether completes it afterward, with greater knowledge of her situation.

While he affirms himself as a moral American and an imaginative observer who has witnessed a great deal and who interprets for himself, Strether still fails to make a fundamental change. That is, he makes some revision without choosing intimacy, even after he sees that it can occur on a different basis from the American examples he has observed, where the female controls the male. His rejecting marriage for himself is significant. Strether's telling little Bilham to " 'Live!' " seems to be close to "marry," for when he puts his advice to little Bilham into practical terms, twice he suggests marriage, first with Jeanne de Vionnet and then with Mamie Pocock (21:277, 22:166). He understands that Chad and Madame de Vionnet cannot marry, but he urges Chad to continue their relationship, and he honors it as if it were marriage.

Strether refuses Maria Gostrey's proposal, not unconsciously as John Marcher refuses May Bartram's offer, but very deliberately. Seeing what he has missed and how he might embrace change, he lacks the courage to do so. In his "Project of Novel by Henry James" (written for his publisher), James says that it is "too late" for Strether.[15] It has also been argued that Strether refuses both women because each is unsuitable, but his statements in the conversations in Book Twelfth seem to foreclose the possibility of intimacy forever, making their unsuitability for him beside the point. Strether chooses still to miss this part of life. He finds courage for other people and courage for himself to see but not to do. Strether is afraid to take a risk, even though he has told little Bilham that it is a mistake not to. He speaks most revealingly with Madame de Vionnet only when he sees her as vulnerable and pitiful, hence less threatening to him and less likely to rebuff him. He admits how much she has meant to him only after he has decided to leave Paris and has therefore precluded a long-term relationship: " 'Ah but you've *had* me!' he declared, at the door, with an emphasis that made an end" (22:289). When he makes his "modest retreat," the process of assessment and reconciliation is over (22:322). Strether chooses to continue as he was before, and he has found a way, with Madame de Vionnet's help, to affirm and be satisfied with "impressions as experience." Her knowing him fully and still feeling regard for him help him to avoid despair and to find value in the life he regretted having led in the early chapters when he first came to Europe.

III

At this point, the process of assessing one's life as it appears in "The Jolly Corner" can be presented quickly. As in *The Ambassadors,* the initial shock involves a journey, but this time, the protagonist, Spencer Brydon, a single man, returns from his home in Europe to his birthplace in New York City in order to complete business transactions involving

---

15. James, "Project of Novel," 415. Fogel, *Henry James,* 45, discusses its being "too late" as James's *donnée.*

his family's property. Brydon is pleased to discover that he has business acumen and worries that he has wasted his talent by living " 'a selfish frivolous scandalous life' " (17:450). As his second shock, an "alter ego" appears to him in his childhood home on the "jolly corner" and shows him the self he might have become had he remained in the United States and been a businessman (17:456). His American self is portrayed as aggressive ("evil, odious, blatant, vulgar") as well as physically maimed (17:477). Even though his alter ego has had "a life larger than his own" and possesses "a rage of personality before which his own collapsed," Brydon rejects this alternate possibility and affirms the life he has led, one that has allowed him to develop sensitivity and taste (17:477).

James retreats from the sensuous and sophisticated female guide, Madame de Vionnet, to portray the guide as a maternal comforter in Alice Staverton. She first subtly encourages Brydon to consider the self he might have become and then does not allow him to deny that he has the potential within him to have become the "awful beast," "a black stranger," a "brute" (17:482–83). Most important, while she does not "like [his potential self] *better*" than Brydon, she does "accept" and "pity" him, thereby implying that no part of Brydon—potential or actual—is repulsive to her (17:484–85). Having aided his vision, her words and actions at the end confirm that Brydon has chosen well. Thus, "The Jolly Corner," which might have been another tale of "unlived life," instead offers a positive ending to the series of stories discussed here, since Brydon sees clearly and prefers the self that he is. He has time before him and a supportive companion. Nevertheless, as in the other short stories, the process is rapid.

Critics, in particular Leon Edel, have pointed out the numerous autobiographical aspects of "The Jolly Corner."[16] For the purposes of the altersroman, it is important to note that James did consider the different shape his life would have had if he had not chosen to live abroad. Although he is not Spencer Brydon, James creates a story in which the protagonist strongly affirms the same choice that the author made.

16. Edel, *Henry James, the Master: 1901–1916*, 315–17. See also Fogel, "A New Reading of Henry James's 'The Jolly Corner.' "

3

"Room to Think"

The Professor's House, by Willa Cather

In Willa Cather's *The Professor's House,* Godfrey St. Peter seems to have had a far richer family and professional life than Strether, yet he ends in despair because he cannot do more than minimally affirm the life he has had. Threatened with having to leave his two special places in his rented house, his study and his garden, St. Peter "review[s] his life, trying to see where he had made his mistake, to account for the fact that he now wanted to run away from everything he had intensely cared for."[1] Although his review seems to center on Tom Outland, his former student and companion, Tom has been gone for about ten years and dead for eight, so that the "everything" that the Professor now wants "to run away from," the true focus of his assessment, is his wife and domestic situation. His most important insight comes from his contrasting his ideal friendship with Tom and his marriage; he realizes that beyond having ceased to love Lillian and to value their intimacy, he no longer respects her. St. Peter asserts that he does "not regret his life" (267); however, he is more convincing when he says that his adult years "were not his life at all, but a chain of events which had happened to him," so distasteful that he decides to go back to being his "idle," "primitive," "solitary," "wise" preadolescent self (263–65). Thus, he affirms only the years of his life before sexuality and responsibility. While still protesting his first shock, having to move from his house, the Professor has a second one, a "temporary release from consciousness" when the gas stove in his study goes out, after which he resolves to adopt his female guide's values and "learn to live without delight" (282). Whereas the second shock in the altersroman usually causes a revision of

---

1. Cather, *The Professor's House,* 275. I have had helpful conversations about Cather's work with Patricia Lee Yongue and Elizabeth B. Cargill.

the protagonist's firmly held version of his life, here, the accident leads to renunciation rather than profound insight. His choosing Augusta, his wife's sewing woman, as his guide and his interpretation of her philosophy, along with Tom's absence and his resistance to his wife, keep Professor St. Peter isolated and help him to stop short of reaching the fullest view of his situation and therefore of being able to come to terms with the life he has had. Because he does not deal directly with the decline of his marriage or Tom's departure to fight in World War I, omitting in particular *his* part in these ruptures, the Professor continues to see himself as a victim, "hurt" and apathetic rather than angry and responsible (283).

Cather has chosen her protagonist's profession with great effect. Looked up to by his undergraduate students, Professor St. Peter is used to believing that he is superior. He stakes out a high moral position in his stance in campus politics, in his choosing to do "uncommercial" research, and in his lecture championing art and religion over science (141). (Interestingly, he ignores his criticism of science when thinking about Tom, whom he acknowledges as a scientist and gifted mathematician, meticulously cataloging his discoveries on the mesa and conducting experiments in the physics lab.) However, arrogance often tinges the Professor's opinions, such as when he reduces science to technology and when he pronounces harsh judgments of everyone, especially women. The Professor is so used to considering himself an authority that it takes numerous assaults, coming one after the other, to penetrate his invulnerability and impel him to assess his life.

St. Peter feels old only at the end of his year of reflection, rather than at the outset, although his wife accuses him of having been "posing" as older than his age for nearly two years (162). The Professor's shock has, instead, three other intricately connected causes: his response to two aspects of his work and his having to move to a new house. First, he has recently finished the eight-volume history of the Spanish adventurers in the Southwest, the work that has occupied his evenings, weekends, holidays, and summers for fifteen years. Its receiving a prestigious and lucrative award honors the work but also clearly marks the original design as complete and the volumes as public objects. The Professor is, as the narrator's main name for him indicates, his position, and he has defined that role for himself. Whereas he could have met his contractual obligations just by teaching, he has also enjoyed his scholarship. His writing has kept him distant from his family, as many of his memories indicate, but it is also what makes him special in his own mind: only one other person at his college, a scientist, has shared his ambition to teach well and to carry on substantial research. Thus, with his major life's work complete, his feeling compelled to assess his life is not surprising.

Second, during the entire year, the Professor is always just about to edit and write an introductory portrait for Tom Outland's diary, an undertaking that also causes him to review his life. Editing places Tom's handwriting on his desk where he can see it all the time and recalls the unrecoverable past. Tom contributed to the last four volumes of the history by retracing the explorers' routes through the Southwest with the Professor; however, his greatest contribution has been the friendship they shared, the "romance . . . of the mind—of the imagination" that he offered the Professor (258). St. Peter's choosing to dwell on this part of his past by setting himself the task of writing the memoir, and then his having difficulty completing it, will be considered later, with Tom's role as the young person for whom the protagonist serves as mentor.

The third factor, moving from their rented house to the new house his wife has just built with the prize money, is the precipitating cause of the Professor's assessment, and it is intricately tied to the other two, since St. Peter must leave the scene of his work and his domestic life, including his daughters' growing up and his meeting Tom. In particular, he will have to abandon the two places where he has spent most of his time, both enclosed spaces. The first is his unconventional attic study where he wrote the history and the second, his walled French garden, his other major project and "the comfort of his life" for more than twenty years, which he associates closely with Tom (14). The carefully designed and tended garden, created as his subtly rebellious response to Lillian's demand that he participate in family life after Rosamond's birth, is the place where he and Tom met, where Tom and the "two little girls" talked, and later, where he and Tom "used to sit and talk half through the warm, soft nights" (112, 124–25, 14–15). In the new house, St. Peter will not have the comforting glimpse of the "innocent blue" water of Lake Michigan, twelve miles away, that he has from the third-floor study window or the view of "the trees that told where the Physics building stood," where Tom conducted his experiments for three years (29, 90). He will no longer be able to pretend that his daughters live downstairs, still harmonious and constituting his family, or that Tom could reenter the garden, as he admits he fantasizes (263). Again, he must acknowledge that time has passed.

Tom Outland reminds the Professor of his age and has literally been St. Peter's student. However, Cather's portrait of Tom differs from the function of the young person as it appears in other novels in this study in three ways. First, Tom's *absence,* not his presence, causes the Professor to feel old. This experience occurs in the present time of the novel, when he accepts that Tom, who has been gone for approximately ten years, cannot return. Earlier, even when he recognized Tom as belonging to the next generation, his student and "an older brother" to his daughters, Rosamond and Kathleen, the Professor perceived Tom not as a reminder of his age but as the occasion of his renewed interest in life (132). Far from resenting Tom's youth, the Professor was grateful that Tom let him live vicariously and renew himself in his company: "Just when the morning brightness of the world was wearing off for him, along came Outland and brought him a kind of second youth. Through Outland's studies, long after they had ceased to be pupil and master, he had been able to experience afresh things that had grown dull with use. . . . To share his thoughts was to see old perspectives transformed by new effects of light" (258). Other passages in which the Professor thinks about Tom are as lyrical as this one, especially when he recalls their being together in his garden, and this marks another difference between *The Professor's House* and the other novels discussed here: the young person is both a more heroic figure and a more intimate companion than is usually the case. For example, when he thinks back to the summer when his relationship with Tom bloomed, while his wife and daughters were away and he was living a "bachelor life," St. Peter idealizes their simplified masculine life, with minimum responsibility and an orderly schedule of work, dining, and conversation:

> [Tom] and St. Peter were often together in the evening, and on fine afternoons they went swimming. Every Saturday . . . he and Tom went to the lake and spent the day in his sail-boat. It was just the sort of summer St. Peter liked . . . . Over a [meal prepared by the Professor] they talked and watched night fall in the garden. If the evening happened to be rainy or chilly, they sat inside and read Lucretius. It was on one of those rainy nights, before the fire in the dining room, that Tom at last told the story he had always kept back. (176)

The Professor's thoughts reveal his sense that he and Tom became intimate friends when "St. Peter got to know all there was behind [Tom's] reserve" (175). Whereas continued contact with Chad causes Strether to see him more realistically, the absent Tom is more difficult to demythologize.

Moreover, recalling their camaraderie allows St. Peter a cover for venting his misogyny, since, in addition to sharing learning, love of the Southwest, and a judgmental attitude, the two men also resist women, with a hint that they must do so to protect themselves. For example, when the Professor muses about Euripides' decision to become a hermit, he blames the behavior of women: "I wonder whether [houses had become insupportable to him] because he had observed women so closely all his life" (156). When they read Lucretius, they consider the goal of imperturbability, being without strong emotions, reached through temperance and retirement from public life (176). In Tom's narrative, peopled almost exclusively by men who teach, pray, employ, nurse, and cook for one another, Tom honors the "self-sacrificing friendship and disinterested love . . . among the day-labourers," while he blames wives for the philandering of husbands, easily accepts the priest's unduly complicated hypothetical reconstruction of Mother Eve as unfaithful wife, and scorns the relationship and values of the only married couple in his narrative, the Bixbys (172). Whereas Lillian St. Peter has been the one to express repeated interest in Tom's life, he refuses to answer her questions and tells "the story he had always kept back" only to the Professor (175).[2] The celebration of male camaraderie and youth, highlighted by its position at the end of the domestic book 1 and implicit throughout book 2, recurs as part of the Professor's resolution in book 3 and will be considered later, after looking at his portrait of Lillian, the companion who remains to him, a portrait that is as harsh as that of Tom is positive, and at the two serious gaps in his assessment.

To sum up, then, by immersing himself in editing Tom Outland's diary, Professor St. Peter seems to have chosen the one task that will

2. The novel has several inconsistencies on this point. For example, earlier the narrator says, "Tom never took up the story of his own life again, either with the Professor or Mrs. St. Peter," whereas in the passage just cited, the Professor recalls that Tom related his entire narrative (124, 175–76). The text seems to indicate that Tom also tells his story to Rosamond and Kathleen, although the difference may be that he tells them his story only in pieces whereas he offers the Professor a linear narrative.

allow him to console himself in the face of change and disorientation and to distract himself from thinking about his present relationships with women, which threaten to overwhelm him. The Professor resolutely sets about reconstructing his memory of Tom, at one point to protect it after his son-in-law Louie has exploited Tom at a meeting of engineers: "With his right elbow on the table, his eyes on the floor [of his study], he began recalling as clearly and definitely as he could every incident of that bright, windy spring day when he first saw Tom Outland" (112). He also conjures up Tom for his project by keeping Tom's Mexican blanket, described as being " 'like his skin,' " available to cover himself when he lies down on the "box-couch" in the study (59, 130). Here, too, revisions as threatening as Louie's occur, since the blanket's originally strong "horsey" smell that recalls Tom is fading after nearly two decades indoors. At the same time, for all the hours he sits at his desk, including Christmas Day, the Professor procrastinates actually editing the diary and writing the introduction because he seems afraid that when he finishes and publishes it, he will have relinquished both his last private tie to Tom and his justification for spending so much time in the old house away from his family. More important, prolonging thinking about Tom allows him to distract himself for a time from considering the issue that he will soon reveal is most on his mind: not the past, but his present situation with Lillian. Don Quixote tries to avoid his thoughts at home by setting out on a quest for Dulcinea, only to have the very goal he chooses force him to confront his central dilemma, lack of intimacy. Likewise, Professor St. Peter's quest for Tom can only temporarily obscure what he is trying to avoid before it makes his assessment of his life impossible to forestall. That is, both Don Quixote and the Professor undertake a quest to avoid the assessment that the quest thrusts upon them. In *The Professor's House,* editing the diary brings St. Peter pain by reminding him of his loss of an ideal companion. His recollection of that relationship serves as a strong contrast with his relationship with Lillian, which has become unbearable.

While mourning his absent companion, the Professor treats the thirty-year companion he does have, Lillian, coldly at best and with hostility at the end. His not wanting to eat with her becomes his not wanting to live with her by the end of his reflection (46, 274). He condescendingly explains Lillian's interest in their sons-in-law, for example, by deciding that "she was less intelligent and more sensible than he had thought her" (79). He never thinks of her uncritically. Even when he finds her attractive at the opera, he compares her "softened" features with her usual look (94). He thinks matter-of-factly that husbands and wives "*always* meet with something which suddenly or gradually makes a difference" so that he does not explore the fact that they are no longer lovers (49, emphasis added). Their estrangement is of long duration, since Tom's graduation in 1910, when Tom replaced her as his companion. He and Lillian do not renew their intimacy after Tom's departure in 1914 or his death in 1916. St. Peter's present decision to go back to being the boy he was ensures that intimacy will not be renewed. Although he admits Lillian's accusation that he has been unfaithful to her with Tom, the Professor is remarkably guiltless about that, even when she surprises and touches him by revealing her pain: "There was something lonely and forgiving in her voice, something that spoke of an old wound, healed and hardened and hopeless. 'You, you too?' he breathed in amazement" (94). He does not consider asking her forgiveness or continuing their conversation. Their communication ends abruptly after her disclosure of emotion, and this is their pattern. The narrator points out that Lillian reaches out to her husband in her thoughts, such as when she "aches for him," understands that Rosamond has hurt him, and worries about his health, but she rarely verbalizes these concerns, and when she does, he either avoids conversation or has a fit of temper.[3] Likewise, when he does express his emotion, wailing, " 'What am I to do about that garden in the end, Lillian? Destroy it? Or leave it to the mercy of the next tenants?' " his wife does not respond but continues her conversation with her son-in-law (77). Although he says that he "got to know all there was" about Tom, the Professor thinks, "[t]he heart of another is a dark forest, always, no matter how close it has been to one's own" when considering Lillian (175, 95). In the shipwreck fantasy he has later on the night that Lillian has revealed her feelings, instead of choosing a time when he and Lillian were happy, he wishes that he could have

---

3. Lillian reaches out to her husband verbally and nonverbally (48, 94, 97, 102, 133, 134, 155, 162–63). Although the reader rarely receives a glimpse of Lillian's thoughts, her comment that " '[o]ne must go on living' " indicates that she has perhaps assessed her life (94). Her actions suggest that while she has chosen to remain with St. Peter, she now focuses on her sons-in-law and daughters for companionship. She has found a way to make her life meaningful despite her husband's aloofness.

stopped time at the moment when he is in the company of a crew of men, without an intimate companion, just after he has envisioned the plan for his histories. (Indeed, the Professor consistently celebrates the beginnings of relationships—his vision of his histories, his courtship, his first sight of Tom, Tom's first meal with the family, Tom's first telling of his and Roddy's story—describing these magical moments in vivid detail while referring casually to daily activities.) He refuses a trip to Paris, the scene of their courtship, with Lillian, in part because *her* admirer, her son-in-law Louie, is arranging it and in part because he will not go with Lillian on the trip that he still regrets that he and Tom never made (260, 163–64). Since he can excuse himself by observing that his wife has now found occupation with her sons-in-law, St. Peter focuses instead on his image of himself as the betrayed rather than the betrayer of Lillian, and it is this feeling that he cannot overcome.

The Professor is typical of the protagonists of the altersroman in that, once embarked on reviewing his life, he peevishly thinks about all that does not satisfy him in order to avoid considering his own role in what has happened. However, ranting about his family's materialism is not simply a distraction, as it seems to be at first, since Lillian's new house, in contrast with the Professor's house, embodies their central conflict. Bought with his prize money, the new house represents his life's work and reifies it, while also being a vulgar display, insulting to the Professor's values. He is offended by Lillian's paying lavish attention to decoration and her purchasing conveniences, such as individual bathrooms, bedrooms, and closets, as well as an electric bell under the dining table to summon the second maid to clear the plates. He ignores his own "selfish[ness] about personal pleasures . . . [and] luxuries," such as sherry, which is at times difficult to distinguish from his wife's love of comfort, except that bathrooms are more mundane (26–27). The new house has been Lillian's project, apparently without much consultation with the Professor, since, *after* they have moved, she asks him to " 'admit that [he likes] having [his] own bath' " and separate bedroom (34). The point is that, so long as he dwells on the ostentation of their new house, St. Peter can focus on the difference between his and his wife's values and can blame her for their lack of intimacy, enjoying indignation and disgust rather than feeling grief and responsibility for what he has lost. The other new house in the novel, "Outland," Rosamond and Louie Marsellus's Norwegian country manor, made possible by Tom's intellectual pursuits, also allows the Professor to rail against materialism and Louie's appropriation of Tom. Outland is a showy house as well, extravagant enough to preserve Tom's laboratory as a museum exhibit, static space, unused but kept intact. The Professor's reaction is contradictory, if understandable. He chooses to remain distant by disdaining others for their materialism, only to complain that he has indeed become isolated and lonely, even in the midst of family.

The Professor seeks to place the blame for their estrangement on Lillian's materialism, while the novel also blames the Professor's arrogance, idiosyncrasies, and coldness, commonplace reasons. St. Peter's thoughts after reading Tom's diary and just before his accident reveal a more complex aspect of their relationship, however, when he describes Lillian: "Her nature was intense and positive; it was like a chiselled surface, a die, a stamp upon which he could not be beaten out any longer. If her character were reduced to an heraldic device, it would be a hand (a beautiful hand) holding flaming arrows—the shafts of her violent loves and hates, her clear-cut ambitions" (274–75). The images of Lillian that the Professor uses, phallic and warlike, deceptively beautiful, describe destructive forces that crush, pierce, burn, and cut. In his image, he is the victim of her force, being "beaten out" and having his features obliterated by her imposition of her own pattern. The images clearly express his sense that he must do as she wishes, that he is living her life. She shapes his life as surely as she has designed the new house. He must escape or she will overpower him. Whereas earlier he thinks that "he must school himself to bear" her increasing intolerance, here he concludes "that he now wanted to run away from everything he had intensely cared for" (35, 275). In addition to some direct evidence of Lillian's control, the chief preparatory clue that the text offers to explain such hostile imagery is the Professor's observation that Lillian now lives in the careers of her sons-in-law "as she had once done in his" (79). That is, her personality is devouring. The imagery of this late passage is unambiguous, and it becomes part of the Professor's justification for holding himself apart at the end. On the other hand, however forceful, the Professor's images present but do not explore his hostility and his feeling like a victim. His response here resembles his easy admission earlier that Tom came between them, which does not constitute a full assessment of the state of his marriage before Tom arrived. In neither case does he look at what he has contributed, or failed to contribute, to the marital relationship. In sum, St. Peter imagines himself as acted upon. He seems to review his entire life, but he spends time reflecting upon wrongs done to him and does not look closely at places where he might be to blame.

Before turning to the help his female guide offers and the resolution of his year of reflection, it is worth noting the second issue that the Professor sidesteps, his day-to-day relationship with Tom and Tom's departure, because it too shows his habit of looking at what happened to him rather than at what he has done. The strong emotion evident in the Professor's recapitulation of his and Tom's relationship in books 1 and 3 attempts to conceal that it omits their words and thoughts during the four years that he and the Professor are so intimate that they make Lillian jealous. The engaging narrative in book 2, "Tom Outland's Story," also encourages the reader not to notice the crucial gap in *The Professor's House*. Only once does the Professor think about their customary meetings during these four years in the "alcove" on campus and Tom's visits to his study, which are especially remarkable since his daughters and wife have not been welcome there (173). Neither do the Professor's reminiscences include conversations during their two trips to the Southwest.

Most significant, though, is the brief treatment of Tom's abruptly leaving the Professor and his fiancée, Rosamond, to fight in World War I. Tom's leaving for the front is a socially acceptable, even heroic act that the Professor cannot complain about or call a betrayal easily. Tom's motivation may indeed be altruistic and have nothing to do with the Professor. However, several features of the Professor's clinical description of Tom's leaving with his former teacher bear scrutiny. "The rugged old man stayed in Hamilton only four days, but in that time Outland made up his mind, had a will drawn, packed, and said good-bye. He sailed with Father Duchene on the *Rochambeau*" (260). To take the items in this brief account in order, first, Tom's former teacher replaces St. Peter as his mentor. Although the Professor says that their relationship had gone beyond the cordiality between teacher and student, Tom's relationships with Roddy, Father Duchene, St. Peter, and Dr. Crane suggest that he needs a paternal figure, even in his late twenties. It is as if the only way that Tom can break away from one powerful figure is to switch to another. Second, Tom's haste to join the foreign legion before the United States has entered the war is also remarkable. While he repeats the common view that Tom is impulsive, the Professor also argues that he was purposeful (61). After all, Tom has

engaged in the extended negotiations necessary to secure the patent
for his gas, refusing a trip to Paris with the Professor to do so (259).
Thus, the text allows the possibility that Tom's leaving, while hasty,
is not simply an impulsive response to Father Duchene's fervor. Still,
this view of Tom's haste as running away is barely suggested, since
it is Louie, who never met Tom, who uses the strong verbs "dashed
off" and "bolted to the front" that mean to escape (40). Third, Tom
takes time to make a will naming Rosamond as his heir, but he does
not marry her, as was often the case with young men preparing to go
to war. Tom probably gave St. Peter his blanket at this time, but his
saying good-bye is omitted, as is a direct statement of his motivation.
That the Professor mentions no further communication with Tom, no
letters from the front, for two years, raises the possibility that Tom's
enlisting is an act of disloyalty. Tom may be extricating himself, however
drastically, from a situation he has decided is unsuitable. The Professor
then uses florid language to end the brief description of Tom's abrupt
departure: "[C]hance, in one great catastrophe, swept away all youth
and all palms, and almost Time itself," and concludes that it is best that
Tom is dead (260). Again, as in the metaphoric description of Lillian,
the poetry distracts the reader from the conversations and emotions
that the Professor does not examine.

Motivation is complex and ambiguous in *The Professor's House*, but
in this case, the consequences are clear. The Professor clearly considers
Tom's leaving Hamilton a crucial event in his own life. Whatever Tom's
reasons for enlisting, the Professor feels abandoned and betrayed. Whatever the reason for the gaps in the Professor's account of Tom's departure, for his not being able to look at his part in it, the result is that he
feels acted upon even a decade later. The altersroman traces the process
of the protagonist's revising some habitual way of thinking about his
or her life, an essential part of accepting the life one has had. St. Peter
offers an example of a character who reflects on his memories but is
unable to look closely at what might cause great emotional upheaval,
in this case, his being abandoned and his responsibility. The result is
that he is left in despair. The protagonist always begins with limited
awareness—although the Professor's inability to anticipate any of the
effects that the move to the new house will have is extraordinary—
but he or she sees more by the end. The Professor, however, never
gets beyond feeling that he has been wronged by life. In his review, he
portrays his life as a series of situations in which he has been unable

to have his way: to detain Tom, to separate from Lillian, to stop time, so that he can say at the end, "his family . . . could not possibly be so much hurt as he had been already" (283). He does not accept the consequences of his admission that he has been disloyal to Lillian, and, although he criticizes her intolerance, he does not see his own, nor does he understand that he may be idealizing Tom. His valuing youth as the time of potential, as evident in his characterization of Tom and his selecting a time of vision as his special moment in his shipwreck fantasy, means that he equates growing up with bearing burdens and sees the direction of life as downward. The most depressing passage in the novel is the Professor's implied definition of adulthood that immediately follows his poetic reference to Tom's death. If responsible adulthood means having "many duties" required, writing "useless letters," framing "false excuses," managing money, being the partner of an increasingly "exacting" woman, and making "meaningless conventional gestures," then a promising youth may, indeed, be better off dead (260–61).

Also notable is how little anyone else seems to care about the Professor, except his younger daughter, Kathleen; her husband, Scott, in a minimal way; and Lillian, at times. Even then St. Peter refuses Scott as a confidant (72). He does try to talk about Tom with Kathleen: " 'Can't you stay awhile, Kitty? I almost never see anyone who remembers that side of Tom,' " referring to Tom's exploring the mesa, but she goes "quickly down the stairs" (132). His and Lillian's inability to complete their expressions of concern for each other has been discussed. Rosamond's criticism, " 'Papa, I don't like to have you working in a place like this [the old study]. It's not fitting,' " shows more regard for appearance than for his needs. She seems unable to understand his reply: " 'Habit is such a big part of work,' " perhaps because she has only recently begun her own work as a homemaker and perhaps because his remark conceals more of his feelings than it reveals (59). Thus, St. Peter is left on his own, without either support or correctives, to reflect on his life. He is not close enough to anyone who might hold him accountable and help him explore honestly the part of his life that so threatens him, and, with his choice of female guide, he further safeguards his choice not to look.

At the beginning of book 3, after he finishes rhapsodizing about Tom and consoles himself that he would have lost him anyway when Tom assumed adult responsibilities, the Professor indicts his own sexuality, his "conjugating the verb 'to love,' " for having determined the entire course of his life, and then rejects all his adulthood when he proposes to return to being the preadolescent Kansas boy he once was (264). He has called having to leave Lake Michigan with his family when he was eight years old the most wrenching "anguish" of his life and says he "nearly died" of the move to Kansas (30–31). Thus, the Professor must choose to become "the Kansas boy" not to return to the place but to regress to the age he was then. Since he moved when he was eight and he sees adolescence as a time of drastic personality change, "graft[ing] a new creature into the original one," he seeks to return to the years between eight and twelve, the age of sexual latency. He calls this time "the realest of his lives," before he became a "social man" and before the possibility of sexual betrayal existed for him (264–67). This view of the self, with sexual development called " 'cruel biological necessit[y]' " and considered not as an organic development but a graft or imposition of personality entirely new and foreign, grants terrifying power to sexuality, so much so that St. Peter feels that he must repudiate it (21). He specifies that the boy is "not a scholar," "had never married, never been a father," thus rejecting his public and domestic adult roles (265). That the boy is "solitary" is uppermost for someone who sees life as a series of betrayals over which he has little control. (The Professor's feelings about sexuality and the long list of betrayals in the novel, which occur to the Professor and to every character, will be taken up at the end, with the discussion of autobiographical echoes in *The Professor's House*.) The Professor may be able to protect himself if he is not involved sexually, emotionally, or intellectually with anyone or any ideas. Returning to the age between eight and twelve has other advantages as well. It occurs after the age of reason, so that thought is possible, but before a child is given much responsibility. Freud named this period latency because violent drives are normally dormant.[4] St. Peter feels no obligation to his family and wants no pressure, just time to daydream and observe nature (281, 265). Finally, for a moment at the beginning of his regression, the Professor at last acknowledges that Tom cannot return (263). After this moment, when "another boy . . . the original, unmodified Godfrey St. Peter" comes

---

4. Erikson, *Childhood and Society*, 260. In Erikson's model, the task of latency, learning industriousness, is crucial, but not nearly as threatening as consolidating ego identity in puberty. See Blanche H. Gelfant's discussion of St. Peter's desire to return to his real and original self "before he realizes his sexuality" (*Women Writing in America: Voices in Collage*, 112–13).

"through the garden door," he does not think of Tom again, except to consider a visit next summer to "Outland country" (263, 270).

St. Peter says that he has had "good luck" to have had the life he has had, but he acts now as though, with his good fortune in the past, he is ready to quit (258). When he returns to consciousness after Augusta saves his life, St. Peter feels as if he has "let something go . . . something very precious," vague words followed by other vague pronouns that refer not to a definite memory or person but to his desire that he should care deeply for anything, his need for passionate joys and griefs (282). Believing that no such renewing relationship as his and Tom's is possible again and certain that his and Lillian's intimacy cannot be reconstituted, the Professor resolves to "live without delight" during the time remaining to him alongside the corrective, "outward bound" Augustas (132, 282).

Whereas the Professor has cultivated his relationship with Tom, observing him from a distance during his four undergraduate years, he grasps at a female guide when he needs someone to affirm for him, without discussion, his sense that life consists of a series of betrayals. Augusta fulfills the function of helper in book 3 physically, when she is fortuitously present to drag him from the gas-filled study. She becomes his guide philosophically when he reevaluates her attitude that life is harsh: "[S]he was the bloomless side of life that he had always run away from,—yet when he had to face it, he found that it wasn't altogether repugnant" (280). His esteem for Augusta at the end of his assessment is a remarkable revision. Earlier, his setting her up by inquiring about the Magnificat and then mocking her naive belief that an illiterate woman composed a Latin prayer are indicative of his usual treatment of her (99). Even though he repeats that his father was Catholic like Augusta and keeps time by the bells ringing in her church, St. Peter has not been religious. On the contrary, he admonishes Augusta that she will not convert him, makes disparaging remarks about religion to his college students, equates art and religion in a class lecture, and makes no formal religious observance, working on Christmas Day (24, 99, 69, 98). He is "amazed" to learn that Augusta had expectations of life beyond "grow[ing] grey" as his family's servant that have not been fulfilled (23). In sum, the Professor has taken her presence for granted and has felt superior to her dour comments and limited life, until now, when he sees a use for her as a model who can be made to justify his decision to "learn to live without delight" and to imbue that surrender with the sanction of religion, even though he does not seem to be considering religious conversion.

In some desperation, St. Peter now determines with hindsight that Augusta has been his unacknowledged and distant female guide all along, one who has reminded him of the prayers and holy days of his father's religion and has given him "some wise observation or discreet comment to begin the day with," sayings that "were heavily, drearily true, . . . [but] good for him" (280). In shaping his recollections of her for his use, however, Professor St. Peter oversimplifies and emphasizes the surface of her life. He mentions her church attendance, her involvement with others in her church community, and her frequently performing works of mercy, such as sitting with the sick and the bereaved, but he does not seem to pay much attention to her faith that motivates these activities. He acknowledges Augusta's religion only in that, in his observation, it provides structure for her life and seems to endorse living without delight.

St. Peter puts his guide's spiritual direction to emotional use in two ways instead. First, Augusta offers a model for stoic acceptance of betrayal. Under the influence of members of her church, she has been duped by a copper-mine scandal, but she accepts her loss and refuses charity (128–29). The Professor is paternalistic toward his family's servant when he considers redressing her financial loss. He admires Augusta's pride in trying to refuse a restitution, and he has been surprised by her one slip from stoicism when she wonders about other courses her life might have taken. Interestingly, he does not seem to have high regard for Lillian's similar stoicism in the face of his infidelity, marked by her words cited above, " 'One must go on living' " (94). His feeling guilty about his lack of integrity in his marriage, along with his surprise, could account for his not being willing to acknowledge Lillian's statement. It is a significant change, then, that in the end the Professor is willing to be advised by the asexual woman from the working class toward whom he feels paternalistic, but not by his wife.

Second, Augusta also offers a model for living alone without passion. The Professor remarks on her self-sufficiency and what he calls her "matter-of-factness," a term that describes her as dull, prosaic, and unimpassioned (281). One of the aspects of life that she has relinquished is sexuality. In the Professor's description, she is asexual, except for her thick wavy hair. She is a "spinster," with a body that is "flat and stiff." She has "a strong arm" and hands that are capable but not graceful, unlike Tom's and Lillian's (23, 278). Thus, even in the company of others under intimate circumstances, Augusta is present to minister to spiritual needs, but otherwise, she remains apart, reading her prayer book, for example. She shows that she remembers her station by protecting the Professor's reputation with Dr. Dudley and the neighbors and by calling him "sir" even as she sits by his bedside. Augusta reassures the Professor that she will not threaten him by demanding an emotional response. In fact, she counters his revelation, " 'I seem to feel rather lonely,' " with a pat answer, " 'That's because your family are coming home,' " to forestall further embarrassing remarks, just as he has cut off further revelation about her expectations of life with " 'Well, well, we mustn't think mournfully of it, Augusta' " (279, 23). In *The Ambassadors* guidance from a woman while he assesses his life enables Strether to look at painful aspects of his life. Here, however, Augusta supports the Professor's *not* looking, because of decorum and because she has always accepted the "sadnesses of nature" (281). In choosing to regress and to esteem Augusta, St. Peter chooses resignation over responsibility. She suits his purpose by not requiring much of him while offering him a way to describe the rest of his life and justify it.[5]

Professor St. Peter regards his regression and his relinquishing desire as his earned "right" because he has fulfilled his obligations for thirty years, because no one will notice, and because he believes that he will be the one who suffers most, being the one who has been "hurt" more than his family has (275, 283). He uses his interpretation of Augusta's life to justify his response further, without acknowledging that being single is not his state in life, as it is Augusta's. The Professor says that "he was not the same man," and indeed, the "apathy" he says that he experiences, the absence of passion and a lack of interest in life, predicts a dull physical existence and does not constitute a satisfying guiding vision, however positive his phrase "outward bound" may sound (283).

---

5. In contrast, many critics present positive views of Augusta as offering the Professor renewed contact with life (David Laird, "Willa Cather and the Deceptions of Art," 57–58); new appreciation for his spirituality or "religious understanding" (Frank G. Novak, Jr., "Crisis and Discovery in *The Professor's House*," 130–32); and a "new story" or narrative strategy that helps him make sense of his life and thus will allow him to survive (William Monroe, "Scripts and Patterns: Stories as 'Equipment for Living'— and Dying," 304, 306–9). Michael Leddy argues that the Professor *may* be about to "construct" a "new adult life," but all the reader can say with certainty is that he has let go of his need for delight ("*The Professor's House*: The Sense of an Ending," 445, 449).

The pain of such drastic suppression of emotions seems to be a high price to pay for protection from encroachment by Lillian and from other betrayals. However, apathy is actually economical, because it allows the Professor to give up the old house and live with Lillian, whom he cannot bear. Apathy also allows him to live with himself despite his unworthiness, proved by his having been abandoned by Tom, and despite his guilt over not being able either to love or to leave Lillian. Despite his not exploring his part in the deterioration of his marriage, once the Professor finds a way to view his life and embark on his new course, his assessment of his life reaches closure. His resignation and renunciation are not positive, but the novel suggests a source of hope. The Professor has at least been able to affirm a small part of his childhood, even though he rejects the thirty years of his life that have seemed important to him. He has thought about the future, next summer, when he may make a trip to the Southwest and encounter Tom's spirit.

More than with any other work in this study, understanding auto-biographical references is crucial to clarify the ambiguities in *The Professor's House*. While Cather cannot be identified with her protagonist completely, that the novel has autobiographical aspects is unmistakable. Cather and the Professor are fifty-two; she had written the same number of books as he had and had received a prestigious financial award, the Pulitzer Prize; she had been residing with a devoted companion for many years; she had been "dragged" by her family to live in the Midwest from Virginia when ten years old; she had used an attic study also occupied by dress forms and had to move from it. This study was in the home of Isabelle McClung, "her primary love, her 'best companion,'" according to her biographer, Sharon O'Brien. Cather was devastated by Isabelle's marriage to Jan Hambourg in 1916. O'Brien interprets Cather's remark that the world split in two around 1922 to refer to her personal crisis during a visit to France to the Hambourg household. Cather had been living with Edith Lewis in New York before Isabelle's marriage, and her initial grief at her parting from Isabelle was somewhat under control. Still, O'Brien argues, seeing the permanence of the Hambourg household might have "sharpened her sense of exclusion."[6]

6. O'Brien, *Willa Cather: The Emerging Voice*, 352, 240. James Woodress discusses the "spiritual malaise of Professor St. Peter/Willa Cather" and summarizes other

This renewed sense of loss resembles the Professor's renewed grief for Tom as he delays editing Tom's diary and moving from the places he most closely associates with him. Like the Professor, Cather can no longer deny that the significant person is gone. Thus, despite dissimilarities in sex and profession, Cather has an emotional investment in the Professor, and her reflection focuses—in code—on her comparison of her intimate relationships with Isabelle McClung Hambourg (Tom Outland) and Edith Lewis (Lillian).

On the one hand, Cather is remarkably generous toward Isabelle in her portrait of Tom, praising her involvement in life and excusing her abandoning Cather for the more socially acceptable role of wife by transposing that departure into the heroic act of going off to war. In Louie Marsellus, she paints an ambiguous portrait of Isabelle's husband as a man who is florid, acquisitive, and overbearing at times, yet who can win people's regard for his thoughtfulness and generosity, a portrait that seems to reflect Cather's opinion of Jan Hambourg. As the Professor points out, Louie's (Jan's) skills enhance Tom's (Isabelle's) gifts, so that the two are complementary. On the other hand, the coded message to Isabelle is a harsh judgment: Tom (Isabelle) has betrayed a close friend, and, as a result, the Professor (Cather) will never love again. Intimacy in the future is not possible.

Instead, the Professor (Cather) is left with Lillian (Edith Lewis). While Cather wrote eloquently to others about Isabelle, she rarely mentioned "Miss Lewis" in her letters and always in reference to practical matters.[7] Various biographical details support the comparison of Lillian and Edith Lewis. Reported to be both protective of Cather yet dependent and clinging, Lewis performed domestic and secretarial tasks that, while helpful, might have seemed at times encroaching. She resembles the wife whom her partner can neither leave nor respect. Further evidence of Lewis's possessiveness may be found in her memoir, her version of Willa Cather. Although written after Cather's death, its sycophantic and sentimental tone may reflect Lewis's habitual attitude

---

autobiographical parallels in *Willa Cather: A Literary Life,* 367–69. See also Janis P. Stout, *Strategies of Reticence: Silence and Meaning in the Works of Jane Austen, Willa Cather, Katherine Anne Porter, Joan Didion,* 88–94, and "Autobiography as Journey in *The Professor's House.*" Stout locates an autobiographical resonance between Augusta and Edith Lewis (*Strategies of Reticence,* 91).

7. O'Brien, *Willa Cather,* 356.

toward Cather. Appropriately titled *Willa Cather Living*, the biography allows Lewis finally to possess Cather, to keep her "living" and under control by rewriting her life.[8] These biographical details suggest that, while she was writing *The Professor's House*, Cather may have mourned again her loss of Isabelle and may have considered emotional retreat to resist her possessive companion of sixteen years.

Although the Professor is the source of most of the criticism of women in *The Professor's House*, he may not speak for Cather on this point. However, it does make sense for the novel to judge men less harshly and to belittle the narrow, confining domesticity of women, since that seems to be what Cather is chafing against in her current predicament. She criticizes women who are in some ways dependent yet are petty and manipulative, as well as the circumstances, including the difficulty of having a career, that encourage wives to be possessive of their partners. At the same time, the novel's criticism of St. Peter's aloofness and arrogance may reflect Cather's concern about her stance in relation to Edith Lewis.

The novel portrays life as a series of betrayals, and it names sexuality as the source of the protagonist's present difficulties. Public betrayals include the federal government's failure to subsidize an expedition to the Southwest, the university's decreased commitment to science, the humanities, and academic values generally, and the scandal of the Kinkoo Copper Company. People are also betrayed in private, including, in Tom's narrative, Tom by Roddy and vice versa, Roddy by women, and Mother Eve's husband by Mother Eve, and, in book 1, the Professor by Langtry, Crane by Tom's will, Tom by Rosamond's forgetting him so quickly and by his being "all turned out chemicals and dollars and cents" by the Marselluses, Kathleen by her sister's lack of consideration, Louie by Scott's blackballing his club membership, and Lillian by her husband (132). Bad luck that might be called betrayal by life includes the destruction of the mesa civilization, the defeat of the French army (in which St. Peter's grandfather fought) in Russia,

---

8. Patricia Lee Yongue discusses Edith Lewis's "desire—the utter need—to possess and control [Willa Cather]" ("Edith Lewis Living," 13). Although she does not view their relationship as sexual, Yongue discusses Lewis as "the 'wife' any professional woman needs, [who] performed invaluable domestic and technical services for Cather" ("Willa Cather and Edith Lewis: Two Stories, Two Friends," 187, 208–9). See also O'Brien, *Willa Cather*, 354–56.

Tom's being orphaned and his dying in World War I, the death of Henry, the cook, on the mesa, and the Professor's being moved from Lake Michigan as a boy. Two points can be drawn from these lists. First, intimacy seems impossible to sustain. Even though they have worked closely together and care for each other, Roddy and Tom have misunderstood each other's attitude toward the very work that they have shared. Disloyalty is the norm. Involvement with others causes pain. Second, this catalog, never foregrounded but touching all the relationships in the novel, suggests a negative view of life. People are victims. That the outcome of nearly every situation is negative certainly reflects the Professor's current state of mind, but betrayal also seems to be part of the author's view, in this novel, of the human condition.

Only a few of the betrayals in this catalog are directly sexual, yet *The Professor's House* suggests that such is the ultimate source of St. Peter's disappointment with life, since it is his sexuality primarily that he renounces. He portrays his marrying Lillian as an impetuous act, done without thought due to biological necessity, and his reminiscences imply that Tom did not fully reciprocate his feelings, but found another mentor in Dr. Crane and an object of affection in Rosamond, before leaving the Professor's circle altogether. Judith Fetterley offers an interpretation of Cather's treatment of sexuality in *My Ántonia* that bears on *The Professor's House*. She argues that in the earlier novel, Cather creates a narrator, Jim Burden, who also "long[s] for a time before definition, . . . a past before the domination of sexual definition where one might be a tomboy and love one's Ántonia to one's heart's content." Glorifying latency (in Jim Burden's case) or returning to latency (in St. Peter's case) as the safest and happiest period of life, when the possibility of sexual betrayal is remote, seems to be a solution to Cather's "lesbian dilemma," although such longing entails great sacrifice. The two novels differ in one important respect. As Fetterley points out, Lena Lingard exists in *My Ántonia* as a sexual being and as Jim Burden's muse: Cather "locate[s] the source of poetic inspiration in the figure of Lena Lingard—the unconventional, the erotic, the lesbian self retained against all odds."[9] For the Professor, being "outward bound" with "a world full of Augustas" means voyaging to a new world. However, this seems to require leaving behind the unconventional

9. Fetterley, "*My Ántonia,* Jim Burden and the Dilemma of the Lesbian Writer," 55, 57.

and the erotic, anything that would disturb apathy and challenge the necessity of learning to "live without delight" (281–82). Cather creates an altersroman in which the protagonist, at times, feels satisfied with his professional life, but her writing a novel in which the protagonist affirms the personal, domestic life she or he has had is difficult, when the friend she has preferred has abandoned her and when she may no longer love the companion she has.

In contrast to the resignation so prominent in *The Professor's House,* Cather has selected two operas for the Professor to attend or re-call that speak both subversively and optimistically about intimate relationships.[10] The Professor hums "his favorite air" from the opera *Il Matrimonio Segreto,* by Domenico Cimarosa, based on an English play, *The Clandestine Marriage,* by George Colman the elder and David Garrick (106). Play and opera show marriage as an economic exchange, with love secondary to the social ambition of the bride's father. The prognosis for the outcome of the sanctioned marriage that occurs is not a good one. However, the plot involves the discovery of an irregularly contracted secret union, and in the opera that union is celebrated in the end. In Ambroise Thomas's *Mignon,* the opera that Lillian and the Pro-fessor see in Chicago, the love triangle initially causes great pain (92). Taken from an incident in Goethe's *Wilhelm Meister,* the opera puts the woman Mignon in the lead. Wilhelm Meister, a wealthy young man, inadvertently hurts Mignon, the woman who loves him best and who in the opera recalls a better past. The plot involves a betrayal, jealousy, and gender ambiguity, with Mignon dressing as a man to pursue her beloved as a servant, but ends with her justification. Wilhelm recognizes Mignon's devotion and returns it, doing so primarily because of the force of her love for him. Unlike life portrayed in *The Professor's House,* both operas have a happy ending. Both sanction loving devotion in untraditional or unlikely partnerships, and perhaps are included as the author's wistful wish.

10. See the discussion of the operas in Richard Giannone, *Music in Willa Cather's Fiction,* 161–63. See also his discussion of the Brahms *Requiem* that the Professor ponders at the beginning of book 3 (165–68).

4

"Soon . . . as we get used to it"

The Mansion, by William Faulkner

Lambert Strether and Godfrey St. Peter avoid assessing their lives. Strether insists that the adventure is Chad's and allows himself to be fooled at times by the Parisians. St. Peter meditates on Tom Outland and argues against the materialism of those around him. However, both have had their ordinary routine upset and find themselves with ample time for reflection, so that, as the novels progress, their reviewing their lives seems to be inevitable. In *The Mansion,* Faulkner's protagonist Gavin Stevens, the county attorney, also resists reviewing his life, filling his time with his quest for justice and believing that what he does for his guide, Linda Snopes Kohl, does not touch him. Significant changes in Gavin's life, such as his trip to New York City to witness Linda's marriage, his own marriage, and his move to his wife's house, do not affect him, as Strether's trip to Paris and his broken engagement and St. Peter's move to the new house do. Finally, however, Linda's involving him in her revenge against her stepfather, Flem, makes Gavin's assessing his life impossible to forestall.

While the process Faulkner traces in *The Mansion* resembles the process of assessing one's life that *The Ambassadors* and *The Professor's House* depict, a more revealing comparison is one between Don Quixote and Gavin Stevens. Since Faulkner said that he reread *Don Quixote* every year, the comparison is worth exploring.[1] Both idealistic crusaders accompanied by a loyal friend, both bachelors at fifty,

---

1. Gwynn and Blotner, *Faulkner in the University,* 50, 150. See also Faulkner, "1956 Interview with Jean Stein Vanden Heuvel," 251. Faulkner's novels are cited parenthetically in the text and identified by the following abbreviations: *T* for *The Town* and *M* for *The Mansion.*

Don Quixote and Gavin declare devotion to women who are out of reach. The time is past when Don Quixote might have courted Aldonza Lorenzo, as it is for Gavin and Eula Varner Snopes.[2] Both have also escaped their day-to-day concerns with a literary project, Don Quixote's collecting and reading the entire corpus of chivalric romances and Gavin's "translating the Old Testament back into the classic Greek of its first translating" (*M*, 392). Cervantes and Faulkner start by treating their idealists ironically; however, when they resume their stories after a gap in time, they admire them as artists of life. Don Quixote is less assured in part 2 about his role as knight, yet Cervantes shows that he *has* changed his world as a result of his adventures recorded in part 1. Similarly, beginning with *Intruder in the Dust*, Faulkner portrays Gavin as more cautious about imposing his interpretations on others, at the same time that he is more effective in his community. In answering a question about what he liked about Don Quixote, Faulkner answered, "It's admiration and pity and amusement—that's what I get from him— and the reason is that he is a man trying to do the best he can in this ramshackle universe he's compelled to live in."[3] Gavin Stevens is not Don Quixote, but comparing the two while tracing Gavin's review of his life will help explain his reaction to Linda and his affirmation of the life he has had.

Gavin's assessing his life is the central feature of *The Mansion*, yet Faulkner allows him only one section told from his point of view, significant in its placement in the middle of the novel and significant in revealing Gavin's ability to misunderstand Linda and to avoid reflection generally. Faulkner names the three parts for Mink, Linda, and Flem. *The Mansion* begins and ends with Mink Snopes, the sharecropper who has vowed revenge against his wealthy kinsman Flem; Linda orchestrates the main action in the present time of the novel; and Gavin, Ratliff, and Chick Mallison reminisce about their lives and Jefferson's history. This complexity is typical of Faulkner's best work: while Gavin's assessment is central, Faulkner traces the process of assessment twice

2. *The Town* traces Gavin's devotion to Eula Varner Snopes, which begins when he first sees her. She is unavailable for marriage because she is already married to Flem Snopes. Don Quixote never approaches Aldonza Lorenzo, but Eula comes to Gavin's office to offer her body, which Gavin refuses. Gavin remains devoted to his memory of Eula, but the focus in *The Mansion* is his relationship with her daughter, Linda.
3. Joseph L. Fant and Robert Ashley, eds., *Faulkner at West Point*, 94.

more, for Mink and the town. With his review of the life of the town, he expands the more individually focused explorations of *The Ambassadors* and *The Professor's House* to include the characters' sense that their community has a history with stages somewhat like those of an individual's life. Finally, Faulkner's wish to be inclusive in *The Mansion*, reviewing his Yoknapatawpha saga, is yet another version of life assessment.

I

In part 1, Don Quixote has a design for his role as knight: "righting every kind of wrong, and exposing himself to peril and danger from which he would emerge to reap eternal fame and glory."[4] Similarly envisioning his occupation as lawyer and his public office as county attorney as a quest for justice, Gavin has filled his days by trying to protect damsels in distress and to "do something about [evil]" (*M*, 307). Some of the "evil" that he sees is a local phenomenon, the invasion of Jefferson by Snopeses, whom he characterizes as rapacious. Along with his loyal friend Ratliff, Gavin enters a bargain as if with a third party (*M*, 130). Toward the end of *The Mansion*, he describes this plan to Linda: *"I am happy I was given the privilege of meddling with impunity in other peoples affairs without really doing any harm by belonging to that avocation whose acolytes have been absolved in advance for holding justice above truth I have been denied the chance to destroy what I loved by touching it"* (*M*, 363). Gavin and Ratliff will give up the possibility of reward such as wealth in exchange for other benefits. First, they can feel secure in their belief that they are special because they are the only ones able to recognize the "danger" of Snopesism, privileged knowledge gained by watching and drawing inferences (*T*, 106). Second, Gavin believes that he has protection from harmful consequences when he does interfere. This formula satisfies Gavin from 1910 until 1946. He believes that "meddling" freely in the town's affairs yet remaining untouched himself is possible and gives him a full life. This is the delusion that Linda challenges at the end of *The Mansion*, causing Gavin to revise *"without really doing any harm"* to " 'Nobody is [safe], around me. I'm dangerous' " (*M*, 427).

Whereas he has treated Gavin as a figure of fun in earlier novels, Faulkner is more appreciative of a sensitive, idealistic male toward the

4. Cervantes, *Don Quixote*, 27.

end of his career. Beginning his revision by making Gavin more effective in *Intruder in the Dust,* Faulkner makes him sympathetic in *The Town* and *The Mansion.* He elicits the reader's sympathy for Gavin in two ways. He explains how Gavin came to be the way he is, as he has done before with less moral characters, such as Joe Christmas, and as he does in this novel with Mink Snopes. As a well-bred son of one of the oldest Jefferson families, Gavin has been raised to be honorable, valiant, courteous, gentle, and magnanimous (the virtues Don Quixote claims to have acquired at the end of part 1) and to defend the public institutions that the gentry values. However foolish Gavin may appear at times as he tries to live by what he has been taught, Faulkner does not mock or dismiss these traditional humanistic values. He also implicitly praises the lifelong devotion and energy Gavin brings to his plan " '[t]o save Jefferson from Snopeses' " (*T,* 182). Second, Faulkner makes Gavin sympathetic by making him vulnerable, more a participant and less an observer in *The Town* and *The Mansion.* His personal life, rather than his public crusades in *Intruder in the Dust, Knight's Gambit,* and *Requiem for a Nun* (published in 1948, 1949, and 1951, respectively), becomes the focus. Readers interpret Faulkner's note to *The Mansion* as a warning not to expect details in this novel to match details in his earlier work, but the note also applies to Gavin, as he becomes subject to " 'living' [which is] motion, and 'motion' is change and alteration."[5]

Like Don Quixote, Faulkner's idealist resists admitting that the passage of time or the actions of others can affect him emotionally. Gavin talks about feeling old and about its being " 'too late for us [Gavin and Ratliff] now. . . . [W]e are just too old . . . too tired . . . . [N]ow it will have to be somebody else [who fights evil]' " (*M,* 307). However, he makes this observation without emotion, which is surprising because he is also saying that his life's work is finished and that he

---

5. Faulkner's interest in the idealist is longstanding and has autobiographical implications. Gavin appears in seven books, is a major figure in five, and changes throughout the twenty-eight years he holds Faulkner's interest. For a more detailed study of Gavin as an evolving character, see Mary Montgomery Dunlap, "The Achievement of Gavin Stevens," and Nancy Eileen Gregory, "A Study of the Early Versions of Faulkner's *The Town* and *The Mansion,*" 74–100, 144–53. For a negative view of the town's values, see Gary Lee Stonum's discussion of "the public forms and institutions which codify human relationships" in the trilogy in *Faulkner's Career: An Internal Literary History,* 162, 156–57. His thesis is that the trilogy "discredit[s] social institutions and cultural forms . . . as both empty and all-powerful" (181–82).

is relinquishing his deliberately constructed role that has made him special. His statement reads like one that he wishes his audience, Chick and Ratliff, to contradict, as Chick does verbally soon after (*M,* 321), and as Ratliff does when he prevents a Snopes from running for the U.S. Senate. Gavin's own actions—marrying, helping Linda Kohl and Essie Meadowfill—also contradict his saying that he feels old. His occasionally frantic activity may be a sign of his anxiety about his insight. Still, his acknowledging the passage of time, by itself, does not cause Gavin to become reflective.

In comparing *The Mansion* with the other novels in this study, the reader might expect Gavin's nephew, Chick Mallison, who is a major voice in *The Town,* to act as a catalyst for Gavin's review of his life. However, Chick plays a minor role in *The Mansion,* in comparison with Chad in James's *The Ambassadors,* for example. Chick's seeing himself as Gavin's rival for Linda and his fighting in World War II show that he is no longer the boy Gavin has helped raise, but an adult. His silently paying tribute to Gavin's guardianship marks the end of that stage of their relationship (*M,* 321). Still, Gavin does not reveal much emotion in response to his nephew; he pats him on the head when Chick taunts him and plans Chick's European tour (*M,* 230, 353).

Instead, two other characters, V. K. Ratliff and Linda Snopes Kohl, shock Gavin and guide him to review his life. As James does in *The Ambassadors,* Faulkner divides this guiding function between two characters. Just as Maria Gostrey helps Strether understand his responses to Madame de Vionnet, Ratliff helps Gavin understand what is going on between him and Linda, acting as a buffer between Gavin and experience while not forcing more information on his friend than he thinks he can handle. In *The Town,* Ratliff brags to Chick that Gavin " 'still missed it [that Flem desires respectability]. And I can't tell him. . . . Because he wouldn't believe me. This here is the kind of a thing . . . a man has got to know . . . himself. He has got to learn it out of his own hard dread and skeer. . . . So I got to wait for him to learn it . . . himself, the hard way, the sure way, the only sure way. Then he will believe it . . .' " (*T,* 258). Ratliff also resembles Maria Gostrey in that he serves as an aid for readers, directing them to wonder why Linda has returned to Jefferson and what she will ask of Gavin. " 'She aint going to marry him. It's going to be worse than that' " (*M,* 256). In contrast, just as Madame de Vionnet's revelations make Strether feel as if he is drowning, Linda's threats to Gavin's code of respectability and gallantry terrify him, although she intends her guidance to be enriching. Linda tells Gavin how limited his life has been.

With the exception of *Mrs. Dalloway*, *The Summer before the Dark*, and *Jazz*, the protagonist's guide in the altersromane considered here is a person of the opposite sex. In *The Mansion*, Faulkner uses a guide of each sex, and then he explores traditional ideas of masculinity and femininity, making the gentler guide a man and the bolder guide a woman, changes that probably reflect his own relationships, which will be discussed later. He takes some pains to emphasize Ratliff's affinity with the feminine. Chick and the narrator repeatedly point out that the bachelor Ratliff cooks, sews, and keeps his house "immaculate." In the final scene, at Frenchman's Bend, Ratliff hands Gavin "the immaculately clean, impeccably laundered and ironed handkerchief which the town said he not only laundered himself but hemstitched himself too." Listening more than he talks, Ratliff is comfortable as the only male in a group of gossiping women. He is intuitive and works indirectly, such as when he goes secretly to Parchman to witness Mink's release and when he gets Clarence Snopes out of the Senate race without confronting him.[6] Whereas Faulkner portrays two male characters in his early fiction who have qualities associated with the feminine, Horace Benbow and Quentin Compson, as unbalanced, he treats both Gavin and Ratliff more favorably. Likewise, several of the strong young women he created earlier in his career are punished (Narcissa Benbow, Temple Drake), but he treats Eula and Linda as having greater vitality than most of the men they know.

Ratliff is a loyal friend who anticipates crises and stands by to support Gavin as well as to prevent him from denying that he has helped Mink kill Flem. To do this, he is alternately compassionate and firm. He allows Gavin to deny, at least at first, that he has done wrong in helping Linda get Mink out of prison two years early, even though everyone expects that he will kill Flem (*M*, 370). Several times in the final scene when he takes Gavin to give Linda's money to Mink, Ratliff offers Gavin formulaic ways to relieve his anguish (*M*, 427–34). He says that Linda just took her turn in a boys' game, Give-me-lief, with her stepfather, implying that these events have been just a game, with fair rules. He suggests that Linda had to avenge her mother. He offers Gavin a refrain

---

6. See *The Mansion*, 168, 206, 231, 319, 431, and *The Town*, 229.

that can be repeated in order to replace reflection, " 'The pore sons of bitches.' " Ratliff uses humor in another verbal construct that sums up Gavin's life: " 'You done already been through two Eula Varners and I dont think you can stand another one.' " He promises his continued friendship: " 'It's all over now, soon that is as we get used to it.' " In sum, he anticipates Gavin's needs and is "gentle and tender as a woman."

On the other hand, Ratliff can be relentless. By himself, Gavin faces that he is an accessory to a murder. However, Ratliff shows considerable rhetorical skill and tenacity (once, with Gavin trapped beside him in the car) when he forces Gavin to listen and respond to what he does not want to face about Linda's intentions. Six times, Ratliff asks the same question: " 'You reckon she really never knowed what [Mink] was going to do the minute they turned him loose?' " (*M*, 419). The first time, Gavin denies that the question matters. The second time, he anticipates the question and hangs up the phone before he can hear it. The third time, Gavin revises Linda's motive from revenge against Flem to " 'pity and compassion and simple generosity' " toward Mink. However, immediately afterward, he admits the extent of his turmoil when he realizes that his former consolation for suffering, translating the Old Testament, will "not suffice any more, not ever again now" (*M*, 391–92). While they are waiting to give Mink the money from Linda, Ratliff presses Gavin three more times. The novel distorts the time sequence. Ratliff asks the first of these last three questions after Gavin has seen Linda's new Jaguar and they have kissed good-bye, but it occurs in the text before the reader has been shown this scene, suggesting that perhaps Ratliff's prodding causes Gavin to reflect on their farewell. Again, three times, Gavin denies Linda's intention to free Mink to kill Flem, although with increasing emotion. Ratliff persists until Gavin finds release in crying.

Far more threatening than Ratliff's questions, Linda's actions challenge Gavin repeatedly during the eight years that she lives as a widow in Jefferson, both in her public behavior and in her private requests. The devastating main shock she gives him, which occurs at their last meeting, has both public and private elements, the sight of the Jaguar and their embrace.

Upon her return, Linda refuses to follow the accepted codes of the town, as if she "perhaps had left the South too young too long ago to have formed the Southern female" attitudes and habits (*M*, 358). Her demanding " 'What line or paragraph or even page can you compose and write to match giving your life to say No to people like Hitler and Mussolini?' " indicates clearly how she ranks words and actions (*M*, 218). Her life thus far shows the risks she has been willing to take in order to live life with passion. Her activity in the town, especially her membership in the Communist Party and her attempts to improve the Negro schools, should have conveyed to Gavin her tough-minded resolution. However, his gallantry encourages him not to take her work seriously, and instead to defend her as a woman needing protection. Thus, for example, he has asked her to promise to leave town if he decides that she is in danger. He asks her not to take a job in California, but to change her destination to Pascagoula because he has some influence there, should the FBI pursue her. Although his requests seem sensible, his language reveals the paternalism behind his courtliness: "I wrote slowly and carefully *You dont have to go I wont ask any more but when I do ask you again to go will you just believe me & go at once I will make all plans will you do that*" and "I threatened to tell the Pascagoula police myself that she was deaf the first time I heard about it [her buying a car]" and "my lawyer friend arranged for her in a car pool" (*M*, 240, 246). His appeal to the sheriff assumes the men's shared values: " '*Tell a woman* that apparently she just finished murdering her father . . . ?' " (*M*, 378, emphasis added). Until he sees the Jaguar and they say good-bye, Gavin has been able to maintain a contradictory view of Linda, choosing to play down her challenges to his idea of what women should be like. That is, Gavin has welcomed the chance to protect Linda, since *his* taking some risks in her behalf keeps his self-image intact. Defending this gallantry and linking Don Quixote and Gavin Stevens, Faulkner said, "It is the knight that goes out to defend somebody who don't want to be defended and don't need it. But it's a very fine quality in human nature. I hope it will always endure. It is comical and a little sad."[7]

When Gavin drives to her house after Flem's funeral and sees her new Jaguar, he has a visceral response:

> and was even walking on when suddenly it was as if a staircase you are mounting becomes abruptly a treadmill, you still walking, mounting,

7. Gwynn and Blotner, *Faulkner in the University*, 141. Gavin is paternalistic toward Mink as well. He believes that he acts for Mink's own good when he decreases the amount of money Linda has given him for Mink, without consulting her: "He [Gavin] would take care of that himself when the time came" (*M*, 426).

expending energy and motion but without progress; so abrupt and sudden in fact that you are only your aura, your very momentum having carried your corporeality one whole step in advance of you; he thought *No place on earth from which a brand-new Jaguar could be delivered to Jefferson, Mississippi, since even noon yesterday* . . . thinking, desperately now *No! No! It is possible! They could have had one, found one in Memphis last night or this morning—this ramshackle universe which has nothing to hold it together but coincidence* . . . . (*M,* 422)

He is so upset when he leaves Linda's house that he abandons his own car and walks back to his office so as not to have to "look at the new car again" (*M,* 427). Gavin's seeing the Jaguar can hardly be called his "second shock," since Linda has given him so many, yet the car does convey crucial information that he has been able to overlook until this moment, namely that she has been acting all along in her own behalf. He has chosen the role of guardian knight; however, she refuses to accept the complementary role of damsel in distress, except as she has revised it. The image of Linda at the wheel, driving herself out of town, especially in a sports car that is expensive, fast, and ostentatious ("fancy," Ratliff says), is a strong one.[8] After he has seen the Jaguar, Gavin begins his usual warning against driving, but he does not continue when she ignores it (*M,* 425). Rejecting his paternalism, Linda challenges Gavin's fundamental image of himself: that he is worthwhile because of his gallantry.

Another aspect of Linda's desire to live fully is her sexual passion, which she expresses privately to Gavin twice, compellingly during their last meeting. Linda's requests for intimacy also threaten Gavin, who prefers a more distant relationship based on paternalism and "devotion." He anticipates and silences her proposing marriage to him. Although she repeatedly tells him, " 'I love you,' " he denies her claim that she has " 'never loved anybody but [him]' " (*M,* 425). He continually pushes her hands away or "break[s] free" when she, as he puts it, "clasps" or "clings" to him, and he routinely changes the subject or leaves when he becomes uncomfortable with her intensity.[9] He

8. Keith Louise Fulton points out the strength of the image of Linda's driving out of Jefferson in "Linda Snopes Kohl: Faulkner's Radical Woman," 433.

9. See Dunlap for a convincing argument that Linda loves Gavin ("Achievement of Gavin Stevens," 221; also 215, 217, 219). In *The Mansion,* see 239 ("clasp" and "cling"). Gavin pushes Linda's hands away (241, 247). He pulls away from her kiss (424) and runs out (241). He changes the subject (238, 239, 241), although he changes the topic from the pardon for Mink to "I love you" (368).

is "shocked" by her saying once whatever unprintable *"bald unlovely sound"* she speaks to describe having sex (*M*, 239). Her using such a word and her affirming that she *"want[s] to"* say clearly that she is not afraid to admit her lust, as he is, since he returns to her Communist Party card as a safer topic. Responding with passion would threaten Gavin's security on two counts: he would have lost control and he would not be acting properly.

Both Gavin and Ratliff respond to Linda as dangerous, but Faulkner emphasizes her generosity and courage.[10] She risks rejection by initiating the kisses and embraces that Gavin reports. When Gavin is unable to respond to her with more than platonic friendship, Linda retreats, reassuring him several times that she will not pursue him: " 'I'm all right now' " (*M*, 241, 252–53). Instead, she tries to get Gavin to engage in life in other ways, for his sake. Her tutoring when he visits her in Pascagoula is gentle and explicit. She hands him the seashell she found her first day there and has saved for him. She makes him stop on the beach to look at the sunset: " 'We were here. We saved it. Used it. I mean, for the earth to have come all this long way from the beginning of the earth, and the sun to have come all this long way from the beginning of time, for this one day and minute and second out of all the days and minutes and seconds, and nobody to use it . . .' " (*M*, 248). Later, Linda interprets what she has shown him: " 'Do you remember back there at the beach when the sun finally went down and there was nothing except the sunset and the pines and the sand and the ocean and you and me and I said how that *shouldn't be wasted* after all that waiting and distance, there should be two people out of all the world desperate and anguished for one another to deserve not to waste it any longer . . .' " (*M*, 250–51, emphasis added). Then she asks him to marry someone else, to experience life for himself rather than vicariously, even

---

10. Dunlap discusses Linda's generosity to Gavin ("Achievement of Gavin Stevens," 222). Dunlap's reading of *The Mansion* is similar to mine, although she argues that Gavin fails to save Linda's humanity (209–41). For other positive readings of Linda's character, see Fulton, "Linda Snopes Kohl," and Sergei Chakovsky, "Women in Faulkner's Novels: Author's Attitude and Artistic Function," 78–79. Judith Bryant Wittenberg argues that Faulkner creates strong women throughout his career and that he affirms Eula and Linda as strong women in *The Town* and *The Mansion* ("William Faulkner: A Feminist Consideration," 327, 329, 335). These positive interpretations represent a major revision in critical opinion. For analyses that criticize Linda, consult the listings in Patricia E. Sweeney, *William Faulkner's Women Characters: An Annotated Bibliography of Criticism, 1930–1983*, 319–42.

if that experience ends in mourning: " 'So that's what I want you to have too' " (*M*, 252). Linda tries to help him find the courage to risk intimacy so that he does not "waste" life. Gavin is reluctant, partly due to anxiety that she will propose marriage to him. He barely looks at the seashell. His concerns about her reputation at the hotel where they stay and about whether she is dressed properly for dinner are comical in the context of the shipyard in wartime.

The woman Gavin marries indicates what scares him about Linda. A former schoolmate of his sister, Melisandre is a more conventional woman of social standing similar to his. Given Gavin's wariness, the reader might expect his marrying at fifty to be the chief feature of his period of assessment; however, his new role as "squire" and escort does not seem to require much adjustment. The novel does not show passion or deep engagement between Gavin and Melisandre (*M*, 383, 363–64). In order to deepen the relationship, Linda offers to make Melisandre jealous, which Gavin brushes off as impossible (*M*, 362–63).

At their farewell, Linda is more insistent than she has been before, kissing him more intensely, "firmly and deliberately." As Gavin begins to respond, he "learn[s] and know[s] not with despair or grief but just sorrow a little," although his feeling quickly turns into "terror." Initially he thinks about "simply supporting her buttocks as you cup the innocent hipless bottom of a child," but he becomes aware that he is not embracing a child: *"so now the thrust of hips, gripping both shoulders to draw me into the backward-falling even without a bed"* (*M*, 423–24). By eliciting a passionate response, Linda shows him what he has missed and what he could have had. Her telling him " 'You always are right about you and me' " is not a compliment, but an accusation that he cannot tolerate her intensity. She accuses him of a version of the failure he has ridiculed in Flem, wasting life: " 'You haven't had anything. You have had nothing.' "

Linda has tried to alter Gavin's carefully constructed role as Jefferson's knight because she believes that with his role, he has had nothing. Fearing that *without* his role intact, he is nothing, Gavin rejects her analysis and affirms his life as he has lived it. He contradicts Linda: *"We have had everything"* (*M*, 425). Whereas at the end of his assessment, Don Quixote repudiates the time he has been a knight and affirms his prior identity as Alonso Quixano, Gavin cannot affirm an earlier period, for he has always tried to live by the Southern code of chivalry. Indeed, Gavin's story in *The Mansion* begins with his devotion to

Linda's mother, Eula, his first glimpse of her in Jefferson, as if his life began at that moment (*M*, 114). Even in the last scene of the novel, Gavin implicitly invokes consistency as the basis of his refusal to admit Linda's guilt to Ratliff: " 'I wont believe it! . . . I wont! I cant believe it . . . . Dont you see I cannot?' " (*M*, 431).

However fragile it may seem, Gavin's affirmation of his entire life is neither naive nor easy. He wills it, despite his disillusionment, and the psychic cost is high. His thoughts reveal that he understands that his claims to superiority and wisdom are delusions. He thinks, *"Yes, I really am a coward, after all"* for allowing Linda to manipulate him to act dishonorably toward Flem (*M*, 378). Later, he thinks about himself in third person: *"the poor dope not only didn't know where first base was, he didn't even know he was playing baseball"* (*M*, 424). Gavin also understands that "his youthful dream of restoring the Old Testament to its virgin's pristinity" cannot console him now, when he feels genuine anguish, as opposed to the embarrassment and longing that he called anguish before.[11] His physical responses in the last two scenes—his sense that he is walking on a treadmill, his terror in Linda's embrace, and his crying in the car—indicate that his two assertions, to Linda and to Ratliff, take a strong act of will. Still, his values are what he has considered best about himself, and he will continue to honor them, whatever effort it takes. Whereas Don Quixote maintains his integrity by privileging his earlier life and renouncing his quest, Gavin affirms his quest as his "real" life, and then, with self-knowledge, asserts that his life has been worthwhile.

On one hand, Gavin's inability to state Linda's intentions to Ratliff may be read as evidence that he will not extend the insights he has had thus far. Linda will not encourage him again. Were he to pursue his observation to Ratliff that " '[t]here aren't any morals,' " he might despair (*M*, 429). Gavin returns to a community of family and friends, as Ratliff implies when he says, " 'soon . . . as *we* get used to it' " (*M*, 427, emphasis added). "Getting used to it" may require reflection, but Gavin's wife and friends have an interest in maintaining the status quo. Despite changes in the town, Gavin's circle approves gallantry. On the other hand, Linda has helped Gavin to change profoundly. He has had more experience and is less insulated from life. Faulkner does not glorify

11. *M*, 427. Dunlap also discusses anguish ("Achievement of Gavin Stevens," 239).

suffering, but he implies that it is better to understand and grow (to be in motion) than to remain innocent. While Gavin's claim that he has had "everything" seems too strong, it may be true in the sense that he has had as much engagement as his "gossamer-sinewed" character can endure (*M,* 128). Immediately after he despairs that morals exist, Gavin adds a way to accept his knowledge that he has participated in what he considers evil, and he forgives himself: " 'People just do the best they can' " (*M,* 429). With this statement, Gavin shows that, although he may continue to act according to his code of gallantry, he is no longer innocent. He no longer sees himself apart from others, above the rest of his community, incapable of doing harm.

The Mansion reflects Faulkner's personal and artistic concern with endings at the time he wrote the book, with some autobiographical echoes in Gavin's review of his life. Gavin Stevens is "approaching" sixty at the end of *The Mansion,* Faulkner's age when he began writing it. According to his biographer, David Minter, Gavin resembles Faulkner's friend Phil Stone physically and Faulkner in his devotion to a romantic love. Pascagoula, where Gavin walks on the beach with Linda, was an important destination, where Faulkner spent his wedding trip and where he spent time with women he loved: Helen Baird, Meta Doherty, Joan Williams, and (as late as 1955 while writing *The Town*) Jean Stein. Gavin's involvement in civil rights and other public issues in Jefferson, the same problems facing Oxford, reflects Faulkner's increased interest in politics.[12]

Faulkner's letters and actions, such as transferring his property to avoid inheritance tax, suggest the stress and awareness of mortality that accompany reviewing one's life. Faulkner expressed weariness in his letters throughout his life, but in December 1956 he wrote more vividly to Else Jonsson that he was working on *The Mansion,* "which will finish [the Snopes trilogy], and maybe then my talent will have burnt out and I can break the pencil and throw away the paper and rest, for I feel very tired."[13] Besides feeling that his life and his career were nearly over,

12. Minter, *William Faulkner: His Life and Work,* 239, 214, 236, 194, 228, 234–35. Phil Stone was a garrulous lawyer, a bachelor until he married a woman sixteen years younger when he was forty-two.

13. Faulkner to Jonsson, December 13, 1956, in Joseph Blotner, ed., *Selected Letters of William Faulkner,* 407.

Faulkner, like Linda, was also saying farewell to Mississippi, moving to a more compatible community where he would not be harassed for his views on integration.[14]

Gavin's relationship with Linda mirrors aspects of Faulkner's relationships with the series of younger lovers he had. Gavin's being involved with Linda while simultaneously drawing back from marrying her recalls Faulkner's maintaining distance and forestalling marriage to any of his passionate younger lovers. However, *The Mansion* does not suggest that Gavin should marry Linda when he feels so strongly that he does not want to. Rather, the novel contains an empathetic portrait of a man who cannot fully commit himself to intimacy. At the same time, Faulkner is also empathetic toward Linda, a strong, sexual woman who speaks for herself and acts in her own behalf. Her courting a reluctant lover recalls a period in Faulkner's pursuit of Joan Williams.[15] Faulkner described Linda and her mother, Eula Varner Snopes, as "two women characters I am proud of," and he called Linda "one of the most interesting people I've written about yet, I think."[16] Faulkner's review of his extramarital relationships occurs at their conclusion, another ending, for he made his final break with Jean Stein early in 1957 and apparently centered his emotional life with his wife, Estelle, in Virginia from this point forward.[17]

What the reader can sense of Faulkner's own assessment as it is transmuted in *The Mansion* and revealed in his letters and actions is

14. For his stance on integration, see Minter, *William Faulkner,* 235. Linda endures the same threats (ibid., 244). After buying a home in Virginia in 1959, "[f]or the rest of his life, Charlottesville seemed almost as much his home as Oxford" (ibid., 242).

15. Ibid., 221–25.

16. Gwynn and Blotner, *Faulkner in the University,* 195; and Faulkner to Saxe Commins, probably in early June 1956 (Blotner, *Selected Letters,* 399–400). Minter notes Linda's resemblance to Stein and Williams (*William Faulkner,* 244). Fulton surmises that "perhaps Faulkner had learned from the young women in his life, Jean Stein and Joan Williams, something of their power and determination ultimately not subject to his control" ("Linda Snopes Kohl," 435).

17. Minter discusses Faulkner's break with Jean Stein (*William Faulkner,* 240). Judith Bryant Wittenberg discusses his return to Estelle in *Faulkner: The Transfiguration of Biography,* 233. Wittenberg sees a pattern in his affairs of "a brief period of intense involvement, followed by slight withdrawal on the part of one or both when it became clear the relationship would always be adulterous, after which the woman married someone else" (228). Wittenberg draws an extended autobiographical parallel in the fiction, saying that Faulkner turned from Meta Carpenter, an early lover, to two much younger women, Joan Williams and Jean Stein, much as Gavin turns from Eula to her daughter Linda (229).

mixed. On one hand, his letters during this period express grief for
what he felt was irretrievably past in his personal life and his career.
His reckless horseback riding, which he described in his letters as a
way of having an intense experience in order to feel alive, does not
suggest acceptance, but desperation and despair.[18] Faulkner certainly
understood what he had given up for his writing. Gavin, an artist of
life who has "presid[ed]" over and tried to see the design of Jefferson,
stands "above" his community, "detached" and "solitary" (*T,* 315–16).
Faulkner wrote to Joan Williams that a necessary part of the writer's
life is "the suffering and the working, . . . the being willing and ready
to sacrifice everything for it—happiness, peace, money, duty too. . . ."
On the other hand, Faulkner affirmed his life as an artist, despite the
cost. In addition to the story it tells, *The Mansion* strives to be inclusive,
with references to nearly all of his Yoknapatawpha saga (although with
a principle of selection that will be discussed later). Thus, in "the last
of [his] planned labors," Faulkner reviewed his work and stamped Yoknapatawpha County as his property once again. Although he doubted
at times whether he had left "a scratch . . . that somebody a hundred, a
thousand years later will see," his assessment of his work, for the most
part, was positive: "Then one day I was fifty and I looked back at it
[what he had written], and I decided that it was all pretty good."[19]

II

The Mansion ends not with Gavin's assessment of his life but with Mink
Snopes's assessment. Mink is the most limited of the protagonists in the
novels in this study, uneducated and without much self-awareness or
breadth of mind, thus showing Faulkner's sense that the life review is
a shared, common activity, possible for many. In contrast, the inability
of Strether's financially successful friend Waymarsh and St. Peter's ed-
ucated colleague Professor Langtry to overcome their rigidity through

18. For discussion of Faulkner's recklessness during the period 1957–1961 when he was
writing *The Mansion* and after its publication, see Minter, *William Faulkner,* chapter 10,
especially pages 245, 237, 241. He also notes Faulkner's grief in 1952, when his affair with
Joan Williams was not going well (ibid., 224–25).
19. Faulkner to Williams, January 13, 1950, in Blotner, *Selected Letters,* 297–98.
"Planned labors" is in a letter to Harold Ober, July 26, 1959, in ibid., 433. "A scratch"
is in Gwynn and Blotner, *Faulkner in the University,* 61. "One day I was fifty" is from
Faulkner to the secretary of the American Academy of Arts and Letters, June 12, 1950,
in Faulkner, *Essays, Speeches and Public Letters,* 206.

reflection, suggests that James and Cather do not regard assessing life as an inevitable process.

In *The Town*, Ratliff calls Mink the only "mean" Snopes, a strong condemnation (*T*, 79). He has the name of a mean animal, and others refer to him as wildcat, wolf, and reptile (water moccasin, rattlesnake, viper). Mink is a sociopath, now termed antisocial personality disorder. His chief emotion is rage over his unmet needs; he shows no remorse and no consideration for anyone but himself. Mink displays furious physical violence during the two prison breakouts and against his defense lawyer. At twenty-five and at sixty, he terrifies two men who are used to imposing their own physical strength and authority, Will Varner and the prison warden. He commits premeditated murder twice to redress what he perceives as wrongs done to him, blaming his victims for "making" him kill them (*M*, 94, 100). Those who know him are convinced that Mink will take vengeance on his kinsman Flem, even thirty-eight years after Flem has failed to act on his behalf during his trial for the murder of Jack Houston. Nonetheless, by telling five sections and part of a sixth in *The Mansion* from Mink's point of view, Faulkner involves the reader and allows Mink's actions to show a logic that makes him both more understandable than the reader might expect a murderer to be and more fully developed than would seem possible.[20]

The variations in aspects of the altersroman that this character offers Faulkner are ironic at times. Like other protagonists who assess their lives, Mink receives a shock that upsets his routine. He has to reenter the world after a thirty-eight-year absence and take responsibility for daily activity. Money and technology offer the most tangible challenges. Mink expects prices to be higher than when he entered prison, but when a storekeeper cheats him, he thinks that the price of bread *"went up another dime right while I was standing there"* (*M*, 263). In a reversal of an earlier scene, Mink walks along the side of a road, this time a highway with "the vehicles now of the rich and hurried who would not even have seen a man walking by himself in overalls. Or probably worse: they probably would have hedged away with their own size and speed and shining

20. See *M*, 374, 392, 411, 415; see 45, 369, 373, 394, 419 for descriptions of Mink as an animal. For discussion of the revisions that make Mink a more sympathetic character in *The Mansion*, see Gregory, "A Study," 126–44. For a positive view of Mink as self-reliant, see Stonum, *Faulkner's Career*, 185–92.

paint any other one of them which might have stopped for him, since they would not have wanted him under their feet in Memphis either. Not that it mattered now" (*M*, 263). Mink is so overwhelmed that he does not recognize the numerous challenges of the cars and trucks that rush past him, yet the narrator describes the vehicles as insulting Mink as surely as the "rich and hurried" Jack Houston did on his stallion on the road to Frenchman's Bend thirty-nine years earlier (*M*, 8).

Often the protagonist of the altersroman loses something of value to him or her. Don Quixote must give up his dream that Dulcinea will come, Strether loses his job and his fiancée, St. Peter has nearly died and "relinquishes" strong emotion, and Gavin has lost "two Eula Varners" (*M*, 434). Having spent most of his life in jail, Mink, a widower who has lost contact with his two daughters, would seem to have been totally divested with nothing left to lose, yet a coworker steals $10 from him. Further, Mink himself has given away $250. Indeed, he feels "rich" upon his release, since he and Flem are still alive, thus giving him his chance for revenge.

The altersroman frequently details the psychology of the characters as they look back over their lives. Mink, however, remains limited. He makes no discoveries about his sexuality or relationships. After murdering Houston in 1908, which he believes he had to do, he has one goal, revenge against Flem, and he makes only one mistake, attempting to escape from Parchman, in reaching it. He thinks that if his escape had been successful, he might have forgiven Flem; otherwise, he acts as if he has not only no choice but also no reason to consider other possible actions. Unlike the more self-aware characters who agonize about their decisions, Mink does not experience doubt. Once out of prison, he barely thinks. He simply has to " 'figger' a little" and repeat his belief that *"Old Moster jest punishes; He dont play jokes."*[21] Rather than ranting and mixing the petty with the serious, as Meadowfill and Jason Compson do in the novel, Mink makes no speeches and performs no wasteful actions. He simply takes one task at a time: get to Memphis, buy a gun, test it, get to Jefferson, and find Flem. His goal is fundamental to him, and his rage is strong, yet his carrying out the revenge is peculiarly unemotional. With the self-centeredness of the antisocial personality, Mink insists that Flem look at him when he fires the gun.

21. "Figger," in *M*, 396. Old Moster, in *M*, 398, 403, 407, 414.

A less humorous variation is that Linda, as Mink's guide, acts as an accessory to a murder. She asks Gavin to get Mink out of jail two years early, provides money, and insists with the Jaguar that she has fully intended that Mink obtain revenge by murdering her stepfather. She literally guides Mink to the door of the house after he has shot Flem.

Even though his seeing himself as a wronged kinsman seems to be a negative identity, Mink assesses his life, on the whole, positively. He feels peace, not letdown, when he has accomplished his revenge. Finally, he has been able to fulfill one intention he has had, and this success is sufficient to allow him to affirm his life. Whereas protagonists in the altersroman often choose to make no change in their lives, Mink plans to make drastic changes: he renames himself and he decides to travel west (*M*, 433–34). Gavin accepts himself as he has been and is, but Mink feels different: "He thought *I'm free now. I can walk any way I want to*" (*M*, 434).

III

In *The Town*, Chick says, "So when I say 'we' and 'we thought' what I mean is Jefferson and what Jefferson thought" (*T*, 3). Since Chick calls attention to the town's voice and since readers speak of Jefferson as a character, the idea that Faulkner looks back over the life of the town is plausible.[22] The assessment of the town in *The Mansion*, which occurs in Chick Mallison's chapters (8, 9, and 11) and in the omniscient narrator's chapters (13, 14, and 15), repeats an important part of Gavin's assessment: change has come, and an earlier way of living is irrecoverable. The review of the town thus contains a third application of Faulkner's prefatory note to *The Mansion*. Although "change and alteration" in the town may be painful, they constitute "living" or "motion." The absence of change is "un-motion, stasis, death." However, the tone of the novel and the characters that Faulkner chooses to mention belie the note's advice to accept change in the case of the town.

Nearly every critic has mentioned Faulkner's recapitulation of his work in *The Mansion* as if the recapitulation were complete. However, the review, which revisits old scenes and characters from novels

---

22. Wittenberg implies that the town is a character (*Transfiguration*, 231). Stonum considers this transitional time as "figuratively the town's adolescence" (*Faulkner's Career*, 163). He sees Chick's narrative as "a record of what has been transmitted."

written throughout his career and includes previously published stories, is neither complete nor unbiased. First, *The Mansion* includes part of the history of Jefferson, but the heroic founders, such as Lucius Quintus Carothers McCaslin, are missing, with only their beleaguered descendants, such as "Uncle Ike" McCaslin, mentioned. Members of the original family still operate the Holston House, but they are "two maiden sisters . . . who were the last descendants of Alexander Holston, one of Yoknapatawpha County's three original settlers" (*M*, 383). The narrator's description is mildly humorous: "The Holston House still clung to the old ways, not desperately nor even gallantly: just with a cold and inflexible indomitability . . . . [N]o man came there without a coat and necktie and no woman with her head covered . . . not even if she had a railroad ticket in her hand." The hegemony of the old landowning families has ended. Of the Compsons and McCaslins, only Jason and Ike remain, both of them ineffective, childless, and propertyless. When Linda searches for relatives of Manfred de Spain in order to return her stepfather's mansion to its former owners, she can locate only two elderly women without heirs. Gavin, the last male Stevens, one of the few remaining old families, has no children of his own. In decline for several decades, the old families have not been vigorous enough to stem the advent of Snopesism in the town.

Second, the novel does not retell, and the characters do not recall, the Civil War stories that were once cherished as tales of courage. For example, the bravery of Col. John Sartoris and his son Bayard during the Civil War, described in *The Unvanquished,* is not mentioned. As Mink walks along the railroad tracks into Jefferson, the narrator points out that the demise of Colonel Sartoris's railroad, now just a minor freight line rather than the grand passenger line it was designed to be, marks a vanquished dream (*M*, 406). Bayard is recalled only as Old Bayard, an old man who was not able to relieve his grandson's pain after surviving combat. The absence of the Civil War heroes is especially notable because so many of the interpolated scenes and chronicles in *The Mansion* involve veterans of war, but this time, World War I or II. The male characters' tone now is sarcastic, particularly in chapter 8, narrated by Gavin's nephew, Chick Mallison, whose war experience includes the hideous absurdity of having endured friendly fire in a German prisoner-of-war camp during World War II. Chick has inherited the facts, but he interprets the story of young Bayard Sartoris's return from World War I, told first in *Flags in the Dust* and retold in *The*

Town, according to what a woman, his mother, Gavin's sister, has told him (*M,* 189–92). Maggie Stevens Mallison is not tempted to "invent [the] vainglory" for heroes, as Miss Jenny describes what men do in the earliest Yoknapatawpha novel, *Flags in the Dust.*[23] Given his source and his own war experience, Chick's retelling is more relentlessly bitter than the two earlier versions. Since World War I, patriotism has required joining the "Yankee army," as Tug Nightingale's story humorously explains, or it is a confidence scheme, as Chick maintains. He repeats his Uncle Gavin's opinion that welcoming parties for the returning soldiers have as much to do with indoctrinating the "next crop of eight- and nine- and ten-year-old males" to be ready to fight the next war as with honoring the veterans (*M,* 180). He also repeats what Gavin has told him, that "war was the only civilized condition which offered any scope for the natural blackguardism inherent in men, that not just condoned and sanctioned it but rewarded it," and that soldiers always come home from war with something to regret (*M,* 189–90). Chick thinks "that the tragedy of war was that you brought nothing away from it but only left something valuable there" (*M,* 354). Although Chick does not speak for Faulkner, the consistency of these observations in chapter 8 and elsewhere suggests a change in Faulkner's attitude toward war: making an exception only of the praiseworthy veteran Devries, narrators in *The Mansion* portray veterans as terribly scarred and do not romanticize war as the occasion for camaraderie and demonstrating valor, perhaps because Faulkner was writing the novel shortly after the less popular Korean War. The point is that when Faulkner told the stories of Jefferson's founding and the Civil War in earlier novels, the narrators and characters spoke with awe for heroes and reverence for the past. *Absalom, Absalom!, The Unvanquished,* and *Go Down, Moses* do not deny Sutpen's obsession, Sartoris's ambition, and McCaslin's cruelty, but the narrators portray the men as having been larger than life. Present-day characters such as Devries, Essie Meadowfill, and Linda Snopes Kohl still face life with courage, but neither the omniscient narrator nor the first-person narrators in *The Mansion* can summon the innocence for hero worship.

The portion of the past that is recounted instead begins in 1908, the "Summer of the Snopeses," when Mink killed Jack Houston, when

---

23. Faulkner, *Flags in the Dust,* 427. This is the novel begun in 1926 and published in 1929 as *Sartoris.*

Eula and Flem arrived in town with Linda, when Ratliff and Grover Winbush lost their café to Flem, and when Gavin was a young student (*T*, 4). This year is important not only in Gavin's life but also in the life of the town, for Gavin and Ratliff date the shift from feudalism to capitalism with the move of Flem, a sharecropper, into the town. The changes that occur to Jefferson between 1908 and 1946—radical shifts in the class structure, the economy, and the town's small scale and appearance—have transformed Jefferson.[24] Even though characters refer to Wallstreet Panic Snopes as an exception in his greedy family, he has opened the first wholesale grocery, the kind that puts small family-owned stores out of business. The old Compson place, a great piece of land formerly owned by one family, is now the site of a housing development with a name, "Eula Acres," that covers the old name of the land. GIs from elsewhere move in to raise families in these "standardized Veterans' Housing matchboxes . . . hutches as identical (and about as permanent) as squares of gingerbread or teacakes" (*M*, 332–33). Thus, fewer residents share the town's history, since they have not "inherited the old facts" (*M*, 381). These changes threaten the town's coherence. The collective voice "the town," a coherent voice as recently as Faulkner's last novel, called *The Town*, is noticeably diminished in *The Mansion*. However, that Linda's educational reforms do not succeed shows that the townspeople are prepared to act as a community to resist some changes. The town's life is ongoing. Jefferson may find a new collective voice, revised as it includes the newcomers, and it may affirm some of the values honored in the past. Nonetheless, the only way that the novel seems able to address the life of the town is not to celebrate "motion," but to note that an era has passed.

Another possible significance of the year 1908 is autobiographical. Born in 1897, Faulkner might have become aware of the town as an entity when he was eleven years old. From the perspective of autobiography, the assessment of the town reveals sadness that the town's history is rapidly being lost with the changes after World War II, while its racism thrives. Chick and the omniscient narrator may speak with sarcasm, but they avoid disgust. The references to the scheming Jason

---

24. See Daniel Joseph Singal, *The War Within: From Victorian to Modernist Thought in the South, 1919–1945*, for a discussion of the changes in the South, particularly the introduction and chapter 1 (3–33). Joseph W. Reed Jr. notes the "chaos of a community which has outgrown its identity" (*Faulkner's Narrative*, 248).

Compson and the less able Ike McCaslin and the Sartoris men implicitly judge the direction of change to be downward. However, by excluding the grandfathers of mythical stature, the assessment of the town in *The Mansion* also resists emphasizing the innocent view that people were once braver or stronger and that the past was a better time.

5

"The Truth Is Like a Lizard"

Angle of Repose, by Wallace Stegner

Angle of Repose traces the assessment of a character who clings to his delusion about his life as firmly as Lambert Strether and Gavin Stevens do and who feels that he is a victim as Professor St. Peter does. Stegner's novel recalls the detailed psychology of *The Ambassadors.* Like Strether, Lyman Ward feels that he is old and alone. Whereas he once had a privileged place in a family and in a university community, he is now divorced, has a grown son who does not share his values, and is retired. Within the last two years, he has had to deal with the shocks of his wife's deserting him, the amputation of his leg and the progression of his degenerative bone disease, and the contradiction between his abundant leisure time and his awareness that he may not have long to live. Lyman returns to his grandparents' home, Grass Valley, California, where he felt "safe" as a child, to reflect on his own life and to compose a "hundred year chronicle of the family" dealing mainly with his pioneer grandparents.[1] His narrative, dictated into a tape recorder and transcribed by a secretary, traces his learning that his version of what has happened in his life and in their lives is faulty. Like Strether, who learns about himself in part by observing closely the development of a younger man, Lyman learns by "liv[ing] in [the] clothes" of his grandparents when they were young (13). Lyman's rhetorical purpose for writing is twofold: he wants to use his grandparents' maintaining a difficult marriage for many years as a weapon against his ex-wife and to justify his life by showing his

---

1. Stegner, *Angle of Repose,* 174, 176, 12. Hereafter cited parenthetically by page number in the text.

resemblance to his beloved grandfather. However, his aim becomes impossible to sustain once he reads all his grandmother's letters and reminiscences, which show him how mistaken he has been. Indeed, given his anger at his ex-wife and grandmother and his intention of praising his grandfather, it is a wonderful irony that Lyman is limited to a woman's point of view, since his grandmother wrote the major portion of the records he uses. She becomes his female guide as he assesses his life, and he shows great courage in not destroying or distorting paper records. Nonetheless, the disjunction between Lyman's purpose and the point of view available to him makes him a tricky, self-conscious narrator for most of the novel.

An important difference between James and Cather, on the one hand, and Stegner, Didion, and Morrison on the other is that the three later writers create self-conscious first-person narrators, and before proceeding it is worth considering the effect of the decision about point of view. Although the reader is in Strether's and St. Peter's consciousness, neither is trying to influence the reader's response to his story. Their process of assessing their lives is internal. They seek to justify themselves and their lives to themselves primarily, although Strether has an important audience within the text, Maria Gostrey and Madame de Vionnet. Of course, James and Cather are trying to shape the reader's response, and their characters deceive themselves, so that these books are as difficult at times to interpret as those with a first-person narrator. However, because Lyman Ward, Grace Strasser-Mendana, and the narrator of *Jazz* seek affirmation from a reader or listener outside their narratives, while simultaneously seeking to understand themselves, their self-awareness as tellers makes their texts full of tricks.[2] In playing with the tension between author and narrator, trying to conceal and reveal,

2. Faulkner's mixing of first person and omniscient narration in *The Mansion* makes it difficult to compare Gavin's assessment in this context. In the criticism of *Angle of Repose*, Stegner's experiment with narrative voice has received the most attention. Audrey C. Peterson discusses his mixing traditional omniscient third-person narration with innovative use of a self-conscious narrator who explores fiction-making and manipulates the reader, in "Narrative Voice in Wallace Stegner's *Angle of Repose*," an article Stegner appreciated (Stegner and Etulain, *Conversations,* 88). Stegner himself refers to "the narrator's buried life, which leaks out through the seams of the narrative" (Suzanne Ferguson, "History, Fiction, and Propaganda: The Man of Letters and the American West, an Interview with Wallace Stegner," 11). Russell Burrows and Michele Moylan say

Stegner, Didion, and Morrison ask the reader to participate in the complexity and elusiveness of self-assessment.

For example, in *Angle of Repose*, gaps are evident in Lyman's knowledge, both because he deludes himself and because he learns as he gathers information and talks; nevertheless, his introductory remarks contain clues that he is not as honest as he would have the reader believe and already understands that his grandparents' story is potentially dangerous unless he can shape it. His misgivings about what he may uncover are obvious in his address to his grandmother's portrait at the outset: "I wonder if you ever reached [the angle of repose]? . . . Was the quiet I always felt in you really repose? I wish I thought so" (19–20). Lyman makes cryptic personal remarks that the reader understands only later as connected to both his grandparents' story and his central concern, "the Ellen business": "I had a wife who after twenty-five years of marriage took on the coloration of the 1960s" (13). He has chosen Grass Valley as his refuge in part because his wife, Ellen, "has no associations with this house" (26). Otherwise, until four-fifths of the way through the narrative, Lyman is careful to avoid any extended mention of his past, which would call attention to his purpose and the similarities between the stories. The only other direct evidence that Lyman controls the narrative is his admission to his secretary, Shelly, that he has hidden information about his grandparents' lives from her, indicating that he has made at least some of his discoveries before he reveals them to her or the reader (150–51).

However, despite his cunning, Lyman's rhetorical purpose of justifying himself while condemning his wife shows up in the discrepancy between what he is doing and what he says he is doing. Although he makes an ethical appeal for himself as teller based on his distinguished career as historian of the American West, Lyman deliberately shapes his study of his grandparents not as a documentary of their life as western pioneers, but as a quest for the secret of their loyalty to each other during their long marriage. After talking with his son, Rodman, Lyman thinks, "What really interests me is how two such unlike particles clung together, and under what strains, rolling downhill into their future until

---

that Lyman Ward learns about himself via the story he tells, in "The Narrative Voice and the Psychology Behind It: Wallace Stegner's *Angle of Repose*."

they reached the angle of repose where I knew them. . . . What held him
and Grandmother together for more than sixty years?" (187). Lyman's
son understands that his father's interest in his grandparents' marriage
is personal. Rodman responds to Lyman's description of his project
with " 'Mother was over yesterday. I think she'd like to see you' " (188),
because he perceives the unspoken part of his father's question: how
did those "unlike particles" remain together when my wife and I could
not? Thus, Lyman's very choice of topic betrays him. His comparing
the two marriages is the central matter that the narrative struggles to
conceal but that continuously breaks through, such as when he uses
the same phrase to refer to Susan Ward's act of disloyalty that he has
used earlier to refer to Ellen's: "She broke something" (506, 395).

In more subtle ways, of course, a teller always reveals himself or
herself in the story. Thus, the reader can look to Lyman's portraits of
the Wards to reveal information about him as well as about his subjects.
Once into his story, Lyman's bias, especially his negative attitude toward
women, becomes clear, although it is not until much later that the
reader understands just what his delusion involves. Lyman claims that
he loved his grandmother, who was a mother to him after his own
mother died when he was two, yet through most of his narrative, he
is as thorough and harsh a critic of her as he is a champion of his
grandfather. He couches this criticism as banter, easy to overlook, so it is
worthwhile to detail its extent. Lyman begins by denying Susan Ward's
written record that she married Oliver for love and instead characterizes
her marriage as her reaction to being jilted by Thomas Hudson (44,
49). Lyman's most serious charge is that his grandmother must be
held accountable for not accepting the consequences of her choice of
husband: marriage to Oliver Ward means living in the West. Susan
initially treats their going West as an "adventure" that would last for
two years, maybe ten (53–54, 59, 156, 166), even though her husband's
lack of formal education and his love of the wilderness mean that he
cannot live in the East (89). Lyman imagines that Oliver protected
her and contributed to her "fantasy" that their life in the West was
temporary with their real life to begin sometime in the future (89).
He also conjectures that Oliver Ward must have been willing to live
in the East, but he has no evidence (330). Although she chose to live
in the West and reaffirmed that decision several times (53, 163, 202,
330), Lyman portrays Susan Ward as creating an unfair argument: if
she chooses Oliver Ward, then she must tolerate living in the West, but

their location is his fault and it is "exile" for her, a word that Lyman attributes to her frequently. In Lyman's portrait, by not acknowledging the consequences of her choice of husband, Susan Ward is irresponsible and sets up a debt that Oliver cannot possibly repay.[3]

Lyman recognizes that his grandmother was strong-willed and that she supported her family financially, but he turns these strengths into flaws. He shows Susan Ward deciding which jobs Oliver should take and insinuates that she felt that her earning money and her self-pity gave her the right to decide where to live in the West. Despite limited finances, she sends her son, Oliver, to school in the East, over his and his father's strong objections. However, whereas Lyman's narrative causes his secretary to judge that Oliver " 'let her lead him by the nose' " (242), other evidence in the text encourages the reader to conclude that, given the information the Wards had at the time, Susan's decisions were always more practical and showed more concern for the family than Oliver's. Besides criticizing her willfulness, Lyman uses his grandmother's career against her by heightening her ambivalence toward her role as sole breadwinner. Here again, Lyman portrays her negatively, as wanting to have it both ways: she enjoys her fame as a writer and illustrator, made possible in part by her western subject, but at the same time she resents that she cannot live in the East and that it is her hard work and money that support the family (384, 386, 445–46).

Susan Ward *has* committed a terrible act of disloyalty to Oliver with her passion for Frank Sargent, one of Oliver's assistants, and her momentary carelessness that causes her daughter's death.[4] However,

3. For further discussion of the Wards as pioneers and Susan Burling Ward as a reluctant westerner, see Stegner and Etulain, *Conversations*, 48, 90–91, 172–73. Melody Graulich looks at the polarized gender myth ("the wandering husband and the nesting woman") to inform her reading of the gender politics in the novel. Lyman's cultural premise that men and women are in opposition causes him to "reduce Susan to the 'type' he was trained to see" ("The Guides to Conduct that a Tradition Offers: Wallace Stegner's *Angle of Repose*," 88, 95). See also Kerry Ahearn, "*The Big Rock Candy Mountain* and *Angle of Repose*: Trial and Culmination."

4. Stegner has relied in part on the letters and reminiscences of Mary Hallock Foote, published one year after *Angle of Repose* as *A Victorian Gentlewoman in the Far West: Reminiscences of Mary Hallock Foote*, ed. Rodman W. Paul. Stegner changed his source to dramatize the rift in the marriage and to heighten the moment of evaluation, the last time Susan Ward decides whether to stay married. He added the adultery and child's death and made clear the hints about the husband's alcoholism, which will be discussed later.

Lyman makes less of this more obvious sin of passion than he might. His anger at his grandmother for her attitude toward her husband and for her snobbery is evident long before he learns her actual transgression. What Lyman resents about his grandmother turns out to have less to do with moral principle than with his personal experience, for he has endured his grandmother's taking in him "a second chance at raising up an ideal gentleman" (279). In recalling her teaching him manners and morals at the beginning of section 5, Lyman describes her as domineering and smothering. She has taken his school assignments and illustrated them with her drawings. She insisted that he name his son Rodman without explaining that this is a name in the family of her best friend, Augusta (27). However, although he complains about his grandmother's "gentility . . . inherited through the female line like hemophilia" and snobbishness (280), Lyman preaches her old-fashioned values to his son and his secretary (57, 82, 28). Like Susan Ward, he expresses himself in writing. Further, he has enjoyed and still values most of what she longed for. Like the well-educated gentlemen farmers of his grandmother's beloved home in Milton, New York, he has intellectual occupation while being taken care of on his similar ancestral estate in California. Lyman is inconsistent when he belittles Oliver Ward's managing the mine at Grass Valley as "a kind of surrender" without also acknowledging that the job has provided him not only with his current refuge, but his childhood home and status in the community as the boss's grandson as well (18, 280). Lyman champions the West without seeming to realize the difference two generations make. The grandson, who grew up in one place and who lives a life very close to that of the squires in his grandmother's eastern home, criticizes his grandmother for holding herself superior to the West as it was in her day and for hating their having to wander from one mining camp to another (243, 246). Still, his sense of injury seems out of proportion to what he "suffered" at her hands, especially given his profession and his preferences, which are like his grandmother's ideals, until the reader understands the subterfuge. Lyman's resentment of his grandmother's domineering is misplaced anger at another woman, his ex-wife, as will become clear. Lyman remains deluded for the greater part of his narrative. He will judge that Ellen Ward's leaving him for another man has hurt him far more than the zealous mothering of Susan Ward, but his grandmother is still a safer target than his ex-wife at this point.

At the same time that he carefully documents and dwells on his grandmother's failings, Lyman is extremely kind to his grandfather, whom he says he "likes" and "trusts" more than anyone (390) and whom he has taken as the model for his own behavior: "I refer my actions to his standards even yet" (25). Lyman associates his grandfather with the mine pump he designed, a machine that is a phallic image in its shape, its "slow, heavy pulse," and the thrust of its strokes (389–90). As a child, Lyman felt reassured by what he describes as the pump's "dependability" in the dangerous mine shaft. It makes the mine safe and is a reminder of his grandfather's "masculine steadiness" (26). The pump's rhythmic sound can be felt and heard, but the pump itself is not actually visible and therefore not showy, as opposed to his grandmother's fussing about.

Although Lyman admits that his grandfather is a failure (246) and that he does not appreciate his wife's need for companionship (89), he turns his other flaws into virtues. He makes Oliver's being easily duped less of a fault by attributing it to his integrity and willingness to trust people. His impracticality and his errors in filing the Idaho land claims and not patenting cement or the automatic weir become evidence that Oliver cannot engage in politics and is so engrossed with great ideas that he loses sight of details (164, 168, 374). Lyman shares his grandfather's contempt for those who made fortunes in the West and praises Oliver Ward for being "a builder, not a raider" (169). Circumstances, Lyman argues, were against his grandfather, the great western-pioneer man, "twenty years" ahead of his time, without the necessary financial backing, which had to come from political negotiation in the East. "[H]e was [not] foolish or mistaken. He was premature" (341). Until the end of the summer, Lyman maintains that his grandfather was a hero, a man of good character hampered by his wife and his circumstances. This praise allows Lyman with one stroke to bolster his self-esteem by showing his similarity to his heroic grandfather and to denigrate his grandmother and, by implication, women in general.

Lyman's research thus far has supported his delusion, and his project looks to be a success. His independence at Grass Valley and use of his grandparents' story as justification for being furious with his wife for divorcing him both seem unshakable. However, two incidents, his audience's response and his reading his grandmother's letter from Idaho, force Lyman first to acknowledge the extent of his deliberate distortion and then to have a startling re-vision. Looking at these incidents briefly in the order in which they occur is necessary as preparation for discussing in greater detail the implication of Lyman's close identification with his grandfather and his blurring his grandmother (mother) and his ex-wife.

Lyman's only audience at this point, his secretary, Shelly, corroborates the reader's feeling that Lyman has been biased toward his grandfather when she admires his grandfather's "magnanimity," a response Lyman sees that his narrative elicits (390). Lyman carefully explains to Shelly that Oliver was never "noisy" or "sloppy" about his drinking, was " '[n]ot a drunk,' " but " 'a drinker' " (389–90). Lyman's denial, which he knows contradicts the common opinion, made directly to Shelly, who has heard the stories of Oliver's alcoholism from her parents, is his most strenuous and obvious bending of the truth, as he admits soon after (421–22). Lyman's success in being able to manipulate his audience turns out not to have the good effect he intended. To his credit, not telling the truth disturbs him. Shelly's praise for *his* "magnanimity," her seeing him as having a quality that he knows he does not possess, also makes him uncomfortable. Lyman is fully aware that, while he has been outwardly supportive of her during their conversations, his private description of Shelly's marital troubles as the "shabby little soap opera . . . playing at my house" is condescending and intolerant (143).

Shelly's response forces Lyman to make a decision. He can end his narrative or continue. Lyman has several ways to avoid facing the unpleasant fact that he has shaped his narrative, perhaps unfairly, in order to justify himself before his ex-wife. One way of ending is to continue drinking, to be "half stoned before lunch," which he rejects (421). His giving up drinking at this point, an important psychological break with his grandfather, indicates that Lyman is willing to look clearly at his own situation and anticipate a future, which he has said earlier that he did not have (20). Pursuing the latter course, continuing, Lyman can easily blame his grandmother entirely, both because her passion is more tangible than the other acts of disloyalty in their marriage and because he controls the narrative, or he can present a more objective view of the evidence. Just as he rejects alcohol, he also rejects lying. His moral position, playing "Nemesis in a wheelchair . . . messing around in her [his grandmother's] guts," in order to write a public record troubles him (391). He shares his grandmother's desire for privacy, which he feels acutely toward the end of the summer when his own privacy at

Grass Valley is threatened. He chooses honesty in part, then, because
of his integrity and genuine desire to understand his situation and in
part, apparently, to ease his mind about continuing his search. His
concern for his grandmother's privacy is an impulse of sympathy for
her, arising from his own experience, but constituted by feeling for
another rather than from consideration of what would best serve his
rhetorical purpose. While he studies the newspapers and letters that
make Susan Ward's passion and the circumstances of her daughter's
drowning clear, " 'the most private things [he] know[s] about her,' "
Lyman thinks about his response to his own wife's disloyalty, *his* deepest
secret, and begins to revise his assessments of both marriages (391).
For the last one hundred pages of the narrative, Lyman responds to
both women, who become more obviously blended together, as are
the two marriages. So, as an act of courage, Lyman stops drinking and
continues writing, moving away from his alcoholic, silent grandfather
and allowing himself to be vulnerable to whatever he may find.

   Lyman's moment of insight has many resemblances to Strether's en-
lightenment when he sees Chad and Madame de Vionnet in the country
and to Gavin's distress when he sees Linda's Jaguar. Suddenly, matters
that the three men might have known all along become inescapable.
Reading one of his grandmother's letters from Idaho, the second cause
of his re-vision, takes away Lyman's gravest criticism of her and his last
defense against his wife and allows him to reinterpret a significant memory from his childhood. In thinking about Ellen, Lyman has lashed out
that "when you take something you want, and damn the consequences,
then you had better be ready to accept whatever consequences ensue"
(395). He has also criticized his grandmother for similar irresponsibility,
but accepting the consequences is exactly what Susan Ward does when
she returns to the West for the last time: "I am going back. Behind all
this anguish, I believe, has been my refusal to *submit*. I do not mean
to my husband only. I have held myself above my chosen life, with
results that I must repent and grieve for the rest of my days. I have
not been loyal. If there is ever a chance that our lives may be patched
together, it must be in the West, since that is where I failed" (473). This
statement is her evaluation of her life. Lyman and Oliver have blamed
Susan for her snobbishness and her refusal to accept responsibility for
her life in the West, and her words and her action of living alone for
two years in the place she most hated both show that, at this point,
she finds their charge just. Lyman judges her, finally, as "responsible,

willing to accept the blame for her actions even when her actions were, as I suppose all actions are, acts of collaboration. . . . She held herself to account, and she was terribly punished" (477). He is fair enough to conclude that if he believes both marriage partners are responsible for the relationship, then he must apply the standard in his own case and revise his conclusion that his wife has been entirely to blame for their divorce.

Lyman's reading a reference in his grandmother's letters to a rose garden in Idaho suddenly makes a childhood memory vivid and allows him a new perspective on it, one that both his grandparents have been careful to deny him before. Susan Ward's letters call the destroyed garden "my punishment," and, she notes, Oliver "meant that [ruined garden] to be before my eyes from day to day as a reminder, and I accept that as only justice" (476). Lyman recalls overhearing his aunt question his grandfather about a destroyed garden in Idaho as a boy, but he did not believe that his grandfather, who loved flowers, could have destroyed a rose garden established with hard work in the wilderness. Stegner uses that overheard question as a tableau, a frozen moment that Lyman's current reflections recall. This question and his grandfather's silently walking away in response troubled the young boy so much that he revised it immediately in an attempt to make sense of and control it. With the reference in Susan's letter and what he now understands about his grandfather, Lyman revises his boyhood denial with an overwhelming flood of insight into his grandfather, and the rose garden becomes the damning piece of evidence: "I, who looked up to him all his life as the fairest of men, have difficulty justifying that bleak and wordless break, and that ripping-up of the rose garden, that was vindictive and pitiless" (483). He gives his memory a new interpretation, which triggers another memory that now takes on significance: in all the time he lived with them, he never saw his grandparents touch (506). What he thought was devotion and respect was deliberately considered distance, intended by his grandfather as punishment.

Lyman has bragged continually that he resembles his grandfather, but with his new insight, he watches the resemblances turn to accuse him rather than justify him as he intended. With grim humor, Lyman refers to himself as "being made of stone." He remains "rigid," unwilling to respond when his son mentions Ellen because "[t]here is too much of grandfather in me" (188–89). Later, he describes his grandfather in a similar way: Oliver Ward "turn[s] to rock" when he has been "betrayed" by those he trusts (497). He points out that they are both stubborn (189). "Like Grandfather, I do a little better without any pushing and pulling" (392). "[L]ike my father and grandfather before me, I am a justice man, not a mercy man" (395). Lyman has believed that people ought to stay married whatever the cost, but when he finds out the terms on which his grandparents stayed together, that his grandfather was unwilling to forgive his wife when she asked, he is horrified at their relationship. He cannot wish Susan's "life-long penance" on anyone, even Ellen (504, 510). He no longer wants to imitate his grandfather, whose rigidity he sees in a new way and whom he now judges as cruel and as less of a person than he had thought.

Lyman's grandmother provides guidance as he assesses his life. Going through her private papers, even with the purpose of criticizing her, gives Lyman insight into a woman's point of view and forces him to listen to a "different voice."[5] In front of her grandson, Susan Ward decorously kept her secrets about her lover and daughter as well as her husband's. Her having remained silent, protecting his grandfather's silence, without asking for anyone to validate her, humbles Lyman. The most difficult lessons that Susan Ward teaches Lyman are that judgment can sometimes entail cruelty and that being in a relationship with an uncommunicative, vindictive partner can cause terrible pain. Two earlier experiences make Lyman receptive to these lessons. As mentioned earlier, he first empathizes with his grandmother when he considers privacy: he is threatening hers just as his own is being threatened. This empathy comes from their having a similar concern. In contrast, he is moved beyond his own concerns when he must consider his grandmother as an unfaithful wife. This image is painful for Lyman, yet not only does he imaginatively re-create her seduction, which might start with just a touch, "the deadliest enemy of chastity, loyalty, monogamy, gentility with its codes and conventions and restraints," but he also applies his reconstruction of that scene to his own wife. The result is that he empathizes with Ellen's loneliness and vulnerability: "When one flesh is waiting there is electricity in the merest contact" (452).

Lyman's new perspective on his silent wife's position is remarkable when compared with his most self-centered reflection just one hundred

---

5. I am using Carol Gilligan's words that refer to woman's viewpoint as distinct, from the title of her book *In a Different Voice: Psychological Theory and Women's Development.*

pages earlier. Lyman readily sympathizes with Susan's isolation when her husband is in the mine (89; compare 91, 153, 375, 435), but until now, he has apparently not noticed that he "did neglect [Ellen] for history . . . [and] did bend her life to fit the curve of mine" (395). He never questioned whether his wife was fulfilled and assumed that she was "quiet" by nature. If Susan Ward, with a career and a reputation, could fear losing her identity (222), how much more might Ellen, without a career outside the home. Lyman has been so self-centered that he does not understand why Ellen could not find as much satisfaction as he does in his achievement. Even during his reflection, he wonders, "Does she remember as I do . . . when I was beginning to get noticed, when all the saturation in books began to pay off for us? Does her mind's eye ever get caught by the image of me coming out of the study after a good four-hour morning? . . . I suppose all the time the life that I thought was sane and quiet and good was *too* quiet for her. It must have made her restless to see me with endless things to do, a lifetime full, and herself with only household routines" (392–93). "For us," "image of me," "only household routines": Lyman's actions have said (and his remembering here continues to say) that he came first, that Ellen was never as important to him as he was, that her concerns were not as worthwhile as his, hardly loving statements. Even though his words reveal to the reader that Lyman is considering Ellen's point of view, he fails here to pursue the implications of his self-centeredness, his contribution to their divorce. He has not valued Ellen, except as an adjunct. He uses the circumstances of her leaving him while he is ill as an excuse not to look for his own faults. "If she had left me when I *was* still a man, . . . I would have hunted among my own acts and in my own personality for her justifications, and would have found them" (395). He repeats here his criticism of Susan Ward: both women knew what their husbands were like when they married, so they should not complain of the consequences. However, his not knowing why his wife left him becomes an indictment of him rather than of her. That is, he has not understood her well enough to know whether she was unhappy. He can only imagine.

Here again is evidence of Stegner's craft. Lyman is appalled when he recognizes his self-centeredness, but the reader has seen him as smug, proud, and judgmental for some time. He has treated others besides Ellen as adjuncts. He says that his son, Rodman, does not appreciate him or share his values, whereas Rodman's actions, although a bit blustery, show genuine concern. It is Lyman who does not recognize or value Rodman as he is, not the other way around. Lyman regards the Hawkes family as there for him, a part of his birthright and the accepted order. He is a snob toward Shelly, whom he regards primarily as a member of the family that has for three generations worked for the Wards (23, 42). His tapes reveal that he is extremely condescending toward her (as well as toward his former students at Berkeley) and judges her harshly, at the same time that he has erotic fantasies about her. In the process of working through the disjunction between his view and the view his grandmother has given him, Lyman's portrait of himself comes to resemble the reader's idea of him.

Typical of characters in an altersroman, Lyman is completely divested by his discoveries. He already feels alone and misunderstood, betrayed by his body, his wife, and his son. He has sought solace at Grass Valley, his "King's X place," where the caretakers and his memory of his ancestors will not betray him as the living have (505). But they all do. Ada Hawkes, his nurse, is old and ill, and her daughter, Shelly, is liberated and nosy and anxious to get away. His grandmother, the proper Victorian lady with the high-necked dresses, was not loyal to her husband, and his grandfather, generous to his employees and grandson, was pitiless and vindictive toward his wife. The public version of their marriage conceals a different reality. His grandparents presented themselves as upholding values that they could not maintain toward each other. Like Joe Allston, the protagonist in Stegner's next novel, *The Spectator Bird*, Lyman has deliberately cast himself in the role of spectator only to find that he is not "quite spectator enough."[6] Although he has been worried about his disloyalty to his ancestors, as his images of himself as a "werewolf" in a "borrowed body," a judge, and "Nemesis" reveal (176, 395, 391), Lyman finds himself telling a story that forces him to revise his version of his life and accept responsibility for his relationship with Ellen.

Because he tells his story to persuade, Lyman has been searching for—and dismissing—possible audiences. He himself is his main listener. Lyman thinks aloud into his tape recorder as a kind of autotherapy or attempt to discover how he really feels. He is so afraid of the only other actual audience he does have, his secretary, that he considers

6. Stegner, *The Spectator Bird*, 82. Hereafter cited as *SB* in the text.

sending certain tapes to a typing pool to keep them from her (143). Shelly scares Lyman because she makes his biases and manipulation clear: " 'You get close to dealing with their sex life, and blip, you turn off the light' " (236), and " 'Was she really thinking of leaving him, or are you guessing?' " (388). She seeks the writer in the text: "Her discussion of Oliver and Susan Ward have this torque in them, they twist toward Lyman Ward too often" (390). Like his son, she reminds him of the generation gap; Shelly is even less like the loyal Ada than Rodman is like his father. Shelly also reminds him of his age and physical condition when he realizes that his hope for a longer, sexual relationship with her is only a "fleeting foolish dream" (466).

Besides these two actual listeners, Lyman has three more potential audiences: the public, Rodman, and Ellen. Lyman has been a publishing scholar, so he may eventually publish this work, but he will have edited his personal dilemma by then. Lyman's ideal of family makes his son the most suitable audience for a family chronicle. He says that he wishes he could talk with Rodman, who has the "largest stake" in the story of his ancestors (42). However, Lyman seems angry with and jealous of his son. As a professor, Rodman has replaced his father in the academy, a reminder that Lyman's academic career is over. Lyman also feels a sense of betrayal, since he believes that a sociologist, even Rodman, cannot share a historian's values or approach his standards of scholarship. At the same time, Rodman refuses to allow Lyman to direct his career. The text also suggests that Lyman sets up this audience to deny it. He dismisses Rodman, not because his son does not care, but because he might understand his father's self-justification too well, as Rodman demonstrates (188–89). Lyman so desperately wants Rodman to side with him against Ellen that the risk of having him as his actual audience is too great.

It becomes obvious that the audience Lyman seeks is his wife. Shelly can react to the narrator's concerns that are within her experience, sexuality and deciding whether to trust someone, but she is inadequate to comment on commitment and enduring loyalty. Only Ellen can say whether she lived a "trapped life" and whether she was "dissatisfied" (452, 393). By the end, Lyman's version of his marriage is, the reader feels certain, closer to Ellen's, but he still needs her to verify it. Moreover, unlike his grandfather, he wants to make some sort of peace with Ellen. Whether he will have a full reconciliation with Ellen remains uncertain, but he has temporarily put aside his anger to understand her desertion and has accepted his share of the responsibility for their divorce. His learning to see his grandmother as a person has been the catalyst for his re-vision. The correspondences between the two women and between his responses to both of them are significant. Reading her words and the reviews of her work, Lyman sees Susan Ward as a well-paid, well-regarded artist, not just his grandmother (mother). He also sees that she has been capable of taking responsibility for her actions, the value he privileges above all others. By ceasing to regard his grandmother as a nurturing mother who ought to be there for him with unconditional love and without needs of her own, he simultaneously revises the image he has had of her as domineering and smothering. Similarly, when Lyman ceases to hold his wife as solely responsible for the failure of their marriage, and therefore as more powerful, he can risk a meeting. Lyman's willingness to be vulnerable, to reapproach intimacy with Ellen, shows that he is braver than either Strether or St. Peter. Moreover, Lyman has reached this reconciliation in greater isolation, in response to a written record without friend or confidant. Less self-centered, Lyman relinquishes his innocent view that his life should be safe because he has suffered so much already. While his last words do not express a firm conviction, they reveal Lyman's wish to try again to have in reality the intimacy he thought he had shared with Ellen: "I lie wondering if I am man enough to be a bigger man than my grandfather" (511).

The title of this chapter comes from a statement by Turgenev that Stegner uses as an epigram for a later novel, *Recapitulation:* "The truth is like a lizard; it leaves its tail in your hand and runs away; it knows that it will shortly grow another one."[7] According to this simile, truth is evasive and regenerative. Although the lizard has one tail at a time, many are possible. The idea of reconstructing a long-held version of the truth in response to some challenge is a central feature of the altersroman in general and of Stegner's later novels as well. Stegner's novels are all autobiographical, or written "too close to the bone," as he says in an interview, so it is not surprising that the concerns of the altersroman first appear in the novels written around the time of his retirement from Stanford University.[8] Stegner began his series in 1967

7. Stegner, *Recapitulation*. Hereafter cited as *R* in the text.
8. Stegner and Etulain, *Conversations,* 17. Although he denies several times that he is Lyman Ward, Stegner does admit that he uses Lyman as a mouthpiece for his concerns (98). For his comments on the undergraduate college students of the 1960s, see also

with *All the Little Live Things*. Throughout that novel, Joe Allston, the protagonist, remains angry, with his problems unresolved. In *Angle of Repose*, published in 1971, Lyman Ward shares Joe's anger and posing, but his review of his life reaches resolution. Returning to Joe Allston in *The Spectator Bird*, published in 1976 and set four years after *All the Little Live Things*, Stegner shows him rejecting his former view of himself as "drifting," going "downstream like a stick," and replacing it with a view of himself as active and responsible (*SB*, 7, 209, 211). Joe risks hurting his wife, Ruth, who also acts as a female guide, in the process of recasting his life story. With *Recapitulation*, published in 1979, Stegner complements his early bildungsroman, *The Big Rock Candy Mountain*, published in 1943, by having Bruce Mason explore his own sexuality, omitted in the early novel, and reevaluate his relationship with his parents as an adolescent. His girlfriend's old apartment, now the funeral home where Bruce's aunt has been prepared for burial, has a stairway reminiscent of the one in James's "The Jolly Corner." However, unlike Spencer Brydon, who courageously seeks and confronts the self he might have become in James's story, Bruce avoids his friend Joe Mulder whom he thinks may mirror the self he might have been had he not left home. He approaches Joe's house in the dark but wanders in the garden instead because he lacks "the nerve to push the doorbell" (*R*, 110–11). Bruce's female guide, a "generous and supportive" voice that he imagines, also allows him to maintain the safe distance from others he has sought since leaving Salt Lake City (*R*, 87). As the etymology of the title, *capit* or head, indicates, Bruce's assessment is private. Completed without checking with another person to verify reality, his review allows him to forgive others for disappointing him and himself for his disloyalty to them by leaving Salt Lake City, but it does not deepen his ability to form relationships or make him seem wiser. This brief overview of twelve years of his career as a novelist shows Stegner's absorption with reviewing and affirming one's life. Like James, he traces several versions of the process, arriving at a different resolution each time.

Stegner and Etulain, *Conversations*, 15, 95–96. Stegner's last novel, *Crossing to Safety*, is more about facing death, a task that occurs later in life than late middle age, when reviewing the life in order to affirm it and make use of the time remaining is the primary task.

6

The "Prudent Traveller"

A Book of Common Prayer, by Joan Didion

In other novels in this study, female characters, such as Stegner's Susan Ward and the narrator and Violet Trace in Morrison's *Jazz,* review their lives, but Didion's *A Book of Common Prayer* is the only novel studied in detail here in which a woman's assessment is the central and singular focus. This novel offers an opportunity to look at a woman's consideration of the kind of delusions that women may have to give up at midlife. Didion reflects Roger Gould's observation that, while assessing intimacy is important, evaluating the way they use power is a more significant concern for women at this stage of life.[1] Like the other protagonists in the altersroman, Grace Strasser-Mendana does not begin her first-person narrative to consider her own life: " '[T]he narrator' plays no motive role in this narrative, nor would I want to."[2] Instead, Grace proclaims that she writes to be a "witness" to Charlotte Douglas, a younger woman from the western United States who has visited Boca Grande, although she really intends to vilify her for being "deluded," the most devastating criticism Grace can imagine (4). She slowly assimilates what has occurred during the year she has known Charlotte as she composes her narrative in the following year. Beginning with a patronizing and sarcastic tone, Grace ends in sorrow and dismay when she realizes that in scrutinizing Charlotte, she has

---

1. Gould, *Transformations,* 246–66. *A Book of Common Prayer* reflects many of Gould's observations about "women's increased mandate to act on their own behalf," but not all of the novels by women with women protagonists studied here as examples of the altersroman do so (246).

2. Didion, *A Book of Common Prayer,* 14. Hereafter cited parenthetically by page number in the text.

also been diagnosing and criticizing herself: "I am less and less certain that this story has been one of delusion. Unless the delusion was mine" (280). At the end of her year's reflection, Grace sees clearly that while she does manipulate others, including the reader, she has done so to allow nearly everyone, again including the reader, to have control over her in ways that she has not understood before. Even her wielding the power of the pen to regulate what she reveals about herself while analyzing Charlotte turns out to have been self-destructive.

A Book of Common Prayer is the most pessimistic novel in this study. On his deathbed, Alonso Quixano praises God that he has returned to his senses in time to affirm, if only for a few hours, his life before he set out as Don Quixote. Although in despair, Cather's Professor St. Peter can find a portion of his life to affirm. Lyman Ward is overcome by remorse by the end of his assessment, but he still wants to try to speak with his ex-wife and perhaps renew their intimacy. On her deathbed, having cleared away her delusions, Grace sees only the negative: how deceived she has been and how much she has lost. Moreover, she is disgusted that the values her culture endorses have encouraged her naïveté, even as an adult, and her arrogance. Her habitual way of thinking about herself has been destroyed, and nothing positive replaces what she has lost. Having failed, by her account, in a long list of roles as social scientist, wife, lover, mother, and "witness," Grace can say that she has been adequate only as a colonial "overseer," an identity she claims to despise (279). Her despair comes in particular from her convictions that she has been arrogant and aloof and has failed Charlotte. She cannot rejoice that now, at least, she sees clearly, nor does she believe that she can change in the little time remaining. Her finding the courage to reach out to a reader offers one note of possibility, which she undercuts with the two confessions of failure that begin and end her last chapter: "I see now that I have no business in the place but I have been here too long to change," and "I have not been the witness I wanted to be" (279–80).

Grace introduces herself to the reader with her delusion intact, that she is perceptive, forthright, and in control: "I do not dream my life. I try to make enough distinctions" (14). Even though she believes that her narrative is not about her, she structures it to begin with the initial blows to her usual way of regarding her life that have come two years earlier, her being diagnosed as having an incurable form of cancer and Charlotte Douglas's coming to Boca Grande. She then promptly denies that either matters. First, she asserts that facing death does not scare her: "I will die (and rather soon . . .) neither hopeful nor its opposite" (14). Grace sets forth all that she has gained with the passage of time, especially status and independence, as if her privilege and accomplishments can somehow shelter and console her. Grace's defenses seem so secure that were it not for the shock that Charlotte offers her usual way of regarding herself, even her illness might not cause her to begin to review her life.

Charlotte's arrival is the second change that precipitates Grace's assessment of her life, although at the outset, Grace thinks that this *norteamericana* from the western United States, young enough to be her daughter, is her opposite: Charlotte "made not enough distinctions. She dreamed her life" (3). Certain that Charlotte has nothing to teach her and will be a safe distraction from her illness, Grace minimizes both her attempt to explain Charlotte and Charlotte's effect on her: "I am interested in Charlotte Douglas only insofar as she passed through Boca Grande, only insofar as the meaning of that sojourn continues to elude me" (14). Grace devotes so much energy to understanding Charlotte that it is worth looking in detail first at her initial fascination and second at her explanation of Charlotte and her lovers and then Charlotte and her daughter, Marin, in order to understand how Charlotte acts as the young person of the same sex who challenges the protagonist. Watching Charlotte "come up . . . against the hardness of the world" penetrates Grace's reserve, as no experience has for many years, and she simultaneously loves and is angry with Charlotte as if she were her daughter (243). Only when she understands emotionally as well as intellectually, as mother and judge, that Charlotte is in a vulnerable position because she has placed herself there, does Grace begin to see resemblances to her own contradictory behavior. Didion emphasizes the role of the young person by having Charlotte threaten Grace not only as a reminder of age but also as a mirror for her own American attitudes and self-destructive, manipulative behavior.

At the outset, then, Charlotte's mysteriousness—her reason for being in Boca Grande, her vulnerability that contrasts with other actions, such as her casually wringing a chicken's neck—inspires Grace's considerable detective activity. Lonely and without as much occupation as she implies, Grace keeps careful track of Charlotte: what she eats for dinner, where, and with whom, her bout with dysentery, her days at the airport.

She readily accepts an assignment from her brother-in-law Victor: " 'As another *norteamericana* you could meet her' " (26). However, Grace's narrative soon reveals that her detective work is not all harmless. As she undergoes cobalt treatment, she seizes on meddling unconscionably in Charlotte's affairs to distract herself. Before she really knows her, Grace treats Charlotte as the subject of one of her experiments, sacrificing Charlotte for her own amusement. For example, Grace mentions Charlotte to her lover, Victor, in front of his wife and after Grace knows that Charlotte has rejected him (36–39). One month later, after Victor has told her pointedly not to see Charlotte again and her son, Gerardo, has specified a guest list limited to family, Grace invites her to the small gathering to welcome Gerardo back to Boca Grande. Her defensiveness about her invitation calls the reader's attention to her meddling: "I cannot now think how I happened to invite Charlotte for drinks that afternoon. . . . I was not yet that close to Charlotte. . . . I suppose I might have invited Charlotte only to discomfit Victor. In fact I have no idea why I invited Charlotte" (202–3). Grace mentions her cobalt treatment as another possible excuse. Since she has witnessed Charlotte's sexuality and she knows that her son is a playboy, she cannot be entirely surprised at the reaction between them. Like Faulkner's Gavin Stevens, who believes that as the town lawyer he is worldly wise and can remain immune to the effects of whatever demands Linda Snopes Kohl may make, Grace, the anthropologist and biochemist, sets out eager to dabble in human affairs, cavalier about her effect on others, and sure that she cannot be touched or held accountable.[3] Thus, Charlotte enters Grace's life primarily as an entertaining diversion and target for her habitual sarcasm, and as only a vague reminder of Grace's age.

Having brought Charlotte into the family circle, however, causes Grace to wonder how much she may be to blame for what she calls Charlotte's "death"/"murder"/"previous engagement" eight months later during the October Violence in Boca Grande (52). Unwilling to plead openly, Grace is still anxious to absolve herself from guilt for Charlotte's remaining behind after everyone else has fled. Her attempt to do so by identifying other causes, primarily Charlotte herself

---

3. For a discussion of Grace's interference, see Patricia Merivale, "The Search for the Other Woman: Joan Didion and the Female Artist-Parable."

(Charlotte "chose to stay"), is difficult because until toward the end, she can think only of adjectives that excuse Charlotte from responsibility: deluded, "hopeful," preoccupied, "reflexively seductive," inattentive, "oblivious," and vulnerable (3, 33, 196, 210). She considers blaming Gerardo, Victor, or Charlotte's husband, Leonard, but can find no convincing evidence. Grace decides, finally, that Charlotte has been in control, that she manipulates others so as not to seem powerful herself, based on two observations: first, Charlotte's deliberate denial that her sexual liaisons in Boca Grande have consequences, and second, her continual and willful misperception of her daughter, Marin, which amounts to her trying to dominate Marin.

First, Grace struggles to reconcile the apparent contradiction in what she has seen of Charlotte's behavior in Boca Grande, her regarding the sexual relationship as serious, while remaining "oblivious to the disturbances she could cause" (210). Grace has evidence that Charlotte acts. Charlotte taps and then rejects Victor. She rents the apartment where she and Gerardo sleep. She also understands the politics. When she must witness Gerardo's former mistress, Carmen Arrellano, destroy American cholera vaccine with a machine gun, she can no longer deny either that it has been misappropriated or that she is vulnerable, as her being "upset" that evening confirms (242–45). She gauges when she is about to be killed, because she mails Grace her emerald ring during her last walk (279–80). However, because she resists all efforts to get her to accept that her actions in Boca Grande have consequences and to get her to leave, warnings that Grace phrases tentatively in March and April and repeats forcefully from July until October, Grace repeatedly qualifies her estimates of what Charlotte knows: "So dimly did Charlotte *appear to perceive* . . . ," and "Charlotte heard . . . but Charlotte *seemed* not to listen" (230, 244, emphasis added). Charlotte insists that she has not been touched emotionally in Boca Grande; nevertheless, by having affairs with two Strasser-Mendana men and snubbing the third and then by staying, she brings about her own death. That is, Charlotte uses her understanding of the ritual scars that she and Grace believe males make on their sexual partners to form a triangle with Victor and Gerardo that destroys her. However much she denies her "connections" and her responsibility, she manipulates her affairs in Boca Grande, as she has before with Leonard, her husband, and Warren, her ex-husband, to let others fight over her. At some level, then, Charlotte never forgets that sex is political and involves power. As Didion said in an interview, "I think there is a confusion between passive and successful. . . . Charlotte is very much in control there in Boca Grande."[4]

Grace's conclusion that Charlotte manipulates men, while claiming to be unconnected, influences her when she examines Charlotte's relationship with Marin and encourages her to consider that Marin is the audience Charlotte wants for her actions in Boca Grande. Grace is upset to see how a mother's attention can be harmful rather than nurturing, serving the needs of the mother and denying those of the child. Marin's rebellion against her mother is extraordinary: joining a terrorist group and hijacking a plane. Based on Charlotte's remarks and her own interview with Marin, Grace deduces that it is precisely because Charlotte's demand is so strong that Marin must react forcefully, even if self-destructively, to break away from her mother's fanciful version of her. She denounces her maternal heritage unmistakably by attaching Charlotte's grandmother's gold wedding bracelet, which Charlotte "insisted" she take at their last meeting, to the firing pin of the bomb (61). Didion pointed out in an interview that Marin "has been misperceived by her mother most of her life,"[5] and Marin shows that she understands this when she tells Grace that Charlotte sees " '[s]ome pretty baby. Not me' " (267). Her words are uncanny, given Charlotte's tearing out a catalog picture of a young girl's dress and saying, " 'This would be pretty on Marin' " (5). She wants Marin to remain a child, willing to allow her mother to dress her, as Charlotte remembers her.

Charlotte replaces her actual daughter with her own version of Marin entirely when she says that the Marin in Buffalo is not her daughter. Grace tells her that with Marin's address in Buffalo she can go to her, but Charlotte says, " 'No . . . I can't exactly. . . . [I]t's not even Marin. . . . Marin would have found Warren [her father and Charlotte's first husband]. Marin would have found me' " (258–59). Charlotte cannot visit her daughter in her own surroundings, for to do so would require that she acknowledge Marin as she is, and Charlotte insists on her fantasy. Finally, however, to deny that her daughter is responsible for any of her actions as a terrorist by calling her a "victim of circumstance" is to deny that Marin is a person (199).

Although she has not been able to nurture her daughter, Charlotte hopes that Marin can meet *her* needs by defying time and space. Not

4. Didion, "A Visit with Joan Didion," 20. See also Didion, "Joan Didion," 350, for similar remarks.
5. Didion, "Cautionary Tales," 23.

only must Marin remain a child, but she must also stay at her mother's side. As Grace reconstructs the past, she says that when Charlotte has felt that she and Marin are becoming separate, "she fought it, she denied it, she tried to forget it" (111). She wants "never to let go" (65). Charlotte is so emotionally insecure that she is incapable of being alone, and she has arranged her life so that she is always accompanied. For example, Charlotte never really leaves home to go to college, since she sleeps all week and returns home every weekend. She "erases" the memory of her mother "when Warren [comes] to her door" (114). Later, taking Marin, she leaves Warren. She is involved with Leonard before she is divorced from Warren. She leaves Leonard for Warren, and she leaves both again with the baby that she hopes can take Marin's place. (Leonard understands immediately that, although they have not had sexual intercourse for some time, Charlotte insists on it in order to get pregnant after Marin leaves [86–89]. She wants to have another child because if she is a mother, then she has an identity, she will not be alone, she is not old, and she cannot die.) She shares her apartment in Boca Grande with Gerardo. None of the connections that Charlotte forges with others, however, is as strong as the one she has with Marin. She tells Leonard, *"'I don't have to see Marin because I have Marin in my mind and Marin has me in her mind'"* (263). Charlotte's claim that "'Marin and I are inseparable'" is certainly crazy, not because it is false, as Grace thinks at first, but because Charlotte believes that she has incorporated her daughter.

Charlotte also asks Marin to be her savior.[6] Gerardo tells Grace that at the moment of her death, Charlotte "cried not for God but for Marin" (66, 276). Charlotte says that she "adores" Marin, using a word that in one sense is properly reserved for God and in another means to idolize (65). Grace expresses Charlotte's certainty that Marin will join her as an act of faith: "That Marin would turn up in Boca Grande Charlotte did not literally believe but never really doubted" (199–200). When Grace reconstructs Charlotte's protectiveness of Marin, she states Charlotte's belief in the reciprocal: "that when she walked through the valley of the shadow she would be sustained by the taste of Marin's salt tears, her body and blood" (65–66). The full verse in Psalm 23 is "Yea, though I walk through the valley of the *shadow of death,* I will fear no evil: for

---

6. Also noted by Katherine Usher Henderson, *Joan Didion,* 75–76. In *Prisoners of Childhood,* Alice Miller discusses how parents try to have their children meet their own needs.

thou art with me; thy rod and thy staff they comfort me" (emphasis added). Charlotte wants protection from death. Under the guise of maternal love, the bargain Charlotte proposes is terrifying: she wants Marin to remain by her side to "sustain" her with "tears, body, and blood," just as Charlotte has lived for her.

If Charlotte's purpose in refusing to leave Boca Grande involves sending a message to her daughter, several interpretations are possible. Charlotte wants to die because she realizes on some level that Marin is changed and will never join her. Or her staying and perhaps, as Merivale suggests, providing money for guns may be an attempt to prove her devotion and her loyalty. By dying on the right side in a "people's revolution," Charlotte can show that she honors Marin's choice in order to be reconciled with her.[7] If Charlotte intends her remaining in Boca Grande as a political message to her daughter, it is certainly ineffective, at least during the time of Grace's narrative. On the other hand, if she can get Grace to carry the image of her dying in a place to which Marin could have gone without fear of the FBI, then perhaps Charlotte can touch Marin in a way that she cannot when alive. Her staying is neither "oblivious" nor heroic, but an aggressive and vengeful act, part of her attempt to dominate Marin, even at the cost of her own life. Grace's judgment that Charlotte "chose to stay," acting deliberately and destructively in relation to men, supports the conclusion she reaches after she visits Marin in Buffalo that Charlotte has also been in control while appearing to wait for Marin.[8]

Charlotte and Grace appear so dissimilar and Grace seems so disdainful that the reader wonders what inspires her maternal affection. Grace mocks Charlotte's prayer that " 'it' turn out all right" as expressing a foolish and irresponsibly optimistic view of life, until she judges that she has shared what she considers such a stupid assumption (56). Informing their behavior is their innocence, based on the attitude they learned as middle-class girls growing up in the western United States that encouraged them to believe they are superior by class and nationality

---

7. Merivale, "Search," 137–38.

8. 201; cf. 260–63, 238–39. For another discussion of how Grace's response to Charlotte shifts, see John Hollowell, "Against Interpretation: Narrative Strategy in *A Book of Common Prayer*," 169, 172–73. I see Grace as understanding more finally than either Henderson, in *Joan Didion,* 73, 80, or Leonard Wilcox, in "Narrative Technique and the Theme of Historical Continuity in the Novels of Joan Didion," 79.

and, because of their gender, they will be taken care of. When she recognizes during her year of reflection that they have been raised with similar values, "give or take twenty years," and thus admits kinship by heritage, Grace becomes vulnerable to fondness for Charlotte as a daughter and later, to a more thorough comparison (57). She discovers by the end that the charges of delusion and manipulation that she has leveled against Charlotte apply to her as well. Initially, however, because Charlotte seems dissimilar enough so as not to be personally threatening, she catches Grace off guard and sets her up to learn from Leonard, the topic of the next section.

Even with the threats to her complacency that her illness and Charlotte offer, Grace would probably not learn as much about herself as she does if not for Leonard Douglas's revelation that her husband financed the Tupamaros, Marxist urban guerrillas active in Uruguay in the 1960s and early 1970s. Grace is so visibly shaken by what Leonard tells her that he later apologizes (255). Like Charlotte and Marin, she first tries to ignore what he has just said—" 'Where's Charlotte?' I said abruptly" (247). Grace's narrative reveals her shock, but she forces the reader to reconstruct the two reasons that the deception bothers her. First, with a single statement, Leonard destroys her view of herself as clever and alert because his fact tells her that if she never knew that her husband, Edgar, financed revolutionaries, then she also must have been ignorant of other information that people have tried to hide from her. Leonard's revelation shatters Grace's pride: "I had no idea. I *prided myself* on listening and seeing and I had never heard or seen that Edgar played the same games Gerardo played" (247, emphasis added). What is worse, Grace sees that she has been duped by the men whom she has treated with disdain. Being a *norteamericana* in Boca Grande has not meant that she is superior but *"de afuera."* Grace must also consider that Edgar's giving her the power of attorney in his will has as much to do with his desire to thwart his two younger brothers' desire for power and to ensure his son's inheritance as it is a compliment to her skill. The second reason for her reaction follows from the first. Because she has never viewed Edgar as a revolutionary, she apparently never considered his role in the assassination of his brother Luis. Leonard's fact tells Grace that Edgar may have been responsible for the death of Luis, whom she seems to have loved, out of jealousy.

The biggest leap the reader must make is to understand Grace's hints that she loved her brother-in-law Luis. The chief clue is that her treatment of this brother-in-law in her narrative differs significantly from her mention of everyone else in the family. At the end of parts 2 and 4, Grace intones the full name of the Boca Grande airport: "El Aeropuerto del Presidente General Luis Strasser-Mendana. Deceased" (141, 192). The repetition, the placement at the end of two sections of her narrative, the length of the name in contrast with the short "deceased," and setting off "deceased" all call attention to the name while she lingers over it. Grace provides few specific dates, but she does give the date of Luis's death, April 1959 (12). Grace has regularly eaten lunch at the decaying foundations of the city Luis planned, Progreso, even on the day her husband died (120). That is, after Luis's death, but while her husband was still alive, Grace has returned to a place some distance from her home that is associated with Luis. She does not mention a wish to get away or to enjoy the scenery in her reflections about Progreso, only her memory of its designer, Luis. She calls Progreso his "grand design" and "toy," but she displays wistfulness rather than the sarcasm she uses to describe the "rather wishful machismo" of Gerardo and the "touchiness of command" of Victor and Antonio, for example (10, 13, 25). Grace laments his having placed himself in such an exposed position as president, where he lasted only fifteen months, until Leonard's revelation forces her to see that *she,* not the presidency, has been the cause of his death.

Grace dismisses men summarily throughout her narrative, so it is galling for her to have to take a lesson from Leonard. Nonetheless, despite the gap concerning Luis in Grace's text, the truth of Leonard's information is never in doubt. She believes him readily because she has long possessed all the information needed to draw such a conclusion about her husband's activity. She has told the reader that all the revolutions in Boca Grande "are made . . . entirely by people we know," that Edgar survived Luis, and that these two older brothers had no fear of their younger brothers, Victor and Antonio, thus eliminating them as Luis's assassin (22, 12). Grace halfheartedly accuses Victor, but says she has no proof (214).

Grace's response to the shock Leonard gives her can be measured in another way as well. Even though she has been manipulative and her text has been convoluted and private, Grace uncharacteristically exposes herself on the last two pages (only thirty pages after her report of Leonard's news) to confess to the reader her failure as an egalitarian and as Charlotte's witness. Just as the reader must work to infer her affair with Luis, so too, trying to understand how Grace suddenly discards her delusion about herself and why she makes such a revealing confession sends the reader back to the beginning, to reconsider her career, her position in Boca Grande, and her relationship with her audience. Reviewing Grace's narrative in light of the last two pages allows the reader to understand how drastic a revision her confession is, both as an act and in its content. Grace realizes, in general, that she has power, although not the way she thought she did, and that she has used it, sometimes unwittingly, to hurt herself and others. She ends in despair in particular because she sees that, although she disdains men, she has helped to sacrifice Charlotte, a younger woman, a daughter, to men's whimsy that nonetheless has terrible consequences.

To begin to untangle the contradictions between what she asserts and what her narrative reveals, then, Grace has insisted until shortly before Leonard's arrival that she is "egalitarian" (234, 10, 14, 170). She seems to bristle at the words *aristocrat* and *gentleman,* and she has "slapped [Gerardo's] face" for referring to someone as " 'in trade' " (170). However, at the same time, Grace is positive that she is superior because of her heritage, career, and nationality. First, she has tried to elicit her reader's respect for her connections from the outset, when she gives her birth name without explaining that she is from an influential Denver pioneer family. Instead of divesting herself of names, as she does for Charlotte, Grace lists her names as important to her identity: "My name is Grace Strasser-Mendana, *née* Tabor" (8).[9] She would consider it unseemly to brag about her heritage, although it is clear that she relies on the reader to recognize a name still visible on buildings in Denver. The significant specific resemblances between Grace and the real Horace Tabor's granddaughter are that both only children lived privileged lives on the western frontier, growing up in the Brown Palace Hotel, and faced disruption of their lives due to scandal when they were about ten years old. Because she is a Tabor and because she wants recompense for having been abandoned by her parents, Grace learns to

9. See also my "The Tabors of Colorado and *A Book of Common Prayer*" for further discussion of the relevance of Horace Tabor, his son, and granddaughter to this novel. In contrast to the way she identifies herself, Grace seeks Charlotte's identity in her surnames, but ends simply with "Charlotte" (84).

demand deferential treatment and the show of protectiveness, however inadequate, such as the Brown Palace staff offers with the "éclair and cocoa" (120).

Similarly, Grace lists the names of the professors with whom she has studied anthropology, recognized leaders in the field, to impress the reader. Even as she claims not to have learned anything using anthropology, Grace is pointing out with pride that she has had a career and written "well-regarded studies" (4). However, it soon becomes obvious that her career has ended with another kind of abandonment. When she meets Warren Bogart, Charlotte's first husband, he addresses her as "Miss Tabor" and calls her professor Claude McKay an "aristocrat" and a "gentleman" (170). Grace identifies her professor for the reader as the man whom she "accused [at their last meeting] . . . of publishing [her] work under his name." She immediately confuses, perhaps deliberately, her responses to Warren's words and to the name Claude McKay, and claims to resent these words in general: "When I remember what I was taught in Colorado certain words set my teeth on edge." She then abruptly changes the topic of her memory to Gerardo and obscures what is bothering her by giving all the possible causes for her pique: the weather, her cobalt treatment, fatigue, business negotiations, tension among her hosts, Warren's generally obnoxious behavior. But her angry reaction shows that Warren has cleverly touched a memory that is still laden with emotion for her. Grace has not given her betrayal by her professor as a cause for her leaving anthropology, but she has mentioned it earlier as coinciding with her doing so: "I 'retired' from that field, married a planter . . ." (4). She has confronted her mentor directly, but then she gives up the fight and surrenders entirely, "retiring" (which she emphasizes with quotation marks) and devaluing anthropology by saying that it cannot teach much anyway. Ironically, her work's being stolen both demeans her and proves its excellence. Still, her professional success in the study of culture has not prevented her personal victimization by her professor.

Grace asserts that as a result of her next career, marriage, she achieves wealth and power. She negotiates the Strasser-Mendana family's North American contracts for copra and brags that she has "putative control of fifty-nine-point-eight percent of the arable land and about the same percentage of the decision-making process" in Boca Grande (165, 12). Although she berates her American father-in-law for calling himself "Don Victor," she acknowledges his ability to make a fortune in Boca

Grande and contrasts his (and by their shared nationality, her) American practicality with Luis's dispensable "design" (10). Since she never says that she loved her husband or that she mourns him, Grace seems to have been motivated to marry by reasons other than affection. On the rebound from the betrayal by Claude McKay, Grace has sought vindication and protection in marriage to a wealthy landowner and solace in the private ("amateur") study of physical science, where she looks for more predictable and manageable cause and effect.

As *"dueña,"* as a Tabor married to a millionaire in an undeveloped country, status and security seem ensured. Thus, far from denouncing aristocracy, as she asserts, Grace has sought the privilege she has been denied in North America and in her profession. Moreover, as her exchanges with Victor, Elena (Luis's widow), and Gerardo show, Grace stoops to exercise power slyly within the family. She refuses to accept the risk of any position more public than administrator of the family's estate, while she privately provokes her in-laws, since even their hostility, which cannot diminish her financial power, acknowledges it. Her text reveals that Grace exploits the "interior" of Boca Grande—its natural resources and the family—for her own needs (11). She can never get enough status or power to allay her fear of death and betrayal—especially by men—but, in response to the affronts she has received, she can disdain others in an effort to feel superior.

Grace may have gained wealth, but she has gone from one dependent relationship to another. Indeed, she seems compelled to repeat what has happened in the past by putting herself in situations in Boca Grande in which she is under men's control and denied autonomy and in which she will be betrayed again. She never gets out of this self-destructive cycle, as Leonard makes clear, neither with Edgar nor with her son, Gerardo. For example, she bestows favors, such as Charlotte, to keep Gerardo in her court. He fulfills their bargain to some extent, such as when he contributes to Grace's reputation by warning his Aunt Elena not to anger Grace because she might " 'cut off [Elena's] clothes allowance' " (76). But he treats his mother ironically, as when he annoys her by "tracing his line" through his father (14), and he dismisses her concerns entirely when he does not protect Charlotte from being shot in the back (276). In the end, Grace sees that she has neither controlled Gerardo nor won his love or regard, but has submitted again to a man who is implicated in the murder of someone she loves, a woman who has become like a daughter. She has been procurer, not puppet master.

Asserting that she has chosen to stay where the light is bright in order to see things as they are and not be fooled again, Grace has chosen the opposite: a home where the blinding light makes seeing problematic and where her American innocence allows others to take advantage of her easily.

Finally, Grace attempts to control her reader and her text, only to find that she has not had her way in that arena either. Despite her disclaimer at the end of her introduction that she includes facts about herself only out of consideration for the reader, Grace has actually tried to shape the reader's response reflexively, out of her deep need to manipulate (14). That is, while she does not understand how deluded she has been or all that she has revealed in her narrative until she reaches the end, Grace uses subtle rhetoric from the outset, with a covert, contradictory appeal to the reader's emotions. She presents herself as a confident narrator, a woman made "prudent" by her experience, one who has already discarded ineffective methods of learning about people (4). However, while demanding respect as a shrewd, liberated woman from the western United States, a Tabor, an anthropologist, and the head of the Strasser-Mendana family, she simultaneously asks the reader to treat her with deference because of all she has suffered. For example, even though she mentions her cancer and cobalt treatments in passing, she reminds the reader often enough to be asking for sympathy. Grace uses this rhetorical stance throughout her narrative, but her introduction is a paradigm. The first fourteen pages of her text, supposedly her introduction of Charlotte, also contain the attitudes and the events in her own life that she considers important, and her selection, intended as her ethical appeal, can be read more convincingly as her insinuation that whatever has happened to her has not been her fault. Her introductory list is a long succession of losses: her parents, her home, her profession, her belief in her profession's assumptions about how much people can know about others or about themselves, her country, her brother-in-law, her husband, her son, Charlotte, and, soon, her life. Later, she recasts these losses as betrayals for which she has not been entirely responsible: betrayal by what she has learned as a child, by her father's murderer, by Claude McKay, Edgar, and Gerardo, and by her body's cell mutations. Yet even in her introduction, as she seeks to shape the reader's response, denying a "motive role in this narrative," Grace undermines herself by reminding her audience to question why she takes all the trouble to write (14).

With her opening sentence, Grace asserts the power of the pen to shape her text: "I will be her witness" (3). The tension between this opening assertion of control and what she will confess with her final words at the end of her year of reflection, "I have not been the witness I wanted to be," breaks through briefly at the beginning of chapter 2 with her command, "Call this my own letter from Boca Grande" (280, 9). This early in the process, she can simply revise: "No. Call it what I said. Call it my witness of Charlotte Douglas," and distract the reader with "one or two facts" (9). After she reports the shock that Leonard gives her and Charlotte's death, she can no longer impose herself on her text in this way.

The end of *A Book of Common Prayer* is difficult to interpret, since Grace seems to lay aside her manipulation of the reader in favor of honest disclosure. Her confession, which leaves her vulnerable before the reader, may be read as the worst bit of self-destructive behavior she has shown yet or salvific. To begin with the negative interpretation, in the last two pages, divested of nearly everything, Grace destroys her remaining delusion, her characterization of herself as the betrayed, when she admits that she has fooled herself: "You will notice my use of the colonial pronoun, the overseer's 'we.' I mean it. I see now that I have no business in this place but I have been here too long to change. I mean 'we' " (279). "I see now" begins a potentially liberating statement. After "but," Grace closes possibility. She can neither affirm her life as overseer, nor can she see the possibility of change. Usually, after seeing their delusion, characters who have assessed their lives can find a way to affirm the life they have had. In some cases, they become reconciled to a part of the life, as Professor St. Peter affirms his eight-year-old self or as Don Quixote affirms his years as " 'Alonso Quixano, whose way of life won for him the name of Good.' "[10] In other cases, they feel that some part of their identity has been special, as Gavin Stevens feels honored to have served Eula Varner and fought Snopesism in Jefferson and as Strether decides that he is glad to be an American and to have the regard of Madame de Vionnet. Shedding the delusion is painful, but gaining the knowledge is perceived as a benefit, even by St. Peter. In contrast, Grace finds no consolation in knowledge, only pain. She cannot, like Alonso Quixano, wish for more time to live with her clear vision.

10. Cervantes, *Don Quixote,* 826.

Grace implies that she would prefer not to have had this experience or gained this insight, that she would be better off not knowing Leonard's revelation, so that she could still hold herself superior to Charlotte and others. She presents her discarding her illusions only as loss: she has less self-esteem rather than clearer vision.

Additionally, she has no friend like Ratliff or Augusta to stand by her side. The "overseer's 'we'" identifies her with a group, but Grace feels utterly alone. Her household is not filled with loving family and a servant she trusts, as Alonso Quixano's is, but with Gerardo and a "dim Mendana cousin" as nurse (52). She has reached out to those around her and no one has been able to satisfy her need. Gerardo denies responsibility for anything that has happened. He is too cold about people, including Charlotte, so Grace says she does not speak much with him anymore (52, 13). She does not trust her youngest brother-in-law, Antonio, and Victor is more concerned with his own loss of power. The most Leonard Douglas can do to console her is to say that the identity of Charlotte's murderer does not matter, implying that fixing blame—achieving knowledge and justice—is, finally, neither possible nor useful (276). Grace goes to Buffalo as Charlotte's ambassador to speak with Marin, but she remains hostile, too severely wounded to accept what Grace says, so they have nothing to share (266, 280). Like John Marcher in James's story "The Beast in the Jungle," whose insight comes one year after the death of the woman who loved him, Grace expresses horror that her insight has come too late and that the only person who might have cared is dead.

In several ways, the process of Grace's review does not feel like those in other altersromane in this study. She has had a revelation of enormous significance, and it lays bare her assumption about American innocence, which in turn changes how she views her life, yet it does not change her life. It is a revelation that destroys, and Grace does not reach the point where she can see what might come next or what else she could do with her insight. In this way, besides its resemblance to James's story "The Beast in the Jungle," *A Book of Common Prayer* also seems at first to resemble Faulkner's *The Mansion*, which ends with Gavin's sobbing in recognition of the way he has deluded himself. Gavin has been just as naive and is just as embarrassed. He, too, has helped a murderer and feels duped. Neither he nor Grace can ever see themselves in the same way again, nor can they see, at the moment, a way to go on, with their most precious truths proved wrong. However, two differences between these novels explain why *A Book of Common Prayer* seems more negative. First, Gavin ends by crying, a spontaneous emotional release, whereas Grace ends with a confession, which is a kind of release, but one that relies on carefully crafted words as well as feelings. Although divested of her usual defenses, she has had time to process the shock and prepare her address to the reader in the last chapter. Second, and more important, Gavin is accompanied by his friend Ratliff, who cares about him and will stand by him. Ratliff may allow Gavin to rationalize his participation in Linda's plot against Flem, but he will not permit him to ignore his lesson altogether. He knows Gavin and Gavin's naïveté, but he will not use that knowledge to take advantage of him. They have been friends for many years, and he still regards Gavin as his best friend. Grace's narrative feels negative in part because she is so alone. She has potentially had such a supportive friend in Charlotte, but she is implicated in initiating the events that have led to Charlotte's murder. Everyone in the family that she already knows would use knowledge of her insight against her. Even though her world (as she depicts it) has few people in it, she could have a broader horizon. She visits Miami easily, for example. Still, she can think of no one anywhere who would help her affirm who she is, this new version of herself. She excludes any such possibility when she summarizes these ideas and insists that they cover the present, the past, and the future: "I am *de afuera.* I have been *de afuera* all my life," and "I have been here too long to change" (52, 279). Gavin and Ratliff belong to a community that has been and will be supportive, even though Gavin is temporarily embarrassed before it. Readers, Grace's community of attentive strangers, as opposed to a close companion throughout adulthood, cannot converse with her or help her through the day, and they may not be as familiar with her heritage and situation or as sympathetic.

Considered in this sense, Grace's final chapter is a complete surrender, with closure and an admission of failure. On the other hand, despite her grief and despair, it may also be read as Grace's attempt to rescue her assessment with a confession that creates an audience who can help her affirm her life. In *Confession and Community in the Novel,* Terrence Doody defines confession as "a deliberate, self-conscious attempt of an individual to explain his nature to the audience who represents the kind of community he needs to exist in and to confirm him."[11] Given

11. Doody, *Confession and Community,* 4. Most critics see Grace as achieving redemption through her love for Charlotte. Janis Stout's view that Grace writes her narrative to

that the people around her have been inadequate, Grace can address only unknown readers if she wants to create a community that will honor her getting rid of her illusions and acknowledge her accepting responsibility. She is no longer hiding.

Moreover, after some struggle, Grace decides not to give in to the temptation to excuse Charlotte as a product of her culture and time, hence a victim, which would also allow her to excuse herself. In the two passages that are the furthest forward in time, chapter 1 in part 2 and chapter 5 in part 6, Grace softens her indictment of Charlotte slightly by observing that people do what their mothers taught them as children and that Charlotte's dreams about "sexual surrender and infant death" are "commonplaces of the female obsessional life. We all have the same dreams" (53, 280).[12] But she resists such pleading for herself when she asserts that she has been responsible, that she is "the *dueña*." Grace asserts instead that we cannot afford dangerous and innocent illusions like those that she and Charlotte have held: children can meet their parents' needs for love that they have not gotten elsewhere; people from the United States are egalitarian and, hence, superior; women are owed protection; the safest way to wield power is by manipulation; one can feel secure and safe. Instead, Grace creates an audience who will pay careful attention when she writes, "You will notice," which is a command to the hasty reader and a compliment to the attentive one. Attention is necessary if her audience is to understand her confession.

Two nineteenth-century German altersromane, Stifter's *Der Nach-sommer (Indian Summer)* and Fontane's *Unwiederbringlich (Beyond Recall)*, present resignation and renunciation *(entsagung)* as suitable attitudes toward the passage of time. Among the novels in this study, *The Professor's House, The Mansion,* and *A Book of Common Prayer* portray resignation, but this response looks negative in comparison with the affirmations of Alonso Quixano, Strether, Lyman Ward, and Violet and Joe Trace in *Jazz*. Nonetheless, despite the possibilities that resignation may be appropriate and that Grace sees her delusion and reaches out to the reader, *A Book of Common Prayer* is still pessimistic since she cannot affirm her life. She wishes for death (51). In the little time she has left,

---

atone for her failed mothering and as an act of martyrdom is closer to mine (*Strategies of Reticence*, 171, 174).

12. In "On Morality," Didion notes, "For better or worse, we are what we learned as children" (161).

it seems unlikely that she will overcome the despair that she feels after reviewing her life.

When interviewed by Susan Stamberg, Didion described her novels as "cautionary tales. Stories I don't want to happen to me. *A Book of Common Prayer* to some extent has to do with my own daughter's growing up. . . . I think that part of this book came out of the apprehension that we are going to both be adults pretty soon."[13] Reading her novel as Didion's warning to herself, the twofold prophecies she makes are devastating, and the threatened punishment for failing to take heed is death. First, with Charlotte's story, she warns that a mother who is overly involved with her daughter will push the child away. A mother who misperceives her child, putting her own needs above those of her child, will disable the child and make communication between them impossible. Second, with Grace's story, she warns that a person who is judgmental and smug about her superiority, certain that she is right but unwilling to display her talents openly for fear that she might be held accountable, cannot achieve intimacy and will hamper any group she is involved with. A woman who remains deluded, refusing to admit such unpleasant truths about herself, will be duped by others again. Both sets of lessons are cast as warnings against self-destructive behavior. The isolation of Grace and Charlotte is terrifying.

Women at three stages of life are dead, or in Marin's case, psychologically dead since she speaks only words memorized from a political tract. While it is possible to read their fate as evidence of Didion's despair, her killing off these destructive parts of herself—the inadequate mother and the hopeless, judging voice—may also be therapeutic. At the same time, although she creates Grace as a first-person narrator, she is not Grace, as she reminds the reader: "[I]n adopting Grace's (the narrator's) point of view, I felt much sharper, harsher. I adopted a lot of the mannerisms and attitudes of an impatient, sixty-year-old dying woman."[14] *Grace* confesses failure and disgust with what she sees at the end of her narrative. Didion can take a lesson from what Grace sees, even if her character cannot.

13. Didion, "Cautionary Tales," 23.
14. Ibid., 22.

$$7$$

"Grown People"

Jazz, by Toni Morrison

Like Stegner and Didion, Morrison portrays the protagonists' childhood experiences as predicting the issues that they must deal with at this stage of their lives. These three writers insist on the importance of mothers and mothering. Lyman revises his judgment of his grandmother and learns to respect her in *Angle of Repose.* In *A Book of Common Prayer,* Grace remains bitter that she, Charlotte, and Marin have not received adequate nurturing. Morrison, however, shows characters grieving, then acting to rectify loss that would seem insurmountable. The three protagonists in *Jazz* reenact the task of the earliest stage of life, dealing with their sense that they have been abandoned and learning to trust. Finding a way to be nurtured by women, Violet and Joe Trace can recover from having been rejected and betrayed, so that they can see themselves as worthy once again and, hence, deserving of love from a beloved. Then, as people who can choose a beloved and can be chosen, they are able to reconcile themselves to the life they have had, reenvisioning it as worthwhile. The Traces are able to affirm their marriage and renew and deepen their intimacy while they still have time together, despite the violence and betrayal they have experienced.

The optimism of Violet and Joe's story contrasts with the outcome of the story of the third protagonist in *Jazz,* the first-person narrator, who also assesses her life. Choosing to "trace" Joe and Violet's story and believing proudly that this story is one that she alone can predict, the narrator embarks on a quest that threatens her habitual way of thinking about black American experience and about herself as a superior recluse observer. After she is shocked by observing the healing that Joe and Violet experience, the narrator recognizes that choosing to live "in [her] mind" after having been "left standing" has not been the only choice she has had.[1] She also sees that her community has understood and honored her unspoken request to help her fool herself that she is involved and wise. With their story as her guide, the narrator imitates Joe and Violet and finds a way to receive maternal nurturing, in her case by imagining a mother who will "understand" her, extend "her hand," and touch her (221). The narrator appears vulnerable before the reader and expresses her desire for intimacy in the last section, but her final cry, "If I were able I'd say [*that I have loved only you*]," is as far as she moves towards change (229).

The narrator conceals her own story throughout most of her text, although she reveals her presence as she assesses the black experience in the South after the Civil War and in Harlem from 1906 until 1926, the present time of *Jazz*. Her catalog of U.S. history provides a context for the Traces' story. The narrator's celebratory "Here comes the new" and Joe's descriptions of himself as having " 'changed into new seven times' " and being " 'a new Negro' " are references to ideas prevalent since the late 1890s and current in Harlem in the 1920s.[2] She juxtaposes the hopes of black Americans at the beginning of their "new" life in the North, as they constitute themselves as the "New Negro," with the reality of the continued "want and violence" that they find (33). Items in the narrator's catalog reflect this tension repeatedly: "clarinets and lovemaking, fists and the voices of sorrowful women" and "Nobody wants to be an emergency at Harlem Hospital but if the Negro surgeon is visiting, pride cuts down the pain" (7). Other public events, particularly the antiblack riots in St. Louis and New York, are more directly relevant to the protagonists, causing significant changes in their lives. Like the other writers considered here, Morrison understands that however intense one's personal reflections in late middle age are, an individual does not assess his or her life in isolation, apart from the social context. Finally, Morrison's signifying, or "read[ing] and critiqu[ing] the texts of other black writers as an act of rhetorical self-definition," becomes in terms of this study the fourth version of

1. Morrison, *Jazz*, 9. Hereafter cited parenthetically by page number in the text.
2. Ibid., 7, 123, 129, 135. *The New Negro: Voices of the Harlem Renaissance*, ed. Alain Locke, is the name of the 1925 anthology of poems, stories, plays, and essays by black Americans. For further discussion, see the introduction by Arnold Rampersad in the recently reissued edition of *The New Negro* and Houston A. Baker Jr., *Modernism and the Harlem Renaissance*, 71–98.

confirming identity as part of assessing the life one has had.[3] Recalling and revising Douglass, Hurston, Petry, and Ellison, among others, as part of her text is Morrison's confident affirmation of herself as writer.

Violet's and Joe's assessments are so intertwined that it makes sense to look at them together and then consider how their story guides the narrator. Like *A Book of Common Prayer, Jazz* begins after the protagonists have their second shock, Joe's shooting his eighteen-year-old lover, Dorcas Manfred, and Violet's finding out about the affair and trying to mutilate the corpse at the funeral. After this second shock is revealed at the outset, the plot moves in two directions, working back to the beginning of their desire to assess their lives while showing how, in the present time of the novel, January until spring, "sweetheart weather," the Traces free themselves from the desires that have been crippling them. In comparison with the outrageous second shock, the beginning of Joe and Violet's almost simultaneously feeling old is ordinary. Quite simply, ten years earlier, when Violet turned forty, she regretted her decision not to have children. "[M]other-hunger had hit her like a hammer," and she sleeps with a doll and takes a baby from his carriage (108). Joe says that Violet has become silent, and the narrator describes her as no longer being energetic and "determined," but as sitting down "in the middle of the street" and "stumbl[ing] onto the cracks," the "dark fissures in the globe light of the day" (22–23). In the present, at fifty, Violet asks Dorcas's aunt, Alice Manfred, " 'Where the grown people? Is it us?' " as if surprised to find that she is a member of the generation who could be parents or grandparents (110). That is, while Violet's feeling old comes as a result of her inability to have children at menopause, paradoxically, until this time, her repeated decision not to become a mother has kept her a daughter, allowing her to feel younger than her age and to ignore the passage of time that raising a child would impose. She tries to reconcile her early prediction of her life and her prediction of the way she would feel about her life with what she sees her experience has actually been. That her life has been " 'different from what I thought' " is her conclusion (111). Violet reviews the decisions she has made, not only about maternity

3. Henry Louis Gates Jr., *The Signifying Monkey: A Theory of African-American Literary Criticism*, 122.

but also about staying with Joe. His affair so shocks her out of her self-involvement that she asks, " 'Do I stay with him? I want to, I think. I want . . . well, I didn't always . . . now I want' " (110).

Left to himself as Violet withdraws, Joe also becomes reflective as he wonders how to console himself for his loneliness. The second spur to his assessment is his feeling emotionally dead. He fears that old age will be "not remembering what things felt like" (29). Initially, Joe feels as though his life has not been satisfying because he has always followed Violet's lead, accepting her having chosen him, moving to the North at her behest, and moving from the Tenderloin district to Harlem. Of course, their falling in love has been mutual, he has imposed his choice of New York rather than Violet's Baltimore as their destination when they leave the South, and he has chosen the time when they move, as he accepts later on. He says at first, however, that he has made only one choice, to have an affair with Dorcas (29–30). Joe's choosing Dorcas renews him because he sees that he *can* choose and feel, because he can attract a young woman, and because Dorcas, who has experienced violence and been orphaned by the East St. Louis riots, knows, like him, "what that inside nothing was like" (38). Confident of being understood, he can "tell his new love things he never told his wife" (36). However, just as Violet's seeking maternity causes her to confront what she has not had, so too, the goal of Joe's quest, Dorcas, becomes the source of his disillusionment.

The most disturbing event in *Jazz* is Joe's shooting his lover. The stated motives, anger and jealousy, are clear, as is Joe's admission to Felice that he has been afraid of his vulnerability in the face of their intimacy. He says that he shot Dorcas because he was " ' "Scared. Didn't know how to love anybody" ' " (213).[4] His action is compulsive. Despite having been schooled by Hunters Hunter, his mentor, that he must not " 'kill the tender and nothing female' " and that people are not prey, Joe tracks Dorcas in New York with a gun, although he is sure that he is not going to shoot her (175, 180). Against great odds, he finds her at a party. Then, although he is an excellent marksman shooting at close range, with a gun so simple to use that "you'd have to fight your own self to miss," he merely wounds her in the shoulder and is allowed

---

4. These double quotation marks, which occur in the seventh and eighth sections of *Jazz*, are accurate and will be discussed as part of the narrator's assessment.

to leave (181). Joe's explanation of the events as reported make more sense, however, when Dorcas is considered as a representative as well as a character.

Dorcas is a young person who makes Alice, Joe, and Violet aware that they are middle aged, and Morrison's portrait of her emphasizes what has been true of other young characters in these novels: she is both a realistically portrayed character and a symbol for the characters who are assessing their lives. Dorcas is a "bold" eighteen-year-old orphan, grieving for her parents and rebellious against her Aunt Alice's control. As Joe's lover, she has guided him to experience greater intimacy than he has had recently in his marriage, although she has become tired of his devotion. She speaks for herself in the eighth section, where, whether seeking "attention or the excitement" or perhaps fulfilling a romantic notion of dying for love, she ensures her death by refusing medical treatment to stop her hemorrhaging (205). Until the eighth section, however, Dorcas's story is told by others, first as part of Joe's story, in his first section (the novel's second) and then as part of her Aunt Alice's (in the novel's third section). Her not being allowed to tell her story at the outset is appropriate within the novel, for, besides being niece, lover, and corpse, Dorcas represents an array of roles for these three adults: the sexuality that Alice Manfred fears, the youth Joe tries to regain and the mother he seeks, and the daughter Violet wants, a sexual rival, and the kind of light-skinned black whose looks she believes her grandmother admired.

In a 1985 interview, Morrison discussed two historical incidents that troubled her and became the basis for *Beloved* and *Jazz*, Margaret Garner's killing her child out of love, rather than see her child live in slavery, and an eighteen-year-old New York woman's dying for love. Her description of the second incident reflects the tension just described between the realistic detail of a young woman's death and the idea of a model or representative:

> [A]pparently her ex-boyfriend . . . had come into the party with a gun and a silencer and shot her. And she kept saying, "I'll tell you tomorrow" because she wanted him to get away. And he did, I guess; anyway, she died. . . . A woman loved something other than herself so much. She had placed all of the value of her life in something outside herself. . . . And that this woman had loved a man that she would postpone her own medical care or go ahead and die to give him time to get away so that, more valuable than her life, was *not just his life but something else connected with his life*. . . . And I thought,

it's interesting because the best thing that is in us [women] is also the thing that makes us sabotage ourselves, sabotage in the sense that our life is not as worthy, or our perception of the best part of ourselves.[5]

In naming the young woman in the novel that calls her back to speak, Morrison uses the name of a woman the apostle Peter brought back to life (Acts 9:36–41). In Morrison's telling of the young woman's story, she interprets "the something else connected with his life" as something the lovers have shared, something connected with the story of Wild, something that makes Dorcas feel special and powerful.

Hunters Hunter has hinted to Joe that a strange woman called Wild who lives in the countryside on the fringe of the community is his mother (175). Three times as a young man, Joe has tracked Wild, who has always eluded him, to ask for a "sign" that she is his mother. He has responded to rejection by performing intense physical work, by turning to Violet for consolation (although he never tells her about Wild), and, finally, by leaving the South. Dorcas's reciprocating his love makes him want her to be Wild, revised into a responsive woman. Her seeking risky behavior, such as meeting him at Malvonne's and wanting to appear together where others will see them, also causes Joe to associate her with Wild, who risks being cut when she approaches the men harvesting cane. Invested by Joe with such a powerful association, Dorcas can give him that sign and "fill . . . [his inside nothing] for him" just by listening to and understanding his story of how he sought a sign from his mother (37). In sharing his feelings with her, he experiences feeling again, which is part of the reason that her rejection tortures him. Her flight reminds him of the similar response of Wild. Now, however, he does not try to ignore his feelings, and his anger toward Dorcas is intensified because it includes anger toward Wild that he has not faced. When Joe shoots Dorcas, he is expressing anger at her and at Wild, as the novel emphasizes in four ways. Joe no longer owns his prized Virginia hunting rifle, with which he has fired blanks at Wild in the country, but he uses its city replacement, "a fat baby gun" that he "pawned his rifle for" (181). The hunts for the two women are juxtaposed at the end of the seventh section,[6] Dorcas calls herself his " 'Mama,' " and the

5. Morrison, "A Conversation: Gloria Naylor and Toni Morrison," 584–85 (emphasis added).
6. Doreatha Drummond Mbalia ("Women Who Run with Wild: The Need for Sisterhoods in *Jazz*," 630–31, 641) and Terry Otten ("Horrific Love in Toni Morrison's

image of the blood on Dorcas's shoulder recalls the redwings found near Wild (193, 224–25). Joe does not shoot to kill. However, Dorcas embraces death and gives that act significance with her last message: " ' " 'There's only one apple. . . . Tell Joe' " ' " (213). The content of her message tells him that what they have shared is important. As an act, sending a message grants his wish for a sign of recognition from her and from Wild. She is dying with him " ' "on her mind" ' " (213). Crying for "more than Dorcas" Joe grieves for all his losses (221). Besides guiding Joe to experience intimacy again, Dorcas also enables him to exhaust both his anger at Wild for refusing to nurture him and his grief.

Because Morrison portrays the assessments of a male and female character as well as the narrator, some characters fill more than one role within the structure being described here. *Jazz* does not subvert the conventions of this structure, but Morrison redistributes the functions. The character of Dorcas, for example, plays different, multiple roles in Violet's assessment. Because she is the age that one of the children Violet miscarried would be, Dorcas replaces the younger children who have been distracting Violet, the infant in the carriage and the young child in her client's lap, and becomes the daughter Violet might have had. However, while Dorcas is young enough to be Violet's daughter, she is also old enough to have a sexual affair and is, in fact, Violet's rival. When Violet decides to try to regain Joe's love, she studies Dorcas as a young guide in order to discover the kind of woman Joe desires and, hence, she thinks, the kind of woman she should look like or try to become. Just as Dorcas reminds Joe of his quest for Wild, her appearance reminds Violet of the young man whom she has never seen but whose appearance and behavior were the favorite topic of her grandmother, True Belle (97). Apparently for the first time, during her reflections following the shock of learning about Dorcas, Violet fights against what she now recognizes as insidious damage caused by her grandmother's devotion to the light-skinned, blond mulatto Golden Gray, devotion that Violet has absorbed and interpreted as a rejection of her " 'very very dark, bootblack' " self (206). That recognition begins when Violet sees Dorcas. She is first a sexual rival, and when Violet tries to cut her, she aims her knife "at

---

Fiction," 661) note that the two hunts are conflated. Otten also discusses Dorcas as a representative (661–63).

the neckline just by the earlobe" because it is a special place for a lover, she says, and it is a vulnerable place, near an artery (95). Once Violet sees her, that place where her "high-yellow skin" and "long wavy hair" meet has added significance (97). That is, although Dorcas and Golden Gray do not literally resemble each other, both have mixed heritage that gives them light skin, hair that does not need to be straightened in Dorcas's case, and curly blond hair in the case of Golden Gray. Dorcas accepts the wound intended by Joe for Wild and receives the one intended by Violet for Golden Gray. Joe and Violet work to uproot old hurtful desires that are interfering with their life. In shooting Dorcas, Joe attacks his own need for a mother. In assaulting her corpse, Violet attacks an ideal that she can never match (208). Joe and Violet come to understand these matters gradually during the second half of the novel, after Violet has consulted Alice Manfred.

Whereas Joe's guide, Dorcas, appears almost by magic—"there she was"—to fill his need, Violet chooses her guide, and she persists, even when Alice Manfred refuses to open the door (29). Initially, Violet visits Alice to learn about Dorcas, but she also seems to feel that, with a reputation for being anything but "vague," Alice might provide a haven, a safe and organized place to "sit down" (71, 80, 82). During their first series of exchanges, Alice is not equipped to be the wise, strong, nurturing guide that Violet seeks, until Violet's demands help Alice to reflect on her own life. As haphazard as Violet's reflections on her life have been thus far, she inspires Alice to a comparatively rapid assessment of her life. Violet helps Alice see what she has done by trying to control Dorcas and to measure how little she has had of life after she gave her unfaithful husband the ultimatum "Choose." After being deserted by her husband and then suppressing her rage, Alice has limited her life in order to preserve her sense of herself as in the right and to limit her vulnerability. She has held herself superior to other black Americans, those darker skinned, violent, and promiscuous, "the embarrassing kind"—a description of Violet—but Violet, by her presence and with her words, forbids Alice either to stereotype her or to be condescending toward the prostitutes whose hair Violet grooms (84–85). Her conversations with Violet force Alice to admit that her righteousness has cost her not only her husband but also other possibilities for intimacy and community (79, 85).

Once Violet's probing releases Alice's anger, at the end of the third section of *Jazz*, she fulfills Violet's desire to understand what it means

to be a middle-aged woman: " 'We born around the same time, me
and you . . . . We women, me and you. Tell me something real. Don't
just say I'm grown and ought to know. I'm fifty and I don't know
nothing' " (110). During their second series of conversations, reported
at the end of the fourth section, Alice's advice—to accept reality, to
live fully and not to miss life, to love—is reminiscent of what Strether
has learned and what Linda wants for Gavin. When Violet says, " 'He's
[Joe] what I got,' " Alice disagrees: " 'Doesn't look so' " (111). When
Violet complains, " 'I want some fat in this life,' " Alice responds harshly,
" 'Wake up. Fat or lean, you got just one. This is it' " and " 'Nobody's
asking you to take it [any wrong or hurt from Joe]. I'm sayin make it,
make it!' " (110, 113). She encourages Violet to love: " 'You got anything
left to you to love, anything at all, do it' " (112). Most important, Violet
can count on Alice not to pity her or to condone self-pity: " 'Don't
get pitiful. I won't stand for you getting pitiful, hear me?' " (110).
Alice encourages Violet's strength, her self-reliance and energy, not
her plaintiveness.[7]

Guides sometimes perform acts of hospitality and domesticity that
show acceptance and nurturing. Madame de Vionnet welcomes Strether
to her home, which he regards as a precious revelation of her private
life. Augusta straightens Professor St. Peter after she saves him from
asphyxiation, and she keeps watch by his bedside. Ratliff cooks for
Chick and Gavin and offers Gavin a handkerchief when he cries. In
Jazz, during both series of conversations, Alice's providing a place to sit
down, serving "settling tea," and sewing nurture Violet. In particular,
the domestic act of mending Violet's dress and coat lining symbolizes
Alice's helping to restore Violet's emotional order with the restoration
of her garments. Alice's gruff words—" 'Give me that coat. I can't
look at that lining another minute' "—contrast with her fine sewing
that not only makes Violet appear less unkempt but also imitates and
supports Violet's bringing together "the thread[s] running loose" of

7. Warnings against pity and self-pity throughout *Jazz* reinforce Alice's advice. Characters mention pity as an undesirable emotion (125, 210, 220). Felice's father says that he wants respect, not pity (204). Violet refuses to go crazy like her mother out of self-respect (97). Joe names himself (124) and chooses Dorcas as his assertive reactions to wounds. In his essay, "The New Negro," Alain Locke writes, "Sentimental interest in the Negro has ebbed. We used to lament this as the falling off of our friends; now we rejoice and pray to be delivered both from self-pity and condescension" (*New Negro*, 8; cf. 10, 11).

her "frayed" emotions (82, 110–11). Although she has meditated in general on "black women [who] were armed" and in particular on "[t]he woman who ruined the [funeral] service," Alice's hospitality is remarkable and implies her forgiveness or, at least, her acceptance (75). Appreciating the welcome she has forced, Violet also turns from thoughts of violence to forgiveness when she tells Alice she wishes that she could have had mother-daughter conversations with Dorcas and could have used a different sharp instrument, her scissors, to fix Dorcas's hair (109). She tells Alice, " '[A]nother time I would have loved her too' " (109).

This emphasis on the partnership or the reciprocity of the relationship between Alice and Violet, guide and protagonist, is exceptional in *Jazz*,[8] and no moment shows it more than their laughing together. Alice and Violet's conversations culminate unexpectedly in laughter after Alice has ruined her shirtwaist that she has been ironing so systematically by burning a hole the shape of a "black and smoking ship" (113). The two unlikely companions are comfortable enough to laugh at one's mistake. Violet begins, and Alice joins her, as Violet teaches her the healing laughter, a response "[m]ore complicated, more serious than tears," that she first experienced when her grandmother, True Belle, came to their home. It is spontaneous and shared, and allows them release. This special moment of communication and sisterhood, in the center of the novel, reverberates throughout the text. It reminds the reader of the narrator's vignette of the two women who laughed but, once alone, the second woman's laughter turned to tears (16–17). It is also the turning point for the characters and the narrator. Violet recalls one positive childhood memory (True Belle's laughter) that will help assuage her anger with True Belle for establishing Golden Gray as an ideal in her mind. No longer embarrassed or taking herself so seriously, she can laugh at herself for the spectacle she made at Dorcas's funeral. Although in that vignette Violet imagines watching herself, shortly after, she is no longer divided but has put herself back together, confirming the efficacy of Alice's mending: "She . . . noticed, at the same moment as *that* Violet did, that it was spring" (114). Once Alice and Violet are recovering, Violet can share her feelings with Joe and, later, with Felice. Their conversations and their laughter also affect the

8. See Mbalia, "Women Who Run," 632–34, for a discussion of their mutual help.

narrator, who opens herself more to the reader from this point, which will be discussed later.

Although *Jazz* includes the characters' recollection of what has led up to the second shock, Joe's and Violet's assaults on Dorcas, the present time of the novel is January until spring in 1926, the time when Joe and Violet complete the assessment of their lives. Morrison portrays the resolution of their reflections in great detail. At first, the Traces deteriorate during this time. Violet talks to "*that* Violet," and Joe cries for three months. When the Traces no longer feel confident that they can trust each other or like the way their lives are going, they face not only that crisis but also the reappearance of the crisis of the earliest stage of life, finding some way to experience nurturing and unconditional love in order to trust others again. However, this is the third time that their early need to know that they are loved recurs. The novel suggests that as infants they received such affirmation from Rose Dear and Mrs. Williams. This need resurfaced a second time when they were about to become adults. Psychologists and psychiatrists point out that, even though completed at the appropriate time of life, the crises of earlier stages of life reappear for review at moments of transition from one stage to the next.[9] The crisis of becoming adults was heightened, moreover, for Joe and Violet by antiblack violence and the absence of a mother to whom they might return briefly for reassurance. Initially, they were mother substitutes for each other. Joe admits that he married Violet " 'just because I couldn't see whether a wildwoman put out her hand or not' " (181). He had tracked Wild before, but the "dispossession," the burning of Vienna done by whites to force blacks to move, makes him desperate to receive a sign while/if Wild is still alive during the two days before he must leave. Similarly, Violet chooses Joe and changes her work habits because he shows at their first meeting that he can help her through the nights, "talking her through the dark" that reminds her of the dark well where her mother committed suicide just a few weeks earlier (104–5, 99). (Rose Dear's suicide is not literally due to violence, but the narrator offers a list of such possible causes and her husband's having to stay away from his family because of his membership in the Readjuster Party is another [101]). When she marries, Violet stops

9. Erikson, *Life Cycle Completed*, 61–66. See also Erikson, *Childhood and Society*, 250, 267, 271–72.

grieving for her mother and feels that she is worthy of being loved. She acts with purpose. Even though he tracks Wild to receive a sign from her once after he is married (and that final rejection is the precipitating cause of his decision to leave the South), Joe and Violet do meet each other's need for affirmation, and this provision has worked for them for years.

Morrison insists on the importance of being nurtured by women, a recollection of unconditional mother's love, as the crucial factor that brings about the resolutions of Joe's and Violet's assessments of their lives. Violet feeds herself by sucking fortified malteds through a straw. More effective, the conversations and laughter that Violet shares with Alice halt her disintegration and strengthen her so that she can look fearlessly at how her life has been different from what she expected and affirm the life she has had anyway. She can then reach out to others, first, trying to engage Joe and, later, offering to fix Felice's hair and cooking for her. Although Joe has strengthened himself by having chosen Dorcas and by having been open with her, he becomes reconciled to the life he has had in response to Violet and Felice, when their conversations and nurturing help him stop crying. Mothering is the basis for psychological well-being in the present in *Jazz,* as it has been in the past, although it is not without problems. True Belle's coming, her laughter and organization help save her daughter's family and are more effective than her son-in-law's presents, but Violet must forgive her for presenting Golden Gray as an ideal.

Careful not to portray the Traces' search for a mother as regressive, Morrison emphasizes choice and responsibility. Twice, Joe insists on his responsibility: " 'Don't get me wrong. This wasn't Violet's fault. All of it's mine. All of it. I'll never get over what I did to that girl. Never,' " and " ' "It was me [who killed Dorcas]. For the rest of my life, it'll be me" ' " (129, 212). Violet does not blame anyone else for her actions when she tells Felice, " ' "I messed up my own life . . . . Forgot it was mine. My life. I just ran up and down the streets wishing I was somebody else. . . . White. Light. Young again" ' " (207–8). She also announces, " ' "Now I want to be the *woman* my mother didn't stay around long enough to see. That one. The one she would have liked and the one I used to like before" ' " (208, emphasis added). Violet does not want to regress to being the *girl* who had not yet been abandoned by Rose Dear or filled with stories by True Belle. Rather, she wants to recapture the mature attitude of taking charge and the vitality that she feels certain Rose Dear would have admired. Violet and Joe no longer view themselves primarily as people to whom things have happened.

The Traces find their quest fulfilled, even though it is reversed altogether, so that instead of remaining close to a mother, they accept a daughter. The narrator is surprised to see that Felice fills the vacancy left by Dorcas's death and that she reconstitutes the triangle. Although the girls have been unlikely friends, "fly and buttermilk," with different moral values, Felice does seem to be a resurrected version of Dorcas as daughter when she enters their apartment. She comes after Violet has returned the photograph of Dorcas to Alice, as if to take her place. At different times, Violet has the same thought about doing the girls' hair (15, 109, 214). Felice becomes the recipient of the Traces' need to nurture and give advice to a young person (197). Just as Strether tells little Bilham to "live all you can," Violet tells Felice to be true to herself, and Joe affirms her name (208, 215). They help Felice to cry and grieve for her best friend so that she does not remain resentful and angry. In another reflection of the scene in which Alice and Violet laugh together, Felice gradually feels comfortable enough with the Traces to laugh at them in their presence (214).

The Professor's House, A Book of Common Prayer, and *Jazz,* the three books by women, generously acknowledge what the other books hint at, that the young people are unknowingly a source of insight to the protagonists. The lessons Dorcas offers have been discussed. Joe tells Felice that by telling him that Dorcas " ' "let herself die" ' " and by describing her unromantically as a person who " ' "used people," ' " Felice has helped him reestablish his marriage (212, 209). Putting the idea of being true to herself into words as a lesson for Felice helps Violet understand herself better. Felice says that Violet tells her story " '[l]ike it was the first she heard of the word [me]' " (209). Felice also makes the Traces feel needed. By caring for her, Joe and Violet receive care in return. That they become more supportive of Felice than her parents and grandmother corroborates observations made elsewhere in *Jazz,* that people need more than family to fill their insatiable need for unconditional love and that even in the absence of a mother, receiving nurturing is possible and it is healing. Welcome in their home, Felice enables the Traces to "put . . . their lives together" (221). They get beyond the crisis that caused their need for a mother's affirmation to recur. They forgive one another, make amends, and then look toward the future.

Violet and Joe no longer worry about why Joe had an affair with Dorcas, but accept that it happened, just as they accept that time has passed and they have no children of their own. They have shed some of their obligations and please themselves instead. They renew their sexual relationship and keep their own time schedule. They explore New York City beyond Harlem and talk to people in their neighborhood, even entertaining Malvonne, who has betrayed them both. They baby-sit, activity that keeps them involved with the next two generations in their community. In the altersromane discussed thus far, reconciliation involves the men's becoming more sensitive and concerned about community and the women's becoming more autonomous. In *Jazz*, however, Joe, who has had what are considered feminine qualities, easily joining the women's groups where he sells beauty products, has become more assertive, and Violet, who was the one to take the initiative and has made many of their decisions, becomes maternal and caring. How a person changes in later middle age is less significant than that men and women explore behavior that is unfamiliar, even risky, for them. While the narrator's assessment of Harlem as Zion is mixed, the energy that Joe and Violet have felt and that the narrator describes from her experience and the healing that the characters experience all argue that the shift from southern countryside to northern city has been achieved.

The first-person narrator provides the connection in the novel among three of the stories of assessment in *Jazz:* the Traces' story, her story, and the catalog of historical events involving black Americans. The worldly and cynical narrator begins Joe and Violet's story in a confident, judgmental voice, but she does not specify other personal data, such as gender or age. The reader can infer, however, that since the narrator is present at the gathering of women when Joe first speaks with Dorcas— "If I remember right, that October lunch in Alice Manfred's house, something was off"—she must be a woman, probably middle aged like the others (71). In the sixth and seventh sections, she judges Golden Gray's actions as a mother might evaluate how well a son has learned and will honor the values of their community. Finally, the narrator engages in the kind of reflection on the life she has lived that characterizes the other protagonists in this study, which also suggests that she is middle aged.

When she begins her narrative, the narrator of *Jazz* resembles Strether in *The Ambassadors* and Grace, the first-person narrator of

A Book of Common Prayer. Like Strether and Grace, who believe that they are merely the observers of the main drama of the young person, the narrator claims only to observe the heroes of action. Certain that she cannot be touched by this story of infidelity and violence, that she is safe and in control, the narrator of *Jazz* does not realize that the story she is drawn to tell will affect her and prove revelatory. Strether is not arrogant, but both the narrator of *Jazz* and Grace believe that they are superior to the foolish characters about whom they write. For example, the narrator describes Violet's and Joe's affairs as "that mess" and "Joe's dirt" (5). She brags about her long experience of the city and proclaims that she sees more than most: "I watch everything and everyone and try to figure out their plans, their reasonings, long before they do. You have to understand what it's like, taking on a big city: I'm exposed to all sorts of ignorance and criminality" (8). Like Grace, whose wariness is her response to betrayal, the narrator justifies her watching as her protective response to an injury: "I agree that I close off in places, but if you have been left standing, as I have, while your partner overstays at another appointment, or promises to give you exclusive attention after supper, but is falling asleep just as you have begun to speak—well, it can make you inhospitable if you aren't careful, the last thing I want to be" (9). The narrator wants the vindication of telling the story of another's betrayal. That Joe and Violet's healing is shocking to her suggests that she not only expects but also derives some satisfaction from the predictability of violence and, in this case, its outrageousness.

The narrator's watching may be a harmless precaution, but the presence in *Jazz* of a gossip who meddles in the affairs of others, Malvonne, reminds the reader that watching may mean actively seeking, even imagining information and that telling may have questionable motives and harmful, divisive results. (Morrison heightens the warning by having Malvonne recall Mrs. Hedges, a gossiping madam who does more than simply watch and listen, in *The Street* by Ann Petry, published in 1946 and reissued in 1991.) However, two changes in her narrative suggest that the narrator of *Jazz* is a more sensitive reflector than her tough stance would indicate. The first change shows that she has begun to "come out more. Mix" (9). The fifth section begins with several pages of the narrator's judging Joe and Violet, ending with her wondering whether the outcome would have been different "if [Joe] had stopped trailing that little fast thing all over town long enough to tell Stuck or Gistan or some neighbor." This observation is followed, after a space on the page, with Joe's response, as if the question had been posed to him: " 'It's not a thing you tell to another man. . . . Gistan would just laugh . . . . Stuck would look at his feet . . .' " (121). The remainder of the fifth section is Joe's version of his life, a first-person narration in quotation marks addressed to an unspecified audience, although the implication is that it is a woman, the narrator. The fifth section ends with his version of tracking Dorcas to the party, where Joe first refers to Dorcas as "she," as if explaining himself to a listener. He then addresses Dorcas ("you"), as if his talking about her has called her back to listen (130–35). The eighth and ninth sections are also primarily first-person narratives. After brief introductory sections by the narrator, Dorcas tells her version of the night Joe shot her and Felice tells her life story. These might be re-creations by the narrator, like the imagined story of Golden Gray, but they are in quotation marks that assert their authenticity and imply an audience whose prompts and responses are not recorded. The narrator may have interviewed Joe and Felice. Perhaps she went to seek sordid details, but what she records is Joe's feeling abandoned by his mother and his love for Dorcas, the way Dorcas died and her expression of love for Joe, and Felice's confirmation of Joe and Dorcas's version of their affair and her own observation that the Traces are decent people. Felice makes clear that the triangle Felice-Joe-Violet, which the narrator predicted would end with more shooting, is nurturing (6).

The narrator admits inventing what she does not know when she begins her version of the lives of True Belle, Rose Dear, and Golden Gray in the sixth section: "[I]t's not hard to imagine what it must have been like" (137). Believing that she has another story of violence, the narrator begins to tell how Golden Gray went to confront and kill his father. The second change in her narrative is her admission of error: "How could I have imagined [Golden Gray] so poorly? Not noticed [his] hurt . . . . I have been careless and stupid and it infuriates me to discover (again) how unreliable I am. . . . Now I have to think this through, carefully, even though I may be doomed to another misunderstanding" (160–61). Her revision is a story about how Golden Gray seeks his father to know him, and she credits his having helped Wild with changing Golden Gray's mind (173). In these two changes—the narrator's listening to the characters and her feeling empathy for Golden Gray—the narrator replaces the expectation of violence and telling stories about violence with telling stories about intimacy. Morrison has described jazz music as "open on the one hand and both complicated and inaccessible on the other."[10] Likewise, in *Jazz* the simplest of plots, a love triangle, turns out to be unpredictable because the characters have been "busy being original, complicated, changeable—human" (220). Although her pride and the apparent openness of the story she tells have misled her, the narrator does listen and is able to revise and take the characters' complexity into account. Her listening and empathy occur after she has reported the conversations and laughter "[m]ore complicated, more serious than tears" shared by Alice and Violet (113).

Witnessing the women's sharing, hearing Joe's and Dorcas's expressions of love, and hearing about the Traces' reconciliation all shock the narrator, forcing her to revise her view of what happens in the world and her version of her life. She is divested of her delusion that her role as one who watches the pain of others can keep her safe from further injury to herself. Her reflection proceeds quickly once she sees that she has been deluded and feels the pain of humiliation and loss. On the one hand, the narrator can no longer see herself as being in control or as superior because of her ability to understand others. Even her certainty that she is invisible has been vanity: "[T]hey knew me all along. . . . And when I was feeling most invisible, being tight-lipped, silent and unobservable, they were whispering about me to each other. . . . I thought I'd hidden myself so well as I watched them through windows and doors, took every opportunity I had to follow them, to gossip about and fill in their lives, and all the while they were watching me" (220). The community's "pity" for her mortifies her (220). On the other hand, the narrator has not been an innocent observer, a person to whom life has happened. Her harsh self-accusation, "I was the predictable one, confused in my solitude into arrogance, thinking my space, my view was the only one that was or that mattered," asserts her responsibility for her posture (220). She sees now that her social commentary has been a way for her to distance herself from life. Watching and satirizing the interactions of others have occupied the space where her own interactions might have been. When she realizes that she has been watching others' lives "instead of having one of my own," the narrator mourns for what she might have had (220). Finally, telling the Traces' story convinces her

---

10. Morrison, "An Interview with Toni Morrison," 257. In an interview shortly after the publication of *Jazz*, Morrison said, "I think of jazz music as very complicated, very sophisticated, very difficult. It is also very popular. And it has the characteristics of being sensual and illegal" (Morrison, "Chloe Wofford Talks about Toni Morrison," 75).

that observing others in order to "meddle" or "finger-shape" is neither innocent activity nor an act of community.

The narrator can move beyond her humiliation and her disgust with herself when she recalls and understands not only Joe's compelling need to be acknowledged by Wild, but also Wild's need to remain apart. That is, she empathizes with the mother's need as well as with the son's. When the narrator sees both of these conflicting needs in her own life, she risks inventing for herself the search for "Wild's chamber of gold," for mother and a safe, womblike place, "[t]hat home in the rock," in order to claim a sponsor who understood living on the fringe of society and was wary, protective of her privacy, looking at others while staying out of sight herself (221). Thus, since she and Wild are similar, the part of her that is like Wild affirms the rest of her: "She has seen me and is not afraid of me. She hugs me. Understands me. Has given me her hand. I am touched by her. Released in secret. Now I know" (221). Whereas the narrator uses verbs of seeing, looking, knowing, and believing in the paragraph preceding this one to describe her own artistic activity, here she changes from sight to touch, moving from the intellectual to the physical, even if only in her imagination. She finds a way to obtain what looks to be impossible. Using the story she tells as her guide, the narrator invokes Wild, a flawed figure, not her mother, silent, as the source of the motherly look, hug, and touch that must occur before she can, in her turn, affirm the self she now sees. This invented encounter bolsters the narrator's courage so that she is not silenced but can finish her narrative, her address to her reader. The narrator affirms herself primarily as a storyteller. Set off as a separate paragraph, "Now I know" acts as a colon to introduce a confident epilogue that tells what happens to Violet and Joe, Felice, Alice, and the narrator.

Having no close relationship at the end of the novel, the narrator cannot show that she welcomes intimacy as wholeheartedly as the Traces do. The narrator "long[s] . . . to be able to say out loud" that she loves another. However, intimacy remains hypothetical: "But I can't say that aloud . . . . If I were able I'd say it" (229). As an artist, the narrator is one who has been "chosen to wait" (229). With her statement, "being chosen to wait is the reason I can [wait]," she affirms the different, "wild" life she has had. She has made choices about how she will live, but those do not include being able at this point to "[s]ay make me, remake me. You are free to do it and I am free to let you . . ." (229).

The narrator cannot remake herself entirely in any way that she wants, but must take who she has been into account. This reflection might be bitter or angry, but she seems wistful. Still, the narrator imagines what she might say to a beloved, and, unlike Grace, who is dying, time remains before her.

Morrison has based *Jazz* on her parents' stories of their youth in the 1920s, capturing the " 'gleaming terms of excitement and attraction' " with which they described the era.[11] Like the Traces, her family migrated to the North. Her grandmother moved from the South in the early 1900s, and her father came from Georgia. While Morrison should not be identified with her narrator, certain aspects of this storyteller's situation are instructive. Some of these insights bespeak humility. The narrator of *Jazz* finds that her story takes its own direction, and she becomes somewhat distrustful of the probing that the artist must do. She also pays a high price for having her closest relationship be the one she has with her narrative, rather than with people. Morrison has said in an interview that " 'writing . . . became the one thing I was doing that I had absolutely no intention of living without.' " In a 1979 interview, Morrison discussed her sense of alienation from the community in Lorain, Ohio, where she grew up: "When she goes back now, she suffers the ambiguity of both belonging and not belonging. She chose not to go back when *Song of Solomon* was published. 'I didn't want those people to look at me funny. I didn't want to experience myself as separate from them. I couldn't bear the fact that old ladies who used to tell me, "Chloe, cross your legs" would look at me in any other way than that they had the right to tell me that still.' "[12] Other insights in *Jazz* support the modernist idea that, "wild" and different, the artist is one of the "chosen" and serves a redemptive function for society (229). Like Wild, the narrator knows enough about her sensitivity to protect herself and live apart for her own safety and well-being. Morrison affirms this humble and special storyteller in *Jazz* who can accept the revision of her violent story and remain open to experience.

11. Morrison, "An Inspired Life: Toni Morrison Writes and a Generation Listens," 275.
12. Morrison discusses writing in "Talk with Toni Morrison," 45. The quote about community is in "The Song of Toni Morrison," 59.

In a fourth instance of assessment, Morrison places herself in the context of literary ancestors with references to novels by other African American writers. By signifying on them, Morrison affirms her place in the tradition. Her reference to Petry's *The Street* has been mentioned. To return for the last time to the culmination of Violet and Alice's conversations, the women laugh together after Alice has burned a hole shaped like a ship in the shirtwaist she has been ironing. The image is an accurate description of the shape of an iron's soleplate, while it simultaneously recalls the ships Frederick Douglass watches near Baltimore in his *Narrative of the Life*, the ships that Zora Neale Hurston signifies on at the beginning of *Their Eyes Were Watching God*.[13] Douglass begins with a contrast: "Those beautiful vessels, robed in purest white, so delightful to the eye of freedmen, were to me so many shrouded ghosts, to terrify and torment me with thoughts of my wretched condition." This vision inspires his "apostrophe" to the ships that also proceeds by contrast. "You are loosed from your moorings, and are free; I am fast in my chains, and am a slave! You move merrily before the gentle gale, and I sadly before the bloody whip! You are freedom's swift-winged angels, that fly round the world; I am confined in bands of iron!" His situation contrasts with his dream of freedom, which seems impossible to achieve. Morrison repeats the contrast in the vignettes and events that show the discrepancy between the hopes of the "new Negro" and the situation in the city. Hurston begins her novel with an image of ships that "have every man's wish on board," and then she contrasts men's and women's attitudes toward seeking fulfillment, with praise for women, who never forget their dreams. Morrison uses the image of the ship in a domestic moment, indoors, not as a vision of grand oceangoing vessels with sails. A destructive error becomes an occasion for sharing and healing.

Jazz concerns itself not with the contrast between the dreams of freedmen and slaves or men and women, but between the dreams the characters started out with and the lives they have had. In the tenth section, when Morrison's narrator refers again to ships, "the Baltimore boats [Joe and Violet] never sailed on," she revises Hurston's criticism

13. Douglass, *Narrative of the Life of Frederick Douglass, an American Slave, Written by Himself,* 95–96; Hurston, *Their Eyes,* 9. Gates discusses Hurston's revisions and critique of Frederick Douglass's description of the sailing ships in the Baltimore harbor (*Signifying Monkey,* 171–72).

of men's merely watching their dreams sail away. Even though Joe and Violet have not sailed to all their dreams, their memory of the Baltimore boats survives as an image from their shared past and thus "binds" Joe and Violet (228). Dreams may join and bind men and women rather than divide them. This is the reflection of older people whose dreams have come true in different ways than they expected. In the same section, Morrison's reference to a pear tree, a central image in Janie's sexual awakening in *Their Eyes Were Watching God,* is a second reference to Hurston's text: "The pears they [Joe and Violet] let hang on the limb because if they plucked them, they would be gone from there and who else would see that ripeness if they took it away for themselves? How could anybody passing by see them and imagine for themselves what the flavor would be like?" (228). Whereas an adolescent Janie contemplates the pear tree in bloom, awaiting pollination, with no mention of fruit, Joe and Violet contemplate the mature, female-shaped fruit that appears in a later season. Morrison's characters recall making a generous gesture together by leaving the fruit for the community to enjoy as well. Individual fulfillment, possession, and exclusive enjoyment are not the main goals.

Finally, the story of Morrison's narrator signifies on a male version of hibernation as a response to injury and pain. Reminiscent of another New Yorker, Jack-the-Bear, Ralph Ellison's Invisible Man, even calling herself "invisible," the narrator of *Jazz* creates an initially self-assured, assertive monologue, with direct address to an unspecified "you," that discusses jazz and violence (220). Both brag that they understand the city and are bold enough to "take . . . on a big city" or "to carry on a fight against" those who do not see Jack-the-Bear.[14] Although initially she does not expect as much change as Jack-the-Bear, who uses the word *hibernation* because it is a temporary state, the narrator of *Jazz* experiences a revelation. She finds that her innocence and safety have been a delusion, and she becomes wiser and more authentic. Still young, Jack-the-Bear continues to allow his reaction to others to guide him. While she has learned a lesson from the Traces and her community, the narrator of *Jazz* is directed from within and is true to her innermost self.

14. Morrison, *Jazz,* 8; Ellison, *Invisible Man,* 9.

Conclusion

With the life assessments of nine characters in mind, it is possible to give a more detailed overview of the process by including specific comparisons that could not be made in Chapter 1. This concluding summary highlights the variety present in the seven altersromane considered here, as well as corroborates the view that a common structure for the process of affirming one's life exists. To review that structure briefly, the process begins with the characters' feeling old and experiencing some shock. This combination causes them to reflect on their lives thus far, usually in the presence of a person young enough to be their child yet old enough to be an adult. They are supported in their reflection by a guide, usually of the opposite sex, who exposes them to some aspect of life they have avoided before or who shows them a way to respond to a situation that they have not considered before. A second shock destroys a cherished illusion that the characters have held about themselves, so that they feel divested and without their usual defenses. If the process is completed, the characters find a way to recover from the second shock and to reconcile themselves with what they have learned. They accept their revised version of their lives, forgive some of the faults of themselves and others, and look forward to the future. The age of these novelists and other similarities between author and protagonist suggest that portraying the process of assessing one's life reflects a personal dilemma.

Although beginning to assess their lives catches all the protagonists by surprise, the variety of the original impetus is extraordinary: general dissatisfaction, a trip, the feeling that life is passing by, the move to a new house, finishing a life work, renewal of an old relationship, historical research, a new relationship, and observation of another. In the end, the successful resolution of the assessment relies in part upon the characters' embracing responsibility for their actions. However, the protagonists do not begin with a conscious choice to review their lives. Instead they divert themselves with a search that seems to take them in a different direction, away from their daily concerns: to see Dulcinea or Dorcas Manfred, to help Chad and Mrs. Newsome or to help Linda Kohl, to have a baby, to edit Tom Outland's diary or to study Susan Ward's papers, to write about Charlotte Douglas or the Traces. Each of these quests fails to distract, since each puts the protagonist in a situation in which he or she cannot avoid reflection. More important, the quests fail to distract because each identifies, in a disguised manner, what the protagonists will recognize as an illusion about themselves that they cherish. Yet even while they resist, complaining that others are forcing them to consider painful information, Don Quixote, Strether, St. Peter, Gavin, Lyman, Grace, Violet, Joe, and the narrator of *Jazz*, once embarked, all pursue their initial insight with a sense of urgency until they have acknowledged their illusion and revised their view of their lives to take the illusion into account.

Evidence that the protagonist is no longer young but belongs to the dominant generation often comes from several younger persons, such as Chad Newsome and his circle of friends in Paris and Professor St. Peter's students, two daughters, and sons-in-law. Reactions are complex. Lyman Ward has been disgusted by his college students in the 1960s, he is sexually attracted to his young secretary, Shelly Hawkes, and he feels rivalry with his son, who is at the outset of his own academic career. Gavin Stevens seems less interested in his nephew, Chick Mallison, once he is grown. Joe Trace loves a younger woman, in part because doing so makes him feel young again. St. Peter knows all along that he has learned from Tom, but Grace Strasser-Mendana and Violet Trace put together the lessons from Charlotte and Dorcas only after they are dead. All the protagonists give the young people advice that has immediate application, but is also intended as a legacy of values by which to live. Strether's message is brief: do not forsake the civilizing influence of Paris and Madame de Vionnet for a commercial career. Other advice is as elaborate as Don Quixote's lectures to Sancho Panza when he leaves to govern his "island." St. Peter has acted as Tom's mentor for several years. Gavin's delaying Chick's enlistment to fight in World War II, Lyman's lecturing Shelly Hawkes to warn her against promiscuity and communes, Grace's trying to help Charlotte interpret her vulnerability in Boca Grande, and Violet and Joe's sharing meals and talking with Felice reveal the wish to nurture the younger characters and to protect them from anticipated danger or pain. Offering advice helps the protagonists to affirm that their experience has made them wiser, as well as to earn the younger person's regard.

Each of these protagonists seeks help from others in their distress. The character who advises them, the guide, may be a supportive confidant, as Maria Gostrey and Ratliff are, or may stun the protagonist who is procrastinating. Madame de Vionnet, Linda Kohl, and Leonard Douglas confront Strether, Gavin, and Grace with knowledge they would prefer to ignore, and the Felice-Joe-Violet triangle surprises the narrator in *Jazz*. The guide may be well known to the protagonist, as Augusta and Linda are to St. Peter and Gavin, or a brief acquaintance, as Leonard and Alice Manfred are to Grace and Violet. Dulcinea and Susan Ward affect Don Quixote and Lyman even though absent themselves. Linda, Leonard, and Alice are more devoted to revision than to the protagonists' keeping their unexamined view of themselves intact.

Apart from this variety, several similarities recur. The guide is usually a person of the same age as the protagonist and the opposite sex, so that he or she has experience of life but models a different way of approaching a problem, and thus, potentially, expands the protagonist's repertoire of responses. Madame de Vionnet and Susan Ward's papers help Strether and Lyman to understand intimacy from a woman's point of view. While the guides may be inept or suffering themselves, they understand more about the protagonist in one area. Alice Manfred, for example, has less experience in an intimate relationship than Violet, yet she recommends that Violet love Joe. Some guides pursue the protagonists, but the latter have all sought the contact—riding out to see Dulcinea or inviting Leonard Douglas for drinks—and thus are at least minimally receptive to the insight offered. At the same time, the protagonists are vulnerable to these characters, as Strether's images of drowning and being on the scaffold reveal. Augusta has witnessed the Professor sprawled on the floor unconscious, and he must trust that she will not mention what she saw. Leonard is not fooled by Grace's hard-boiled stance into thinking that she understands power. He does not honor her plea for kind treatment but devastates her with one statement of fact. Several of the protagonists have close friends, but they are less likely to intrude than a guide is. Joe Trace's "male friends passed word of [Violet's public craziness] to each other, but couldn't bring themselves to say much more to him than 'How *is* Violet?' "[1] The person who acts as an adviser or guide often speaks with authority: " 'You have had nothing' " (*M*, 424) and " 'Wake up' "

---

1. Morrison, *Jazz*, 22. Hereafter cited as *J* in the text.

(*J*, 110). The guides in these altersromane, whether as purposely as Linda Kohl and Leonard Douglas, or as accidentally as Madame de Vionnet, are part of the scene of the second shock, if not its source, and, therefore, are closely associated with the protagonists' disillusionment. The protagonist rarely denies or quarrels with whatever devastating information the guide gives, suggesting that the insight is one that the protagonist *could* have had, but has resisted seeing.

The second shock is as varied as the impetus to assessment is: Don Quixote's realization that Dulcinea will never come to him, Strether's meeting Madame de Vionnet and Chad in the country, St. Peter's nearly fatal accident after considering suicide, Gavin's interpreting Linda's buying a Jaguar and her farewell embrace, Lyman's reading his grandmother's letter from Idaho and recalling that his grandparents never touched each other, Grace's learning that her husband ran guns and probably killed her lover, Joe's killing Dorcas, Violet's mutilating the corpse, and *Jazz*'s narrator's discovery of renewed intimacy where she expected violence. Here again, though, whatever the surprise—that an expected event does not occur, as in *Don Quixote* and *Jazz*, or that an unexpected one occurs—the similarity of the protagonists' responses is remarkable. With the exception of St. Peter, they learn some fact about someone else (Madame de Vionnet and Chad are having an affair, Linda is independent, Oliver Ward was vindictive, Joe was unfaithful), and the information impinges upon their complacency enough to trigger an insight into their own situation. More precisely, their discovery causes them to recognize an aspect of their view of themselves that they have been careful to disguise and keep secret. Thus, the second shock strikes the protagonists as an uncanny revelation because it challenges their view of a private and cherished attribute. On the other hand, what they recognize about themselves should come as no surprise, for they have called attention to what has been bothering them at the outset.

In order to understand how the second shock precipitates each character's insight as well as how his or her chief concern is identified at the beginning of the novel, it is necessary to return for a moment to the beginning of the process. During their initial reflection about the life they have had, the protagonists recall success and misfortune and inevitably bring to mind some of their flaws, as well as their virtues. For example, as he begins to assess his life, Strether admits that he is partly to blame for his son's death, and he realizes fairly easily that he has not lived fully. Violet Trace regrets that she did not have children, and she worries about not being as assertive as usual. However, the protagonists name these less emotionally charged errors to distract themselves, the guide, and others from finding their most closely guarded illusion. They want to think well of themselves, so they look at what they consider "safe" flaws, ones that they can acknowledge without too much damage to their positive view of themselves as good people. Strether's admitting that he has been naive and his resolving to see more actually earns him the praise of Maria Gostrey and the more worldly young people in Chad's set. Or the protagonists express strong emotion but concentrate on the flaws of a spouse in order to direct blame elsewhere. St. Peter, Lyman, and Joe admit that they are angry with their wives, but they claim an excuse: Lillian St. Peter is materialistic and foolish, Ellen Ward deserted her husband when he was ill, and Violet Trace ignores Joe. The protagonists reveal only that which does not appear to undercut the implicit, partially conscious persona that they want to present to the world.

The protagonists both know yet cannot recognize for some time that they are protecting a cherished illusion about themselves. Don Quixote's account of Dulcinea's appearance in the Cave of Montesinos, which occurs midway through his assessment in part 2, is a good example of this blend of one's knowing one's central concern at some level, while not being able to face it. The episode in the cave reveals what Don Quixote is not willing to acknowledge: that the world, even at the height of knight-errantry, has never been ideal and that he does not have much power. He feels inadequate for Dulcinea, unable to meet her needs and desires, such as her request for money, or to consider her sexuality, as figured by her offering him her petticoat. However, throughout his account of what happened in the cave, he calls attention to his fears and to what he perceives to be his flaws, which he does not mention again until he is on his deathbed when he tries to prevent his niece from marrying a man such as he has been.

The first and last statements that the narrator of *Jazz* makes about her situation show this distinction between what she is conscious of and what she protects herself from acknowledging in a different way. The narrator admits in the first section that she "mak[es] sure no one knows all there is to know about" her and understands this early in her narrative that she does so because she has been hurt or "left standing" (*J*, 8–9). Only at the end, however, does she understand her arrogance and naïveté and the impossibility of what she earlier praised as her wariness: "And when I was feeling most invisible, being tight-lipped, silent and unobservable, [the people] were whispering about me to each other. They knew . . . how shabbily my know-it-all self covered helplessness. . . . I was the predictable one, confused in my solitude into arrogance, thinking my space, my view was the only one that was or that mattered" (*J,* 220). The narrator reinterprets and renames the same quality when "how to take precaution" becomes "arrogance" (*J,* 8, 220). She seems to admit everything about her flaw when she introduces herself in the first section. However, her opening admission boasts that she knows enough to protect herself, whereas her final one confesses a failing. Thus, the attribute under scrutiny is the same, but the narrator revises her appraisal of it and calls it a flaw at the end.

For several other characters, discarding a cherished illusion involves a similar reversal and a blow to their pride. Like the narrator of *Jazz,* Don Quixote and Gavin believe that they know best for others and that they are honorable and bold, not cowardly, in their pursuit of justice or the truth, two claims that cover their worry that they are inadequate and their fear of intimacy and sexuality. Gavin learns that he is not always noble minded and that he does act with self-interest. Grace does not scorn those around her because she feels superior, as she brags in her introduction, but as a defense because she has been badly hurt by the series of betrayals that began with her parents' deaths by the time she was ten. Worse still, she is not even aloof, but painfully affected by what happens to Charlotte in Boca Grande.

Violet Trace has also been betrayed by her mother's suicide, her father's leaving, her grandmother's stories about Golden Gray, and, recently, Joe's infidelity. She was able to feel loveable when she married Joe, but she loses that when she blames herself for not having children. Violet is able to heal her pain from both old and new betrayals better than Grace, though, partly because of her luck that she and Joe love each other and partly because they are willing to work together to renew their relationship.

Like the others, Strether finds that he has been acting in response to an earlier wound. He knows that he has limited his life for some time, but, witnessing Madame de Vionnet's attachment to Chad, he is shocked to realize just how protective he has been of his emotions after his excess of grief at the death of his wife. He now thinks that he has been not sensitive but timid. Even in his relationship with Mrs. Newsome, he feels, he has done her bidding without revealing much of himself. He has lost a great deal, including his son, as a result. Although Strether says that it is "too late" for him to live more fully, his insight leads to his speaking his mind in his three farewell meetings with Chad, Madame de Vionnet, and Maria Gostrey.

St. Peter, Lyman, and Joe have worked hard and been reliable, only to find that they do not feel as fulfilled as they believe they deserve. They want a villain, not themselves, to blame for misfortune or what is missing in their lives, and they name their spouse or family. St. Peter could speak for all of them when he thinks that his family "could not possibly be so much hurt [by him] as he had been already" by them.[2] In contrast to St. Peter, Lyman and Joe are able to consider their failings and their contribution to the deterioration of their marriages. All his life, Lyman has taken his grandfather's side against his grandmother's gentility and snobbery, but he has also feared Oliver Ward's anger. Learning that his grandfather was vindictive dissolves Lyman's fear of not living up to his grandfather's standard, which he has repeated throughout his narrative. Lyman loses his lifelong hero. When he admits his own similar rigidity and self-centeredness, he is humbled. However, his reinterpretation has a positive outcome, since it frees him to define his own standard and be open to his ex-wife. Joe's response to Violet's preoccupation—his affair and the shooting—makes it difficult for him to ignore his responsibility and blame others for long. Using his legacy, tracking, that his mentor, Hunters Hunter, taught him, he is surprised to find himself perverting Hunters Hunter's values twice by stalking a female and a person. Joe shoots Dorcas, but he is simultaneously lashing out at Wild, merged complexly in his mind with Dorcas, in order to express his rage at her for not acknowledging him as her son and in order to bring closure to his search for Wild and a mother's affirmation.

St. Peter ends his assessment one step sooner than other protagonists. He seems afraid that if he were to continue his conversations with Lillian and pursue her accusation of his infidelity or to admit his rage that Tom left him, he might still be capable of the fury and the pain he experienced as an eight-year-old boy who "nearly died" of being "dragged" from Lake Michigan: "No later anguish, and he had had his share, went so deep or seemed so final" (*PH*, 31). Citing the example of his namesake, his grandfather, whom he has belittled before,

2. Cather, *Professor's House*, 283. Hereafter cited as *PH* in the text.

St. Peter protects himself temporarily from frustration by regressing. He considers suicide, but his trying to escape his gas-filled study while barely conscious convinces him that he wants to live. In the end, adopting the heretofore unpalatable example of self-denial that Augusta offers and secularizing it, he resolves to suppress all emotion rather than explore his flaws and illusions further.

Feeling old and experiencing the initial shock are not small matters, but the protagonists do not display strong emotion at the outset. The second shock, in contrast, fundamentally threatens the security they derive from their version of the life they have led, and they feel that they cannot bear a revelation that challenges it. Don Quixote's physician believes that "melancholy and depression were bringing [Don Quixote] to his end."[3] The narrator of *Jazz* says, "[J]ust thinking about their pity I want to die" (*J*, 220). Gavin cries as he makes an implicit admission of Linda's intentions to Ratliff: " 'Stop it! . . . Dont say it! . . . No! . . . No! . . . I wont believe it! . . . I wont! I cant believe it . . . . Dont you see I cannot?' " (*M*, 431). These characters seem to have lost everything—role as a knight, work (including child-rearing), power, fiancée or spouse or lover, health—as well as their fond view of themselves. What they see about themselves makes their life story less decorous because it now includes pretenses to virtue and other flaws, as well as errors in the past that require forgiveness from themselves and others.

On the other hand, when the protagonists face the illusion about themselves that they have cherished, their gains are significant and consoling. By revising it, they free themselves from the conviction that their life has happened to them. With the exception of St. Peter, they feel less like victims whose lives have been determined or under the control of others. Mink Snopes, the tenth protagonist in this study, who has felt all along that his life has happened to him and that he has no choice except to act as he does, feels in charge once he has accomplished his revenge by killing Flem. The characters seem to be freer and more confident, relieved at not having to protect secrets about themselves. They are less righteous and less concerned altogether with what others think of them. These characters discard encroaching associates and harmful practices and attitudes. Strether distances himself from the

3. Cervantes, *Don Quixote*, 826.

Newsomes. Alonso Quixano resumes his name without pretense of a noble title, rejects his life as a knight, and denounces reading chivalric romances. Lyman, Grace, and the narrator of *Jazz* overcome arrogance, and the Traces overcome injury and self-pity. Don Quixote and Gavin stop hiding behind their poses as knights and relate to others more fully. The versions of their lives at the end of their assessments are inclusive and coherent, and the reader of an altersroman is convinced that the protagonists' revisions more accurately reflect the events.

The idea of innocence frequently appears both in literary studies of development in young adulthood and in psychological studies of assessing one's life in middle age.[4] This recurrence offers a reason to conclude by reviewing how innocence applies to the development of the characters studied here. Don Quixote, Strether, and Gavin are more naive about how the world works than the other protagonists. Also, the characters in these novels have not had equal experience of sexuality and intimacy. However, innocence arises from more than lack of knowledge or degree of involvement with others. It also means individuals' acting on unexamined assumptions about their ability to control their lives, about their own self-interestedness, and about evil. From the outset until the time of their second shock, the characters' attitude toward free will, which they usually do not examine explicitly, is contradictory. On the one hand, they all complain about unwelcome events beyond their control, so that, at times, they deny their responsibility. On the other hand, prior to their second shock, these characters assume that life is fair and, in some way, whether by force of will or reason, controllable. Based on this assumption, a kind of optimism, they also believe that they can bargain with life to insulate themselves from evil and harm in several ways. Some believe that they are invulnerable by right, whether their privilege comes from their education and class (Don Quixote, Gavin, Lyman, Grace) or gender and nationality (Grace) or talent as a

---

4. My discussion of innocence relies on the following sources: Brooks, *William Faulkner,* 296–308, 429; Minter, *Interpreted Design;* and Arthur M. Schlesinger, "What Then Is the American This New Man." Holman's discussion of the American version of innocence in "The *Bildungsroman,* American Style" and Kenneth S. Lynn's analysis of psychic immaturity, particularly in nineteenth- and twentieth-century U.S. fiction written by men, in "Adulthood in American Literature," have also been helpful. In the psychological literature, Gould lists "I am an innocent" as one of the false assumptions that people discard during midlife (*Transformations,* 294–307). Erikson does not use the term *innocence,* but his discussions of integrity cited elsewhere have been helpful.

storyteller (the narrator of *Jazz*) or a pact with "Old Moster" (Mink). With the possible exception of Gavin, they know logically that they have been hurt or ill and therefore are vulnerable, yet some still feel, perhaps even because of the price that they have paid with their suffering, that they have a right to future protection. Strether, St. Peter, Mink, Lyman, Grace, Joe, Violet, and the narrator of *Jazz*, for example, plead that they have been hurt enough already. At the outset, all are striving to feel in charge at the center of their worlds. Grace is confident that she has arranged her life in Boca Grande so that people will watch out for her. St. Peter and Strether believe that they do not have to look at any unpleasantness that they choose to ignore. These three and the narrator of *Jazz* have tried to remain safe by resolving not to become close to anyone again but to be self-sufficient. Don Quixote, Gavin, and Lyman believe that their code of honor will order their lives. Most important, the protagonists act as if all harm comes from the outside and as if the less admirable tendencies in human nature that they have observed in others do not exist in them. Without much reflection, they have assumed that their motives are not as self-interested as those of others.

By the conclusions of these seven examples of the altersroman, the protagonists have moved beyond innocence in several ways. All understand more about the impossibility of absolute safety and about their own self-centeredness and capacity to do harm: in sum, about the complexity of the human situation in which they are full participants. Their being special does not protect them from life, because, they understand, no one is perfect or invulnerable or allowed to be beyond responsibility. *All* people belong to the community of "poor sons of bitches," as Gavin and other characters in *The Mansion* observe. At the same time, even though they have been victims of bad fortune as well as recipients of good, the protagonists acknowledge that they have exercised free will in their responses to their experiences. They end with a more balanced view of what they are responsible for and how much they control. Having had their insights, St. Peter and Grace still try to protect themselves from the risk of being hurt by asking less of life, although Grace does reach out to her readers. St. Peter, who has been responsible throughout his adulthood, seeks to avoid further pain with apathy. The others, however, accept that they cannot insulate themselves completely from the sinister or deny their own ambition, pride, fear of life, selfishness, or vindictiveness. No longer equating feeling special with being invulnerable, these characters are now "safe" to be around, as Ratliff says of Gavin (*M*, 427). If these novels stopped at the point where Faulkner ends *The Mansion*, the reader might wonder what difference relinquishing innocence makes. However, Lyman, Grace, and the narrator of *Jazz* speak and Don Quixote, Strether, Violet, and Joe act after they have accepted their insights so that the reader has a better idea of what maturity following assessing one's life might look like.

Far from proposing physical or mental escape from the vicissitudes of life when control fails, which is another aspect of innocence, most of these novels relish the details of everyday life and relationships. Even if they live alone, the protagonists' interactions with others are portrayed. Their schedules, the routes they walk or drive, the furnishings of their homes or the places they stay, and the food they eat are all described. Indeed, critics point out that Cervantes revised the romance genre by including causal explanations of events, empirical evidence, and realistic details about bodily functions, food, and clothing. To take one example, eating, with the food served described, occurs in each of the novels: Don Quixote's Sunday pigeon, shared with his niece, and his meager meals on the road, shared with Sancho Panza; Strether and Madame de Vionnet's *omelette aux tomates;* the lamb dinner the Professor cooks for Tom and the dinners Lillian plans to please her sons-in-law; Gavin and Melisandre's dinner; Ratliff's recipe for a toddy and the Christmas dinner he cooks for Chick; Lyman's bourbon and sandwiches; Charlotte's dinners of oysters and spiny lobster; Violet's malteds that she sucks through a straw (a replacement for maternal nurturing), the ham she devotedly prepares for Joe, and the catfish she cooks for Felice. Some of these examples are special occasions (Strether's luncheon and the Professor's dinner). Not all meals are shared. Mealtimes are described in *A Book of Common Prayer,* for example, but the characters rarely sit down companionably together to eat, a sign of their misery. Nonetheless, not only does the depiction of preparing and consuming food show both male and female writers' acceptance of the physical, the ordinary activities of life, but it also shows caring, communality, the social linked with the physical.

Throughout *Childhood and Society,* Erik Erikson discusses individual development as intricately connected to the values of the society to which the individual belongs. An individual life is not determined by society, but a person is influenced and supported by the collective values that his or her society holds during his or her lifetime. In this context, a negative note is that the U.S. novelists considered here follow their literary ancestors and include violence as a prominent part of their work, whether in society (war affects characters in the novels by Faulkner, Cather, and Didion; antiblack violence affects characters in Morrison's novel) or in the characters' personal experience, either as physical violence (the Traces, Grace, and Gavin) or psychological abuse (Strether, St. Peter, Lyman, and Grace). These altersromane reflect that violence of all sorts continues to be part of experience in the United States. Erikson further believes that identity within a culture evolves over time as the individual's society advances or declines. On the positive side, this study of characters who accept the lives they have had and relinquish innocence, along with their unwarranted conviction of superiority and invulnerability that innocence has given them, suggests a turn in U.S. society toward accepting maturity as an achievement to embrace rather than escape. In thinking about identity on the western frontier, one of Stegner's protagonists says, "Perhaps it took several generations to make a man."[5] Certainly, in the U.S. novels considered here, it takes nearly a lifetime to mature, to understand the responsibility for oneself that American individualism entails as well as to balance the responsibility to one's community that the human situation requires.

Two more observations remain to be made about the presentation of the social context in which the characters assess their lives, and it is useful at this point to broaden the discussion to consider examples of the altersroman in addition to the seven that have been the main focus. First, while all these novels give the reader a strong sense of the protagonist's place and time, *Mrs. Dalloway, The Mansion,* and *Jazz* have multiple plots and include more direct assessments of their society. The result is that they expand the intense focus on a single consciousness found in *The Ambassadors* and *The Professor's House,* for example. *Mrs. Dalloway* focuses on Clarissa Dalloway's affirmation of her life, and it includes Peter Walsh's assessment of his life and, briefly, Sally Seton's, all in their fifties. *The Mansion* focuses on Gavin Stevens, and it includes Mink

---

5. Stegner, *The Big Rock Candy Mountain,* 563. Erikson discusses the individual's social context in *Childhood and Society,* 268, 277–84. See also chapter 8, "Reflections on the American Identity" (285–325). He discusses "Historical Relativity in the Psychoanalytic Method" in *Life Cycle Completed,* 94–101.

Snopes's review of his life. *Jazz* has three protagonists in late middle age who look back over their lives. Thus, for Woolf, Faulkner, and Morrison, assessing the life one has had is a common activity. The assessment of their society in these novels occurs in two ways. First, characters besides the protagonists critique society in passages unmediated by the narrators. In *Mrs. Dalloway*, Septimus Smith, a veteran of World War I who suffers from what would now be called post-traumatic stress disorder, condemns the machinery of British society that sent young men to war. Gavin's nephew, Chick, is cynical about his experience in World War II. Mink's reflections constitute an indictment of tenant farming and the abuse of privilege. In *Jazz*, Felice's parents comment on their jobs and media coverage of news about black Americans. Second, the narrators interrupt the story to critique their society. Virginia Woolf erupts into the text of *Mrs. Dalloway* to condemn England's worship of Proportion and Conversion, sister "goddesses" that have made England "prosper" but that require submission of will and serve the ideals of imperialism and patriarchy.[6] Like Woolf, Faulkner includes first-person narrators and an omniscient narrator. In a voice that resembles Faulkner's, the omniscient narrator criticizes the unchanged attitudes toward war and racism while worrying about the shifts in the town's social structure and economy that may destroy community. The narrator of *Jazz* refers to episodes of antiblack violence and places the Traces' story within the context of black Americans' migration north. She presents public events as causes for the characters' actions. Dorcas moves to New York to live with her aunt because her parents have been killed during the riot in East St. Louis in 1917. In these three novels, the complexity serves as a vehicle for criticism of the abuse of power, the patriarchy, war, and racism.

The second aspect of social context, the differences that seem to exist between those altersromane written by women and those by men, will require considering Virginia Woolf's *Mrs. Dalloway*, Edith Wharton's *The Mother's Recompense*, Doris Lessing's *The Summer before the Dark*, and Paule Marshall's *Praisesong for the Widow*, in addition to *A Book of Common Prayer* and *Jazz*. In the novels by women with female protagonists, these protagonists consider more diverse guides than in

6. The passage in Woolf's *Mrs. Dalloway* (hereafter cited in the text as *MD*) is in the center of the text, 149–154. See Abel's discussion of the passage, "Narrative Structure(s)," 181–83.

those novels by women with a male protagonist or in novels written by men. The male protagonists all have a female guide (although Gavin Stevens has a male guide as well). With the exception of Dulcinea, the female guide seems to present herself rather than be someone whom the protagonist has sought. However challenging Madame de Vionnet, Linda Snopes Kohl, and Susan Ward's papers may be to the comfort and beliefs of Strether, Gavin, and Lyman, the men are led to give up their initial resistance and to consider a different point of view. With the exception of Grace, even when the women choose their guides, they tailor the advice they receive.

Kate Clephane in Edith Wharton's *The Mother's Recompense* chooses among four guides. She briefly considers consulting a woman, but decides that she cannot trust her.[7] The three men occupy traditional positions of power: the family lawyer, an elderly philanthropist, and the rector of her family's prestigious church who is a candidate for bishop. Although the two men to whom she confesses are initially horrified that she has had a passionate affair with her future son-in-law, both feel compassionate and aid her. The rector puts aside what he considers the proper response, which is to " 'stop this abomination,' " the marriage of Kate's daughter and former lover, in favor of "compromise." Kate may remain silent, he advises her, if " 'she is absolutely convinced that less harm will come to all concerned if she has the courage to keep silence—always. . . . The thing in the world I'm most afraid of is sterile pain' " (*MR*, 211–12). Kate accepts part of his advice because it enables her to avoid the embarrassment of telling her daughter. However, she confesses to her lawyer, Fred Landers, who has also become her suitor. Expecting his shock and rejection, she is in turn shocked when he is willing to overlook her past and pursue his marriage proposal: " 'The time will come,' he said, 'when all this will seem very far off from both of us' " (*MR*, 259). Kate dismisses both of the guides she has chosen because neither man understands her and neither can meet her needs. Kate sees her affair as more significant than the men do and her passion as important to her identity, yet contradictorily, she judges herself more harshly. Too, their compassion and Landers's offer of intimacy frighten her. Although she rejects them, Kate alters the responses of her guides in order to affirm her life based on "the fact of being able . . . to say

7. Wharton, *Mother's Recompense*, 172. Hereafter cited as *MR* in the text.

to herself, whenever she began to drift toward new uncertainties and fresh concessions, that once at least she had stood fast, shutting away in a little space of peace and light the best thing that had ever happened to her [receiving Landers's pity]" (*MR*, 272).

In *A Book of Common Prayer*, Grace Strasser-Mendana finds that her guide understands her very well, but is unable to provide the forgiveness she seeks.[8] Leonard Douglas's revelation that her husband financed revolutionaries destroys her illusion that she knows the political situation in which she participates in Boca Grande. But he does not follow his revelation with emotional support beyond " 'I shouldn't have told you. It upset you' " (*BCP*, 255). When she is trying to reconstruct Charlotte's last hours and place blame for her death, perhaps trying to bring up the topic of her own involvement in the most recent revolution, Leonard dismisses her and her effort: "[T]here are no real points in knowing one way or another" (*BCP*, 276). Part of Grace's despair results from her not being able to find anyone else she trusts to turn to for consolation.

In Paule Marshall's *Praisesong for the Widow*, Avey Johnson seems to be chosen by her guides. The first is her great-aunt, who named Avey and chose her to spend each summer with her in South Carolina at Ibo Landing and who has recently appeared to her in a dream beckoning Avey to walk again to the Landing. The second is Lebert Joseph, one of the elders and "the hub, the polestar" in the Afro-Caribbean community on the islands of Grenada and Carriacou whose "penetrating look . . . marked him as someone who possessed ways of seeing that went beyond mere sight and ways of knowing that outstripped ordinary intelligence."[9] He is a shape-shifter, whom Avey distrusts at first: "He had lied, deceived and tricked her into coming on the excursion. Yet to her amazement she found herself all the more fond of him for having done so" (*PW*, 230–33). She responds to Lebert Joseph in part because he recalls her great-aunt's mission for her, that she remember her ancestors and honor them. She is also prepared to respond because, for the three years since her husband's death, Avey has been evaluating her life and judging that the price the family has paid for material success has been " *'Too much! Too much! Too much!'* " (*PW*, 145). Lebert Joseph, with the help of women in the community

8. Didion, *Book of Common Prayer.* Hereafter cited as *BCP* in the text.
9. Marshall, *Praisesong for the Widow*, 172, 243. Hereafter cited as *PW* in the text.

on the islands, helps Avey to her insight to use the money she and her husband have earned to build a home on her great-aunt's property near the Landing and assume her role as teacher of youngsters, in particular, a responsive grandchild.

In *Mrs. Dalloway, Jazz,* and *The Summer before the Dark,* the female protagonists seek a woman rather than a man, and these guides are more effective than the men who advise Kate Clephane and Grace. Once before, Clarissa Dalloway consulted Sir William Bradshaw, "[a] man absolutely at the head of his profession, very powerful," for "his advice" (*MD,* 278). He is, by coincidence, the physician who has seen Septimus Smith, the veteran who commits suicide on the day of Clarissa's party. Clarissa finds Bradshaw "obscurely evil, . . . capable of some indescribable outrage—forcing your soul, that was it" (*MD,* 281). The novel validates her strong reaction by having Richard Dalloway, Septimus and his wife, and the narrator agree about Bradshaw: "He swooped; he devoured. He shut people up" (*MD,* 154; compare 279, 149, 152). Society authorizes men like Bradshaw as guides, Woolf says, but people are better off *not* consulting them. He destroys his patients, as he has destroyed his wife, by not wanting people to be themselves. In contrast, Clarissa's reflections during the day have leaped forward while she watches the old woman across the way, an unlikely guide whom Clarissa never meets but whom she is watching twice when she considers what is important in her life. The first time, she is wondering what to oppose to the religious fanaticism of her daughter's tutor, Miss Kilman, and the passion of her former suitor, Peter Walsh:

> Love and religion! thought Clarissa . . . . How detestable, how detestable they are! . . . The cruelest things in the world, she thought, seeing them clumsy, hot, domineering, hypocritical, eavesdropping, jealous, infinitely cruel and unscrupulous, dressed in a mackintosh coat, on the landing; love and religion. . . . There was something solemn in it [the old woman looking out of the window, quite unconscious that she was being watched]—but love and religion would destroy that, whatever it was, the privacy of the soul. . . . Why creeds and prayers and mackintoshes? when, thought Clarissa, that's the miracle, that's the mystery; that old lady, she meant, whom she could see going from chest of drawers to dressing-table. She could still see her. And the supreme mystery which Kilman might say she had solved, or Peter might say he had solved but Clarissa didn't believe either of them had the ghost of an idea of solving, was simply this: here was one room; there another. Did religion solve that, or love? (*MD,* 191–93)

Clarissa interprets the old woman as encouraging her to value that which is mundane and concrete. Later that evening, when she is alone at the window trying to make sense of why a young man would commit suicide, she again watches the old woman following her daily routine preparing for bed, which helps her to her consolation: "She felt glad that he had done it; thrown it [his life] away. . . . He made her feel the beauty; made her feel the fun" (*MD*, 283–84).

Alice Manfred is successful as Violet Trace's guide in *Jazz*. Morrison shows Violet accepting all her advice: to love her husband, to face that she has only one life, not to be pitiful. Alice cares about Violet, and her nurturing increases Violet's self-esteem. Morrison also portrays guiding as a reciprocal activity. Alice confronts her own anger and righteousness as a result of talking with Violet.

In *The Summer before the Dark*, Kate Brown regards the men she knows as limited or disappointing, so that it seems appropriate for her to choose a woman to help her learn about life. Kate has "lost respect for her husband," she chooses a young lover who, when he becomes ill, reminds her of her children, and she feels superior to her male employers.[10] However, by the end of her reflection, Kate decides to reject the advice of her guide, Mary Finchley, entirely. Mary insists on having the freedom to have casual affairs as she pleases, even though her behavior hurts her husband, and she does not seem able to understand why Kate would object to her having an affair with Kate's husband: " 'When I ask [Mary] about [her affairs] she says, Oh I can't do with just one man! She looks rather embarrassed—but it's because *you* are a bit thick' " (*SBD*, 226). Because she has felt alive during their irreverent conversations and because she has not confronted her anger at her husband for his numerous casual affairs, Kate has lacked the strength to do more than allow Mary to confuse her. At the end of her summer of reflection, when a young woman tells Kate that " 'It doesn't matter a damn what you do. . . . That is the whole point of everything,' " Kate asserts, " 'I don't believe it' " (*SBD*, 242–43).

The point is that women sometimes have to acknowledge the guides, like Leonard Douglas or Lebert Joseph or Mary Finchley, who present themselves. However, in general, the women seem used to seeking

---

10. Lessing, *Summer before the Dark*, 63. Hereafter cited as *SBD* in the text. See Waxman, *From the Hearth to the Open Road*, 46–59.

and receiving guidance and are willing to consider options. Even with their greater flexibility to alter or reject the advice they receive, the women have a more difficult time endorsing their society. Cervantes and James portray characters who affirm their heritage. Wharton, Faulkner, Stegner, and, to an extent, Cather are nostalgic for the values of an earlier time. Five of the authors, all women, are critical of views they consider dominant in their culture. The patriarchy, war, and racism have been mentioned. Materialism and acquisitiveness that undermine relationships distress the Professor and Avey Johnson. Despite their criticism, protagonists in altersromane by Woolf, Marshall, and Morrison are able to affirm their lives. Cather's protagonist is resigned at the end of his reflections, and Didion's remains in despair.

Making other observations based on the gender of the author or character seems at times to be helpful, but clear distinctions are difficult to maintain. For example, the reciprocity of the relationship between protagonist and young person is remarkable in *Jazz*, and Cather, Didion, and Marshall also credit the young person as a source of insight for the protagonist. In *Praisesong for the Widow*, Avey repeats her youngest daughter's advice in her mind during her review of her life. In contrast, Chad and Shelly anger Strether and Lyman. However, exceptions to this observation come to mind. Kate Clephane's daughter, Clarissa Dalloway's daughter, and the young person, Maureen, with whom Kate Brown converses are primarily a source of concern rather than insight. The same caution not to impose distinctions must be observed when considering the kinds of issues that the protagonists consider when they reflect on their lives. In books by men and women, the male characters consider marriage and evaluate their marriages almost exclusively. Learning to be more open in their relationships is what Joe achieves and what Lyman hopes for, but such vulnerability is frightening to Gavin and does not seem possible for the Professor or Alonso Quixano—or to the narrator of *Jazz*. Many of the other female protagonists have the same preoccupation. Mrs. Dalloway and Violet Trace affirm their relationships. Avey Johnson and Grace Strasser-Mendana reflect on relationships now in the past. Kate Clephane accepts that she made the correct decision when she "escape[d] from the oppression of her married life" and New York eighteen years earlier, even though doing so meant "desert[ing]" her three-year-old daughter (*MR*, 13). She makes a similar decision to leave her daughter's home in New York and to reject a marriage proposal in the present time of the novel.

One difference is that while the men focus on their vulnerability, the women are anxious to learn to assert themselves more. Kate Brown returns home to speak up to her husband. Avey regrets that she did not take the responsibility for calling "Jay" back when her husband became "Jerome" and let earning a good living stifle his spontaneity. Exploring distinctions based on gender can be helpful, but generalizations become difficult to maintain because of the complexity of the altersroman.

The events in the seven novels studied here are not strictly auto-biographical, and the distance between author and protagonist varies in each, with irony serving as a protective disguise. However, the sensibility of the protagonist or some emotional aspect of the conflicts or of the source of regret have somehow been part of the author's experience. The resolution of the transition at midlife at the end of these novels suggests that the altersroman serves a therapeutic purpose for the authors, and their using their creativity in new ways is evident in their subsequent careers. None of these is the author's last novel, although *Jazz* is Morrison's latest. Shortly after completing the second part of *Don Quixote*, Cervantes wrote the *Persiles*, which he considered his masterpiece. In *Beyond Fiction*, El Saffar says that "the *Persiles*, unlike *Don Quixote*, celebrates the achievement of harmony not only among the characters but between character and narrator, dream and reality, fiction and truth."[11] Following *The Ambassadors*, James wrote the other novels of his major phase, *The Wings of the Dove* and *The Golden Bowl*, before writing *The American Scene*, his observations about the United States after a twenty-year absence, and autobiography, *A Small Boy and Others* and *Notes of a Son and Brother*. Outstanding creative work follows in Cather's and Stegner's careers. Faulkner wrote *The Reivers*, his most optimistic initiation story. *Democracy*, written seven years after *A Book of Common Prayer*, is a more affirmative novel. Like their protagonists, these writers seem to have used writing an altersroman as a way to come to terms with their own lives, evident in the surge of energy and creativity that resolution often brings.

11. El Saffar, *Beyond Fiction*, 128–29.

Bibliography

Abel, Elizabeth. "Narrative Structure(s) and Female Development: The Case of *Mrs. Dalloway.*" In *The Voyage In: Fictions of Female Development,* ed. Elizabeth Abel, Marianne Hirsch, and Elizabeth Langland, 161–85. Hanover, N.H.: University Press of New England, 1983.

Abel, Elizabeth, Marianne Hirsch, and Elizabeth Langland, eds. *The Voyage In: Fictions of Female Development.* Hanover, N.H.: University Press of New England, 1983.

Ahearn, Kerry. *"The Big Rock Candy Mountain* and *Angle of Repose:* Trial and Culmination." *Western American Literature* 10 (1975): 11–27.

Alter, Robert. *Partial Magic: The Novel as a Self-Conscious Genre.* Berkeley and Los Angeles: University of California Press, 1975.

Anderson, Ellen M. "Dreaming a True Story: The Disenchantment of the Hero in *Don Quixote,* Part 2." In *Essays on Life Writing: From Genre to Critical Practice,* ed. Marlene Kadar, 171–89. Toronto: University of Toronto Press, 1992.

Auerbach, Erich. *Mimesis: The Representation of Reality in Western Literature.* 1946. Reprint, Princeton: Princeton University Press, 1953.

Baker, Houston A., Jr. *Modernism and the Harlem Renaissance.* Chicago: University of Chicago Press, 1987.

Barth, John. *Chimera.* New York: Random House, 1972.

Barthelme, Donald. *Paradise.* New York: Putnam, 1986.

Beck, Warren. *Man in Motion: Faulkner's Trilogy.* Madison: University of Wisconsin Press, 1961.

Bell, Ian F. A., ed. *Henry James: Fiction as History.* London: Vision Press, 1984.

Blotner, Joseph. *Faulkner: A Biography.* One-volume ed. New York: Random House, 1974.

———, ed. *Selected Letters of William Faulkner.* New York: Random House, 1977.

Brooks, Cleanth. *William Faulkner: The Yoknapatawpha Country.* New Haven: Yale University Press, 1963.

Buckley, Jerome Hamilton. *Season of Youth: The Bildungsroman from Dickens to Golding.* Cambridge: Harvard University Press, 1974.

Burrows, Russell, and Michele Moylan. "The Narrative Voice and the Psychology Behind It: Wallace Stegner's *Angle of Repose*." *Journal of Evolutionary Psychology* 10 (1989): 286–93.

Cather, Willa. *My Ántonia*. Boston: Houghton Mifflin, 1918.

———. *The Professor's House*. New York: Knopf, 1925.

Cervantes, Miguel de. *Don Quixote*. Ed. Joseph R. Jones and Kenneth Douglas. Critical Edition. New York: Norton, 1981.

———. *The Trials of Persiles and Sigismunda*. Trans. Celia Richmond Weller and Clark A. Colahan. 1617. Reprint, Berkeley and Los Angeles: University of California Press, 1989.

Chakovsky, Sergei. "Women in Faulkner's Novels: Author's Attitude and Artistic Function." In *Faulkner and Women: Faulkner and Yoknapatawpha, 1985,* ed. Doreen Fowler and Ann J. Abadie, 58–80. Jackson: University Press of Mississippi, 1986.

Chapman, Sara S. *Henry James's Portrait of the Writer as Hero*. New York: St. Martin's Press, 1989.

Cooke, Michael G. *Afro-American Literature in the Twentieth Century: The Achievement of Intimacy*. New Haven: Yale University Press, 1984.

Didion, Joan. *A Book of Common Prayer*. New York: Pocket Books, 1978.

———. "Cautionary Tales." Interview by Susan Stamberg. In *Joan Didion: Essays and Conversations,* ed. Ellen G. Friedman, 22–28. Princeton: Ontario Review Press, 1984.

———. *Democracy*. New York: Simon and Schuster, 1984.

———. "Joan Didion." Interview by Linda Kuehl. In *Writers at Work: The "Paris Review" Interviews,* ed. George Plimpton, 337–57. 5th ser. New York: Penguin, 1981.

———. "On Morality." In her *Slouching towards Bethlehem*, 160–65. 1968. Reprint, New York: Pocket Books, 1981.

———. "A Visit with Joan Didion." Interview by Sara Davidson. In *Joan Didion: Essays and Conversations,* ed. Ellen G. Friedman, 13–21. Princeton: Ontario Review Press, 1984.

Doody, Terrence. *Confession and Community in the Novel*. Baton Rouge: Louisiana State University Press, 1980.

Douglass, Frederick. *Narrative of the Life of Frederick Douglass, An American Slave, Written by Himself*. Ed. Benjamin Quarles. Cambridge: Harvard University Press, 1960.

Du Bois, W. E. B. *The Souls of Black Folk*. 1903. Reprint, New York: New American Library, 1982.

Dunlap, Mary Montgomery. "The Achievement of Gavin Stevens." Ph.D. diss., University of South Carolina, 1970.

Durán, Manuel. *La ambigüedad en el "Quijote."* Xalapa, Mexico: Universidad Veracruzana, 1961.

————. *Cervantes.* Boston: Twayne, 1974.

Edel, Leon. *Henry James, the Master: 1901–1916.* Philadelphia: J. B. Lippincott, 1972.

————. *The Stuff of Sleep and Dreams: Experiments in Literary Psychology.* New York: Harper and Row, 1959.

Ellison, Ralph. *Invisible Man.* New York: Signet, New American Library, 1952.

Ellmann, Maud. " 'The Intimate Difference': Power and Representation in *The Ambassadors.*" In *The Ambassadors,* ed. S. P. Rosenbaum, 501–14. 2nd ed. Critical Edition. New York: Norton, 1994.

El Saffar, Ruth. *Beyond Fiction: The Recovery of the Feminine in the Novels of Cervantes.* Berkeley and Los Angeles: University of California Press, 1984.

Erikson, Erik H. *Childhood and Society.* 2nd ed. New York: Norton, 1963.

————. *Dimensions of a New Identity: The 1973 Jefferson Lectures.* New York: Norton, 1974.

————. *Identity and the Life Cycle.* 1959. Reprint, New York: Norton, 1980.

————. *Insight and Responsibility.* New York: Norton, 1964.

————. *The Life Cycle Completed: A Review.* 1982. Reprint, New York: Norton, 1985.

————, ed. *Adulthood.* New York: Norton, 1978.

Fant, Joseph L., and Robert Ashley, eds. *Faulkner at West Point.* New York: Random House, 1964.

Faulkner, William. *Absalom, Absalom!* New York: Random House, 1936.

————. *Essays, Speeches and Public Letters,* ed. James B. Meriwether. New York: Random House, 1966.

————. *Flags in the Dust.* New York: Random House, 1973.

————. *Go Down, Moses.* New York: Random House, 1942.

————. *The Hamlet.* New York: Random House, 1940.

————. *Intruder in the Dust.* New York: Random House, 1948.

————. *Knight's Gambit.* New York: Random House, 1949.

————. *The Mansion.* New York: Random House, 1959.

————. "1956 Interview with Jean Stein Vanden Heuvel." Interview by Jean Stein. In *Lion in the Garden: Interviews with William Faulkner, 1926–1962,* ed. James B. Meriwether and Michael Millgate, 237–56. New York: Random House, 1968.

————. *The Reivers: A Reminiscence.* New York: Random House, 1962.

————. *Requiem for a Nun.* New York: Random House, 1951.

————. *The Town.* New York: Random House, 1957.

————. *The Unvanquished.* New York: Random House, 1938.

Ferguson, Suzanne. "History, Fiction, and Propaganda: The Man of Letters and the American West, an Interview with Wallace Stegner." In

Literature and the Visual Arts in Contemporary Society, ed. Suzanne Ferguson and Barbara Groseclose, 3–22. Columbus: Ohio State University Press, 1985.

Fetterley, Judith. *"My Ántonia,* Jim Burden and the Dilemma of the Lesbian Writer." In *Gender Studies: New Directions in Feminist Criticism,* ed. Judith Spector, 43–59. Bowling Green, Ohio: Bowling Green State University Popular Press, 1986.

Fogel, Daniel Mark. *Henry James and the Structure of the Romantic Imagination.* Baton Rouge: Louisiana State University Press, 1981.

———. "A New Reading of Henry James's 'The Jolly Corner.' " In *Critical Essays on Henry James: The Late Novels,* ed. James W. Gargano, 190–203. Boston: G. K. Hall, 1987.

Fontane, Theodor. *Unwiederbringlich.* 1891. Reprinted as *Beyond Recall,* trans. Douglas Parmee. London and New York: Oxford University Press, 1964.

Fraiman, Susan. *Unbecoming Women: British Women Writers and the Novel of Development.* New York: Columbia University Press, 1993.

Frenkel-Brunswik, Else. "Adjustments and Reorientation in the Course of the Life Span." In *Middle Age and Aging: A Reader in Social Psychology,* ed. Bernice L. Neugarten, 77–84. Chicago: University of Chicago Press, 1968.

Fulton, Keith Louise. "Linda Snopes Kohl: Faulkner's Radical Woman." *Modern Fiction Studies* 34 (1988): 425–36.

Fussell, Edwin Sill. *The French Side of Henry James.* New York: Columbia University Press, 1990.

Gates, Henry Louis, Jr. *The Signifying Monkey: A Theory of African-American Literary Criticism.* New York: Oxford University Press, 1988.

Gelfant, Blanche H. "Love and Conversion in 'Mrs. Dalloway.' " *Criticism* 8 (1966): 229–45.

———. *Women Writing in America: Voices in Collage.* Hanover, N.H.: University Press of New England, 1984.

Giannone, Richard. *Music in Willa Cather's Fiction.* Lincoln: University of Nebraska Press, 1968.

Gilligan, Carol. *In a Different Voice: Psychological Theory and Women's Development.* Cambridge: Harvard University Press, 1982.

Gould, Roger L. "The Phases of Adult Life: A Study in Developmental Psychology." *American Journal of Psychiatry* 129 (1972): 521–31.

———. *Transformations: Growth and Change in Adult Life.* New York: Simon and Schuster, 1978.

Graulich, Melody. "The Guides to Conduct that a Tradition Offers: Wallace Stegner's *Angle of Repose." South Dakota Review* 23 (1985): 87–106.

Gregory, Nancy Eileen. "A Study of the Early Versions of Faulkner's *The Town* and *The Mansion.*" Ph.D. diss., University of South Carolina, 1975.

Gullette, Margaret Morganroth. *Safe at Last in the Middle Years, the Invention of the Midlife Progress Novel: Saul Bellow, Margaret Drabble, Anne Tyler, John Updike.* Berkeley and Los Angeles: University of California Press, 1988.

Gwynn, Frederick L., and Joseph L. Blotner, eds. *Faulkner in the University: Class Conferences at the University of Virginia, 1957–1958.* Charlottesville: University Press of Virginia 1959.

Hassumani, Sabrina. "Sex and Civilization in the Novels of Henry James." Master's thesis, University of Houston, 1987.

Helson, Ravenna, and Paul Wink. "Personality Change in Women from the Early 40s to the Early 50s." *Psychology and Aging* 7 (1992): 46–55.

Henderson, Katherine Usher. *Joan Didion.* New York: Frederick Ungar, 1981.

———. "Joan Didion: The Bond between Narrator and Heroine in *Democracy.*" In *American Women Writing Fiction: Memory, Identity, Family, Space,* ed. Mickey Pearlman, 68–89. Lexington: University Press of Kentucky, 1989.

Hollowell, John. "Against Interpretation: Narrative Strategy in *A Book of Common Prayer.*" In *Joan Didion: Essays and Conversations,* ed. Ellen G. Friedman, 164–76. Princeton: Ontario Review Press, 1984.

Holman, C. Hugh. "The *Bildungsroman,* American Style." In his *Windows on the World, Essays on American Social Fiction,* 168–97. Knoxville: University of Tennessee Press, 1979.

Howe, Susan. *Wilhelm Meister and His English Kinsmen: Apprentices to Life.* New York: Columbia University Press, 1930.

Hurston, Zora Neale. *Their Eyes Were Watching God.* 1937. Reprint, Urbana: University of Illinois Press, 1978.

James, Henry. *The Bostonians.* 1886. Reprint, New York: Library of America, 1991.

———. *The Novels and Tales of Henry James.* New York Edition. 24 vols. New York: Charles Scribner's Sons, 1907–1909.

———. *Partial Portraits.* London: Macmillan, 1888.

———. "Project of Novel by Henry James." In *The Notebooks of Henry James,* ed. F. O. Matthiessen and Kenneth B. Murdock, 372–415. New York: Oxford University Press, 1961.

Johnson, Carroll B. *Madness and Lust: A Psychoanalytic Approach to "Don Quixote."* Berkeley and Los Angeles: University of California Press, 1983.

Jung, Carl. "The Stages of Life." In *The Collected Works of C. G. Jung,* trans. R. F. C. Hull, 387–403. Vol. 8. New York: Pantheon Books, 1960.

Kadar, Marlene, ed. *Essays on Life Writing: From Genre to Critical Practice.* Toronto: University of Toronto Press, 1992.

Kohut, Heinz. *The Restoration of the Self.* New York: International Universities Press, 1977.

——. *The Search for the Self: Selected Writings of Heinz Kohut, 1950–1978,* ed. Paul H. Ornstein. Vol. 1. New York: International Universities Press, 1978.

Laird, David. "Willa Cather and the Deceptions of Art." In *Interface: Essays on History, Myth, and Art in American Literature,* ed. Daniel Royot, 51–59. Montpelier: University of Montpelier, 1984.

Leddy, Michael. *"The Professor's House:* The Sense of an Ending." *Studies in the Novel* 23 (1991): 443–51.

Lessing, Doris. *The Summer before the Dark.* 1973. Reprint, New York: Random House, 1983.

Locke, Alain, ed. *The New Negro: Voices of the Harlem Renaissance.* 1925. Reprint, New York: Atheneum, 1992.

Lynn, Kenneth S. "Adulthood in American Literature." In *Adulthood,* ed. Erik H. Erikson, 237–47. New York: Norton, 1976.

Mann, Thomas. *Buddenbrooks.* Trans. H. T. Lowe-Porter. 1901. Reprint, New York: Knopf, 1973.

Marshall, Paule. *Praisesong for the Widow.* New York: Penguin/Plume, 1983.

Mbalia, Doreatha Drummond. "Women Who Run with Wild: The Need for Sisterhoods in *Jazz." Modern Fiction Studies* 39 (1993): 623–46.

Merivale, Patricia. "The Search for the Other Woman: Joan Didion and the Female Artist-Parable." In *Gender Studies: New Directions in Feminist Criticism,* ed. Judith Spector, 133–47. Bowling Green, Ohio: Bowling Green State University Popular Press, 1986.

Miller, Alice. *Prisoners of Childhood.* Trans. Ruth Ward. New York: Basic Books, 1981.

Minter, David L. *The Interpreted Design as a Structural Principle in American Prose.* New Haven: Yale University Press, 1969.

——. *William Faulkner: His Life and Work.* Baltimore: Johns Hopkins University Press, 1980.

Monroe, William. "Scripts and Patterns: Stories as 'Equipment for Living' —and Dying." In the BYU Symposium's *Willa Cather, Family, Community, and History,* ed. John J. Murphy, 301–10. Provo, Utah: Brigham Young University Humanities Publications Center, 1990.

Morrison, Toni. "Chloe Wofford Talks about Toni Morrison." Interview by Claudia Dreifus. *New York Times Magazine* 11 (September 1994): 72–75.

———. "A Conversation: Gloria Naylor and Toni Morrison." Interview by Gloria Naylor. *Southern Review* 21 (1985): 567–93.

———. *Conversations with Toni Morrison.* Ed. Danille Taylor-Guthrie. Jackson: University Press of Mississippi, 1994.

———. "An Inspired Life: Toni Morrison Writes and a Generation Listens." Interview by Dana Micucci. In *Conversations with Toni Morrison,* ed. Danille Taylor-Guthrie, 275–79. Jackson: University Press of Mississippi, 1994.

———. "An Interview with Toni Morrison." Interview by Tom LeClair. In *Anything Can Happen: Interviews with Contemporary American Novelists,* conducted and edited by Tom LeClair and Larry McCaffery, 252–61. Urbana: University of Illinois Press, 1983.

———. *Jazz.* New York: Alfred A. Knopf, 1992.

———. "The Song of Toni Morrison." Interview by Colette Dowling. In *Conversations with Toni Morrison,* ed. Danille Taylor-Guthrie, 48–59. Jackson: University Press of Mississippi, 1994.

———. "Talk with Toni Morrison." Interview by Mel Watkins. In *Conversations with Toni Morrison,* ed. Danille Taylor-Guthrie, 43–47. Jackson: University Press of Mississippi, 1994.

———. "Virigina Woolf's and William Faulkner's Treatment of the Alienated." Master's thesis, Cornell University, 1955.

Neugarten, Bernice L. "Adult Personality: Toward a Psychology of the Life Cycle." In *Middle Age and Aging: A Reader in Social Psychology,* ed. Bernice L. Neugarten, 137–47. Chicago: University of Chicago Press, 1968.

———. "The Awareness of Middle Age." In *Middle Age and Aging: A Reader in Social Psychology,* ed. Bernice L. Neugarten, 93–98. Chicago: University of Chicago Press, 1968.

Novak, Frank G., Jr. "Crisis and Discovery in *The Professor's House.*" *Colby Library Quarterly* 22 (1986): 119–32.

O'Brien, Sharon. *Willa Cather: The Emerging Voice.* New York: Oxford University Press, 1987.

Otten, Terry. "Horrific Love in Toni Morrison's Fiction." *Modern Fiction Studies* 39 (1993): 651–67.

Paul, Rodman W., ed. *A Victorian Gentlewoman in the Far West: Reminiscences of Mary Hallock Foote.* San Marino, Calif.: Huntington Library, 1972.

Peck, Robert C. "Psychological Developments in the Second Half of Life." In *Middle Age and Aging: A Reader in Social Psychology,* ed. Bernice L. Neugarten, 88–92. Chicago: University of Chicago Press, 1968.

Percas de Ponseti, Helena. *Cervantes y su concepto del arte.* Vol. 1. Madrid: Gredos, 1975.

Peterson, Audrey C. "Narrative Voice in Wallace Stegner's *Angle of Repose.*" *Western American Literature* 10 (1975): 125–33.

Petry, Ann. *The Street.* 1946. Reprint, Boston: Houghton Mifflin, 1991.

Pratt, Annis. "Novels of Rebirth and Transformation." In her *Archetypal Patterns in Women's Fiction,* 133–66. Bloomington: Indiana University Press, 1981.

Reed, Joseph W., Jr. *Faulkner's Narrative.* New Haven: Yale University Press, 1973.

Riley, Edward C. *Cervantes's Theory of the Novel.* Oxford: Clarendon Press, 1962.

Rivkin, Julie. "The Logic of Delegation in *The Ambassadors.*" *PMLA* 101 (1986): 819–31.

Schlesinger, Arthur M. "What Then Is the American This New Man." *American Historical Review* 48 (1943): 225–44.

Singal, Daniel Joseph. *The War Within: From Victorian to Modernist Thought in the South, 1919–1945.* Chapel Hill: University of North Carolina Press, 1982.

Stegner, Wallace. *All the Little Live Things.* 1967. Reprint, Lincoln: University of Nebraska Press, 1979.

———. *Angle of Repose.* 1971. Reprint, Greenwich, Conn.: Fawcett Crest, 1972.

———. *The Big Rock Candy Mountain.* 1943. Reprint, Lincoln: University of Nebraska Press, 1983.

———. *Crossing to Safety.* New York: Random House, 1987.

———. *Recapitulation.* 1979. Reprint, Lincoln: University of Nebraska Press, 1986.

———. *The Spectator Bird.* 1971. Reprint, Lincoln: University of Nebraska Press, 1979.

Stegner, Wallace Earle, and Richard W. Etulain. *Conversations with Wallace Stegner on Western History and Literature.* Salt Lake City: University of Utah Press, 1983.

Stifter, Adalbert. *Der Nachsommer.* 1857. Reprinted as *Indian Summer,* trans. Wendell Frye. New York: Peter Lang, 1985.

Stonum, Gary Lee. *Faulkner's Career: An Internal Literary History.* Ithaca: Cornell University Press, 1979.

Stout, Janis P. "Autobiography as Journey in *The Professor's House.*" *Studies in American Fiction* 19 (1991): 203–15.

———. *Strategies of Reticence: Silence and Meaning in the Works of Jane Austen, Willa Cather, Katherine Anne Porter, Joan Didion.* Charlottesville: University Press of Virginia, 1990.

Sweeney, Patricia E. *William Faulkner's Women Characters: An Annotated Bibliography of Criticism, 1930–1983*. Santa Barbara: Clio, 1985.

Tanner, Tony. "The Watcher from the Balcony: Henry James's *The Ambassadors*." *Critical Quarterly* 8 (1966): 35–52.

Tolstoy, Leo. *Tolstoy's Short Fiction*. Edited and with revised translations by Michael R. Katz. New York: Norton, 1991.

Vaid, Krishna Baldev. *Technique in the Tales of Henry James*. Cambridge: Harvard University Press, 1964.

Walton, Patricia L. *The Disruption of the Feminine in Henry James*. Toronto: University of Toronto Press, 1992.

Ward, J. A. "*The Ambassadors* as Conversion Experience." *Southern Review*, n.s., 5 (1969): 350–74.

Waxman, Barbara Frey. *From the Hearth to the Open Road: A Feminist Study of Aging in Contemporary Literature*. New York: Greenwood Press, 1990.

Wegelin, Christof. *The Image of Europe in Henry James*. Dallas: Southern Methodist University Press, 1958.

Weiger, John G. *The Individuated Self: Cervantes and the Emergence of the Individual*. Athens: Ohio University Press, 1979.

Westervelt, Linda. "The Individual and the Form: Maggie Verver's Tactics in *The Golden Bowl*." *Renascence* 36 (1984): 147–59.

———. "The Tabors of Colorado and *A Book of Common Prayer*." *Notes on Contemporary Literature* 20 (1990): 4–6.

Wharton, Edith. *The Age of Innocence*. 1920. Reprint, New York: Penguin, 1996.

———. *The Mother's Recompense*. 1925. Reprint, New York: Charles Scribner's Sons, 1986.

Wilcox, Leonard. "Narrative Technique and the Theme of Historical Continuity in the Novels of Joan Didion." In *Joan Didion: Essays and Conversations*, ed. Ellen G. Friedman, 68–80. Princeton: Ontario Review Press, 1984.

Wittenberg, Judith Bryant. *Faulkner: The Transfiguration of Biography*. Lincoln: University of Nebraska Press, 1979.

———. "William Faulkner: A Feminist Consideration." In *American Novelists Revisited: Essays in Feminist Criticism*, ed. Fritz Fleischmann, 325–38. New York: G. K. Hall, 1982.

Wolfe, Donald, Dennis O'Connor, and Marcy Crary. "Transformations of Life Structure and Personal Paradigm during the Midlife Transition." *Human Relations* 43 (1990): 957–73.

Woodress, James. *Willa Cather: A Literary Life*. Lincoln: University of Nebraska Press, 1987.

Woolf, Judith. *Henry James: The Major Novels.* Cambridge: Cambridge University Press, 1991.

Woolf, Virginia. *Mrs. Dalloway.* New York: Harcourt, Brace and World, 1925.

Yongue, Patricia Lee. "Edith Lewis Living." *Willa Cather Pioneer Memorial Newsletter* 33 (1989): 12–14.

———. "Willa Cather and Edith Lewis: Two Stories, Two Friends." *Willa Cather Yearbook* 1 (1991): 187–211.

Index

Altersroman: psychology important to, x, 20, 25, 43, 141; not new, xi; prominence increasing, xi; name, xii, 20; variety, 20; curtailed examples, 21–23; not a deathbed story, 24; details of everyday life, 159
—autobiographical echoes: recurrence of midlife review stories, x, 20, 72–74 passim, 108; therapeutic, x, 19–20, 149, 167; admitted by author, x, 107; age of author similar to protagonist's, x, 35, 49, 66–68, 83–84, 107; review of career, 88–92, 129–30; surge of creativity following, 167
—distinguishing characteristics, xii, 18–20, 21, 23–24, 149
—guide, 3, 7–9, 15; facilitates insight, 33, 38, 65, 151; often of opposite sex, 38, 76, 151; encourages tolerance, 38; different point of view, 38, 151; speaks with authority, 151; part of second shock, 152
—impetus to review the life, ix, xii, 149–50
—introspection: process resisted, ix, 6–7, 14, 21, 22, 37, 41, 57, 149–50, 152; delusion, ix, 7, 10, 152–53; experiment with new behavior, 6, 7–9, 14–15; recollection haphazard, 24; review earlier developmental crises, 26–29, 138–39; often confused, 42; begins with limited awareness, 60; comes to feel inevitable, 71; incidence, 85–86, 161; urgency, 150
—resolution: revised version of the life, ix, 60, 107; disgust, xii, 110, 116; despair, xii, 110, 119, 126–27; affirmation, xii, 5–6, 16–17, 43–44, 47–48, 49, 72, 81–82, 88, 140–41;

importance of, xiii, 5, 16–17, 19, 29, 156–57; amends made, 5, 14, 17, 140; delusion relinquished, 13–17, 82, 123, 154; consolation, 29, 30, 156; understanding greater by end, 106
—second shock, x, 15; contribution by protagonist, 19; divests protagonist, 87, 105, 123–25, 156; variety, 152; as revelation, 152, 156
—young person: receives lesson about values, 23, 37, 150; source of protagonist's recognition of age, 37, 150; not necessarily pliable, 37; source of insight for protagonist, 140; nurtured, 150. *See also* Narrative technique; Social context; and individual authors and works

Anger of protagonist: in *Jazz*, 133, 155; in *Angle of Repose*, 153; in *The Professor's House*, 153

Authenticity: in psychological literature, 4; in *Don Quixote*, 5; in *The Summer before the Dark*, 26; in *Jazz*, 148

Autobiographical echoes in altersroman. *See* Altersroman, distinguishing characteristics; and individual authors and works

Barth, John, 21, 22
Barthelme, Donald, 22
Bildungsroman: compared with altersroman, xii-xiii; female bildungsroman, xii, 25; psychological development of protagonist in, 21; distinguished from altersroman, 24–26, 29; autobiographical echoes, 35